The Complete Poems and Collected Letters of Adelaide Crapsey

Edited with an Introduction and Notes by Susan Sutton Smith

State University of New York Press

Albany 1977

The Complete Poems and Collected Letters of

Adelaide Crapsey

Adelaide Crapsey (1878-1914) Rome, 1909

Ninety of Adelaide Crapsey's poems were published in the editions of 1915, 1922, and 1934. Thirty-nine poems and sixty-nine letters are published here for the first time.

Published by the State University of New York Press
Albany, New York
www.sunypress.edu

Library of Congress Cataloging in Publication Data

Crapsey, Adelaide, 1878–1914.
The complete poems and collected letters of Adelaide Crapsey.

Bibliography: p.
Includes index.
I. Smith, Susan Sutton, 1943– II. Title.
PS3505.R277 1977 811'.5'2 76–25509

ISBN 978-0-87395-342-9 (hc : alk. paper)
ISBN 978-1-4384-5138-1 (pb : alk. paper)

For my mother & father

Contents

Acknowledgments

The Crapsey family, most recently Mr. and Mrs. Arthur H. Crapsey, Jr., and Miss Esther Lowenthal made this book possible through their generous donations of manuscripts typescripts, letters, and other materials to the University of Rochester Library. Miss Lowenthal and Mr. and Mrs. Crapsey have also been generous in granting interviews and answering innumerable questions. I am also greatly indebted to Jean McKinney Connor (Mrs. Ralph Connor), daughter of Jean Webster McKinney. Mr. and Mrs. Connor have not only assembled their invaluable collection of the poet's manuscripts and a large number of relevant letters from Jean Webster to her fiancé, Glenn F. McKinney, but have also allowed me to borrow these materials and have been kind and patient in answering my questions. Professors Rowland L. Collins and William H. Gilman of the University of Rochester have provided the encouragement and advice without which this book would never have been written but are in no way responsible for its flaws. I wish to thank the library staff members who have given me so much help, particularly Frances Goudy of the Vassar College Library Department of Special Collections, and Margaret B. Andrews, Alma Burner, Catherine D. Hayes, Mary Huth, Karl Kabelac, and Robert Volz of the University of Rochester Library. Professor John Aldrich Christie of Vassar College found Mrs. Connor for me, and I am grateful for his timely introduction. Finally, Margaret A. Mirabelli, W. Bruce Johnson, and Norman Mangouni of the SUNY Press have all been wonderfully helpful and patient.

INTRODUCTION

Life

"a few diffused faint clews and indirections"

Adelaide Crapsey seems to have guarded her privacy. She copied into her commonplace book a quotation from Balzac's *Honorine* that may serve as a *caveat* to her biographer: "Les drames de la vie ne sont pas dans les circonstances, ils sont dans les sentiments, ou si vous voulez, dans ce monde immense que vous devons nommer le monde spirituel."

Adelaide Crapsey was born on 9 September 1878, in Brooklyn Heights, New York, the third child and second daughter of the Rev. Algernon Sidney Crapsey (1847–1928), then an Episcopal clergyman, and Adelaide Trowbridge Crapsey (1855–1950), daughter of a newspaper editor in Catskill, New York. Algernon Sidney Crapsey became rector of St. Andrew's church in Rochester, New York in 1879, and his family followed him to Rochester by Hudson River steamer and canal boat. Six younger children were born in the rectory. In 1893 Adelaide and her sister Emily (born in 1877) were sent to Kemper Hall, an Episcopal boarding school in Kenosha, Wisconsin. Adelaide took a college preparatory course including Latin and French and succeeded her sister as editor of the school magazine and valedictorian of her class. She was an enthusiastic basketball player and referee.

In 1897 Adelaide Crapsey entered Vassar College. Here, too, she was an excellent student; she was graduated with honors and was elected to Phi Beta Kappa. She managed several basketball teams, took the part of Lucy in *The Rivals,* and was a member of a debating team affirming "That England's policy in the Transvaal is unjustifiable." For three years she was class poet and in her senior year was editor-in-chief of the *Vassarion,* the Vassar College yearbook. As editor-in-chief, she approved, if she did not compose, the tart poetic comment printed above the Vassar members of the Daughters of the American Revolution:

> Ye see the daughters set down here
> Wi' pedigrees and a' that
> They count back full a hundred year—
> But are they mair for a' that?
> For a' that and a' that,
> Their family trees and a' that,

The man of independent mind
He looks and laughs at a' that.[1]

This use of Burns has the spirit of another independent mind, Adelaide Crapsey's friend and roommate, and a literary editor of the yearbook, Alice Jean Chandler Webster (1876–1916). The one-line identification beneath Adelaide's portrait in the *Vassarion* reads, "It is a very serious thing to be a funny man," and Adelaide's love of humor is evident in her friendship with Jean Webster. A great-niece of Mark Twain from Fredonia, New York (a small town about 120 miles southwest of Rochester), Jean Webster became the author of popular juvenile novels and sketches of college life, including *When Patty Went to College* (1903), *Jerry Junior* (1907), *Daddy Long-Legs* (1912), and *Dear Enemy* (1915). In a memoir of Adelaide Crapsey, written for the *Vassar Miscellany* in 1915, she recalls her friend's "delightful quality of camaraderie" and "quick, bubbling humor."[2] Mary Elizabeth Osborn states that "Jean Webster said that she had had Adelaide in mind while she was writing *Daddy Long-Legs*" and adds the supposition that "this is probably true of many of the 'Patty' sketches as well."[3]

Two deaths saddened Adelaide Crapsey's college years. Her sister Ruth died of undulant fever at the age of eleven in 1898. Beautiful Emily, the sister to whom she was closest, died suddenly of appendicitis at the age of twenty-four in 1901. After graduation from Vassar in 1901, Adelaide spent one year at home in Rochester and then, during the academic years 1902–1904, she returned to Kemper Hall to teach history and literature.

In about 1903 Crapsey first began to suffer from the fatigue that was a symptom of her fatal disease. In October 1904 she sailed for Europe and studied at the School of Archaeology in Rome until late in 1905. She was able to earn money by working occasionally as a lecturer and guide. When she returned from Europe at the end of 1905, she accompanied her father to Batavia, New York, during his trial for heresy.

Dr. Crapsey's "heresy" was a product both of his own character and of Rochester's rapidly changing social structure. The city's population grew from 144,834 in 1892 to about 160,000 in 1904. Political and religious reforms around the turn of the century succeeded in part because "they harmonized with other rapid transformations in the city's character."[4] The depression of 1893–1896 had drawn the city's religious leaders into social work; once involved, they stayed involved. In the summer of 1889, the frail Dr. Crapsey ("scarcely five feet six" and "weighing hardly one hundred and twenty") was given his first trip to Europe by his parishioners.[5] His tour of the English cathedral towns, with their contrast between the material wealth and grandeur of the organized Church and the poverty and squalor of the people, affected him in ways his parishioners could not have foreseen:

> There never was a sadder man than I when the clerical scales fell from my eyes and I saw the world just as it is, a world of sin, sickness, sorrow, and death: a world of war, pestilence and famine, just as it was before Jesus died; just as it will be until men cease to worship Jesus as a God and begin to care for one another as He cared for the sinful, the sick and the sorrowing while He was yet alive.[6]

Dr. Crapsey later wrote, in the "Prefactory Note" to his autobiography, that "in successive stages of my career I have been influenced by the master minds of Newman, Darwin, and Karl Marx."[7] Influenced by what came to be known as Social Christianity, Dr. Crapsey formed a Brotherhood, which "enrolled many nonchurchmen and opened rooms in a building near St. Andrew's Church in 1893, thus providing a community center for the men of that working class neighborhood."[8]

A social survey completed in 1904 by a committee composed of such clergymen as Crapsey examined the composition of Rochester's 160,000 inhabitants. With "a fourth of the total foreign-born, according to the census of 1900, and more than half the remainder of foreign-born parents, the committee saw a real problem of assimilation. It found, too, 29 per cent of the men between the ages of 25 and 44 unmarried and 28 per cent of the women."[9] Some of Rochester's industries were "light" and employed skilled workers: the growing photographic industry; companies making optical goods, thermometers, and "other instruments for America's unfolding technological civilization,"[10] and companies producing dental equipment, machine tools, and the Cutler mail chute. Rochester's major industries, however, men's clothing and women's shoes, together employed "approximately half the city's wage earners," and the city "ranked fourth or fifth among American cities in the production of both articles."[11] In these industries, fierce labor-management struggles lasted for decades. Many men and women could not marry because they earned so little: in 1890 the average annual wage for the workers in Rochester's shoe industry was $415.[12]

His efforts to reach the workers brought Dr. Crapsey into open conflict with his church:

> Dr. Crapsey embarked on a series of Sunday evening

> lecture-sermons on religion and politics which attracted wide interest and received full coverage in the press. Indeed the practice, followed by several of the papers, of printing lengthy versions, running to one or two columns each, of four or more sermons every week, greatly extended the influence of the more forceful preachers. This practice also involved a danger which Crapsey discovered to his sorrow in February 1905.
>
> After sketching with sweeping strokes the relations between the church and the state down through the ages, Crapsey reached contemporary Rochester in his tenth lecture. His forthright condemnation of the commercialization he saw in both the church and the city seemed a bit too pointed to some listeners, but the real trouble started when the next lecture attacked contemporary churchmen for their failure to bring their interpretation of the Scriptures into harmony with scientific knowledge. This had often been said in a general way, but Crapsey pressed the point home by suggesting the incredibility of the Virgin Birth. The reaction was immediate, both within and without his church. Several ministers rose to defend their doctrines from the pulpit the next Sunday, and Crapsey's final sermon on social gospel went almost unnoticed.[13]

Crapsey and her father had always been close: Arthur H. Crapsey, Jr., a nephew of the poet, recalls his uncle Paul's statement that "discussions at the Crapsey dinner table were chiefly between Dr. Crapsey and Adelaide."[14] She now helped her father to bear up under the strain of the trial and the attendant publicity. In his 279-page autobiography, Dr. Crapsey mentions only one of his children, Adelaide, by name.[15] Almost ten years later, crushed and yet exasperated upon discovering that her parents have given up her teaching position at Smith without her knowledge, Crapsey, in a letter to Esther Lowenthal (7 April 1914) implies her sense of her father's and her mother's unworldliness (for all their social concern) and their general inability to cope with life's more practical aspects. Jean Webster expressed a similar feeling when she noted that Dr. and Mrs. Crapsey weren't the ideal parents for a large family. (See her letter of September 1913, p. 14.)

Dr. Crapsey's account of the unusual ecclesiastical trial indicates by implication some of the forces interested in achieving his downfall:

> . . . the court proceeded with the case; it offered in evidence my sermon, my book, "Religion and Politics," and it called as a witness

> my assistant, Mr. Alexander, who testified that on a given evening I had said that Jesus was born of middle-class parentage and that the doctrine of the later Church, which removed Him from the sphere of humanity by denying His natural birth, was the great disaster of Christendom. My counsel, Mr. Perkins, put this witness through a severe cross-examination, in which it was brought out that Mr. Alexander had applied to the vestry for the rectorship of St. Andrew's in case of my conviction.[16]

In December 1906 Dr. Crapsey was on his own request formally deposed from the ministry of the Episcopal Church, after he had unsuccessfully appealed his suspension by the ecclesiastical court. At the same difficult period, the Crapseys' eldest son, Philip, died at thirty-one of malaria contracted during his service in the Spanish-American War.

From 1906 to 1908 Adelaide Crapsey served as an instructor of literature and history at Miss Lowe's preparatory school in Stamford, Connecticut. Although she accompanied her father to the Hague Peace Conference and on a walking tour in Wales in the summer of 1907, the years at Stamford were ones of increasing physical difficulty. Apparently her problem had not yet been diagnosed as tuberculosis, but she found herself exhausted and often spent weekends in bed to recover from the effort of a week's teaching. The story of this struggle, which she spared her family, is told in a 1929 letter of reminiscences from her Stamford friend, Louise H. Merritt (now in the Rochester collection).

In January 1908 the Crapsey family moved into a new house at 678 Averill Avenue, Rochester, built for the lifetime use of Dr. and Mrs. Crapsey by William Rossiter Seward (1834–1926), Rochester banker and philanthropist. "The roomy home," says Blake McKelvey, "made a hospitable community center":

> A weekly Bible-study group met there. Mrs. Crapsey prepared meals for needy or sick families, sent out numerous baskets at Thanksgiving and Christmas and, with her daughter Adelaide, organized a sewing club to make dresses for poor children out of materials donated by interested friends. In addition, Dr. Crapsey organized a vacant lot gardening movement which secured the free use of numerous lots each summer and parceled them out to scores of needy families. This scheme, patterned after a similar one in Philadelphia, started in 1908 as a relief measure during a period of industrial layoffs, but continued into the good years that followed

> because of the community spirit it nurtured among those who participated. Dr. Crapsey's son Paul took over its direction in 1910 and maintained the program for three more summers.[17]

Failing health caused Adelaide Crapsey to give up teaching and in December 1908 she again returned to Europe, living in Rome, London, and Kent and spending short periods in Fiesole and Paris. In February and March 1909 she was in the Anglo-American hospital in Rome. Since she seldom dated her letters, and since the envelopes (and thus the postmarks) do not survive, the twelve letters to her family from Europe, written between 1909 and 1911, must be dated, if possible, from internal references such as her remarks on the funeral procession of Edward VII (16 May 1910) and by comparing their contents with the information given in Mrs. Crapsey's chronologically arranged extracts.

During her entire stay in Europe, Crapsey was in poor health, yet was trying to live as cheaply as possible. Lower living costs were one of her chief reasons for remaining in Europe. She later told Esther Lowenthal that she had lived on one pound a week in London. This struggle was the source of her characteristically humorous quatrain, "Expenses," dated "London, 1910," and a letter to her mother, probably written late in October 1909, from Herne Bay in Kent, gives details of her weeks in Paris:

> Dont you think my Parisian accounts [she often closes her letters with a detailed account of her expenditures] are most beautiful. I thought they would amuse you all. I had really a very nice little time there—and stayed a few days longer than I expected to. That was because everyones plans were changed because Louise Brigham, Mrs Draper's ni[e]ce came down with typhoid fever. She has been having it all the time . . . . Louise has been getting on as well as anyone with typhoid fever could—so it might all have been worse. Mrs. Draper has spent all her afternoons—at the hospital—in the mornings we kept out of doors. Took small boats up and down the Seine once or twice. Our lunches we got at small Latin Quarter restaurants—finally settling down at one special one where we had napkin rings and kept our napkins for a week, a saving of 2 cents a day. You'll see by the accounts that we were getting quite expert at keeping to the franc and even cutting under.
>
> The poor man who figures on the last was a poor soul walking up and down in front of the restaurant in a driving rain. We were trying

> to be strongminded about street begging but I weakened and gave him a franc—then Mrs Draper and Helen gave in and took a share each. As a matter of fact a penny or two to someone came to be almost a regular part of lunch—but as I usually had such small change with me the little boy with the violin and the blind woman who sang and the rest aren't on the list. Not that are [our] charities were large,—because we were all really and strictly economizing. I had to have my brown dress mended—new selves [sleeves] and yoke—now it will do for another winter. That was $6 material and making. But my one Parisian extravagance—was a pair of made to order corsets—or not really corsets—girdle things that really fit. We had the funniest time over them. We asked the woman if she could make them—she was doubtful—Oh yes she *could* make them but corsets, real corsets, were the proper the only thing to wear, she was eloquent on the subject of corsets. I began to feel as if my past had been a mistake—because I had spent it without corsets—as if my future would be a disaster if I didn't get some at once. However I stood firm—I hadn't, didn't, couldn't, wouldn't wear corsets. Well then she would make me something—something that would please me forever. Well then we got to work—we got rid of steels, we got buttons instead of hooks—we had the lacing loose—in fact we did everything that would strike a Parisian corsetmaker as mere madness,—and the result is excellent. You see she got quite interested in what she called my "miniatures",—and I wish you could have seen the final fitting, when she and her two assistants tried them on. They invented more enthusiastic descriptive terms for that one girdle in four minutes than I could think of in a lifetime for Alps or Cathedrals or Pictures or statues or heroic acts and great events. It really became a Parisian adventure and we were all much amused. Tell Mr Seward—you can tell him can't you even if it is about girdles—that they—I mean it/are/is/my most beloved possession. They didnt cost all of the 30 francs though—only 20 of them but that was quite mad enough. I am so glad to be at Herne bay where houses are $3.50 a week and there are no temptations.

Several letters close with "love to Mr. Seward" (the philanthropist who had provided the Averill Avenue house for the Crapseys), and a later letter to Mrs. Crapsey, dated 11 October 1910, seems to indicate direct financial assistance: "It was dear of Mr Seward. I was getting low and [a] little worried. The reason is that I have *had* to get some clothes. 'Donato

Pietrocupo' simply wont get me through another winter . . . . Much, more, most and heaps of love to you and Mr Seward. I'll write him soon. This is just to let you know that the money is here and how grateful I am. . . ."

In London Crapsey continued her work on the "application of phonetics to metrical problems." In May 1910 she found London weather still bad, "horrid—grey and cold and bleak—it congeals one" and work at the British Museum reading room tiring: "The B.M. is rather strenuous and I use the little library near here as much as I can. At least I am looking at the outsides of books that I ought to have known long ago." On 24 May 1910 she writes happily that she received a letter of encouragement from T. S. Omond, an English prosodist, who wanted her to publish some of her metrical studies in the *Modern Language Review.* Her British Museum reader's slips for April 1910 through February 1911 indicate a widely varied and yet intensive program of reading in poetry, metrics, phonetics, and aesthetics.

The letters from Europe are in one sense a disappointment. Adelaide Crapsey's sojourn in Bloomsbury seems to have left her unacquainted with any of her fellow poets, for the letters never give the slightest hint that she knew the work being done by her fellow Americans Ezra Pound and Hilda Doolittle or by the English members of the group later to be known under Pound's label as "Imagists." Poor health and her engrossing metrical analysis undoubtedly help to explain this isolation.

In February 1911 Crapsey returned to America and began work immediately as an instructor in poetics at Smith College. Among her colleagues and friends at Smith were Mary Delia Lewis of the English department and Esther Lowenthal, then an instructor in economics (now professor of economics and dean emeritus of Smith College). In a memoir of Adelaide Crapsey, Miss Lewis evokes the poet's gray-clad figure, her "indefatigable industry," "a fastidious taste which would admit no standard but perfection, and dominating all, an extraordinary intellectual grasp and power." Miss Lewis speaks also of Crapsey's "instinctive shrinking from any talk which savored of the petty or unkind, and her keen relish for a humorous situation in literature or in life," but her most interesting description concerns Crapsey's combination of sympathy and exquisite reserve, "her power of understanding, arising from her strong belief in the essential right of every individual, however intimate a friend, to unexplained acts and motives."[18]

Esther Lowenthal wrote on 1 May 1969 that Adelaide Crapsey "worked very hard at Smith both at her teaching and at the counting of syllables for the metrics," and Miss Lowenthal later said (in an interview on 8 October 1969) that the poet spent many, many hours in the English Seminar Room, an airless room in the Smith College Library. (Miss Lowenthal believes that Crapsey made some of the numerous copies of her poems in the English Seminar Room when she was exhausted by her work on the metrics.) Often overcome by fatigue, she went to the Smith College doctor, who, without examining her at all, diagnosed her problem as too much time spent indoors and prescribed fresh air. Adelaide Crapsey did as she was told, and Esther Lowenthal accompanied her on a daily walk up a rather steep hill in Northampton. Miss Lowenthal said also that Adelaide Crapsey "was always working very hard on the metrics [pronounced 'mētrics'], counting all the syllables in *Paradise Lost, Samson Agonistes,* the longer poems of Tennyson, [Francis] Thompson, Swinburne, and nursery rhymes."

Adelaide Crapsey seems to have been both an exacting and an inspiring teacher, striving to instill in her students her convictions about the importance of form. A former student, Louise Townsend Nicholl, recalled these impressions of her appearance in a review of the second edition of *Verse:*

> Thirteen years ago, when I was a freshman, I used to see Adelaide Crapsey, a little new English teacher, on the campus, a small figure in gray—gray shoes, gray dresses, gray capes, nothing but gray she wore—walking very softly and quickly. Her arms would be full of books; her smooth head, often hatless, always a little bent; her brown hair heavy on her neck; and her little soft gray shoes moving so quietly, so quickly, so lightly! I have never seen any feet but hers which were really like those mouselike ones about which Sir John Suckling wrote.[19]

Another former student testified to the "scholarly approach" that was her gift to her pupils: "her passion for accuracy, truth and beauty. She never let poetry be only feeling. It had form; it had technique. It, like music, from its very form achieved beauty. A rondel had meaning because of its very form, a ballad became alive like a person—it had its own body."[20]

Some time in the summer of 1911 Adelaide Crapsey visited a doctor and was told that she suffered from tuberculin meningitis, or tuberculosis of the brain lining. She did not tell her family of the diagnosis.

Jean Webster and Adelaide Crapsey, friends as undergraduates, remained close. Crapsey's mother (in a journal now partially excerpted in the Adelaide Crapsey papers) records that in September 1911 her daughter "went to Tyringham [Massachusetts] to visit Jean Webster." The cinquain entitled "Laurel in the Berkshires" in the 1915 edition has the title "Laurel in Tyringham" in the holograph copy. A letter written on 19 June 1913 from Jean Webster to her fiancé, Glenn Ford McKinney, echoes or anticipates the cinquain:

> Tyringham is in bloom—it is the loveliest thing you have ever seen—looking up from our veranda the Gilder pastures are pink—and near at hand, against the dark green of the pines, that mass of laurel is intoxicating.
>
> Smith Commencement is today. Doc. Taylor of Vassar receives a degree and Adelaide Crapsey was scheduled to hood him—but she waived the honor & came away early to join me. . . .

Adelaide Crapsey's Tyringham vacation soon ended; she collapsed on 8 July 1913. Her version of the collapse is given in a letter to Esther Lowenthal dated 17 July 1913, written from the Hillcrest Hospital in Pittsfield, Massachusetts:

> I finished the favorite literature [a playful term for her metrical studies] and sent it off on Saturday the 21st of June. I reckoned that it would take P.E.M [Paul Elmer More, editor of *The Nation*] about 3 weeks to get around to reading his surprise and settled back to rest during that time. It came back on Tuesday the 23d of June—but with (not to employ the method of suspense) a really very nice (if in spots funny) letter. The thing was too long for *The Nation* but I seem to have "hit on a very interesting point"—but the argument was hard to follow (E! that masterpiece of lucidity!) and "it would be a satisfaction to me personally if I could see your argument shorn of all secondary issues and presented in its barest skeleton." Being willing to oblige I sat me down—(after a day or two to get my breath)and ripped the favorite literature up the back and did a condensed version—sending it off to be typed on the 7th of July— I stayed in Tyringham to avoid the interrupting packing + unpacking. Of course in the meanwhile I had written Mr More saying that I would like very much to send the shorter paper—and getting in reply a nice little note with his vacation address—to send the thing to. On the 8th of July as I got out of my bath I leaned over quickly felt a remarkable pain and after a second found it more discrete [discreet] to drop full length on the bathroom floor than to stand up. After a while I got up grabbed a nightdress—and retired again to the floor. No not really fainting—just staving it off by lying flat you know. It was awfully funny. After a moment or two I got back to my room and went to bed and we got—or rather the others got hot water bags +

such and it really was a[w]fully funny—and nothing at all serious—Just one of those things you can do by a queer little twist—the fillament of a muscel or something broke.

She makes light of her "rest cure," but letters of her friend Jean Webster during the rest of the summer dramatize the swiftness with which all desire to "Climb the great pasture rocks/ And dream me mermaid in the sun's/ Gold flood" ends in a tragic certainty. Jean Webster writes to Glenn Ford McKinney on 8 July:

Wednesday
8.30 P.M.
Dear Glenn

Being alone, I'll write to you. I have just returned two hours ago from putting Adelaide in a hospital in Pittsfield! Nothing so serious as apendicitis—but the doctor thinks that three weeks flat on her back in a hospital will improve her—and I think so too. We put her in, at about six hours notice while she was still too dazed to object. I discovered a very nice private hospital in Pittsfield on very high ground (1500 feet up) and a splendid surgeon at the head. She has a very pleasant room with three windows and a very pretty smiling nurse. I am sorry Pittsfield is so ungetatable from here—the only way now, since the evening stage is off, is to motor. But I dare say her rest cure will work quite as well without too many callers—and I left her in a very contented frame of mind. I think at last—after 4 years of silly tonics and rest & fresh air [&] everything else that didn't work—we are going to cure her up!

On 30 July 1913 hope is still alive: "Adelaide is still incarcerated. She comes out in another week though and I hope will have two or three days here before going to Rochester. . . . " A letter written on 5 August strikes a grimmer note:

The Gilders have been most polite of late about putting their car at my disposal. Yesterday they took me to Pittsfield to see Adelaide—and tomorrow they are going to send the car over to bring her back. I didn't find her nearly so well as I had hoped—in fact I am sort of worried about her. She has a dreadful cough and hasn't slept for five nights. I am hoping that when I get her out in the sunshine she will get over it. Unfortunately she can only stay here 4 days. Her family want her in Rochester as soon as she can travel.

And the news of Jean Webster's 10 August letter to Glenn Ford McKinney is even worse.

> I have been having such a dreadfully worrying time over Adelaide. She has been awfully ill since she came back—simply coughed all night long; couldn't lie down a minute. And of course she got terribly tired from being awake. Nothing to do with her lungs I am pleased to say—two doctors have examined her. I have just got her off to Rochester where there is a throat specialist. I hope he will spot the trouble! It seems an awful pity—after working over her all summer—to have to return her worse than I got her. I promised her father on my word of honor that I'd send her back well. . . .

Finally, in an undated letter written from Tyringham in late August or early September, friends and family know the truth.

> Monday morning
> Dear Glenn
>
> I got back to Tyr. yesterday to find most distressing news about Adelaide— She has been examined by two throat & lung specialists and they both say that she has tuberculosis in rather an aggravated form. She has had it for 3 or 4 years in a lurking hard to diagnose way, but it has suddenly burst out into a well developed unmistakable case. She must give up at Smith and go to Saranak immediately for two years at least.
>
> There is a very good Sanitarium about a mile & a half out of the village where it isn't so depressing nor abnormally expensive. I am hoping to be able to get her in there but there's a big waiting list & it requires some pull. I have written to every one I know of who has any interest with the head doctors. I may have to take her up to Saranak myself & make sure that she is comfortably installed with all the queer things she needs for a winter in the open. Her family are not awfully efficient about putting things like that through and of course they are most dreadfully upset. She was just their last hope. All the rest of them more or less have had accidents or illnesses or operations & they are nervously worn-out with 12 years of that strain. Nine children are too many in a nervous family! There is always something awful just going to happen. . . .
>
> It seems to me simply criminal for this to have happened after all the doctors we have had. No one ever suggested Tuberculosis & I had her lungs examined twice in Pittsfield by 2 different men. . . .

Her disease was diagnosed as "well-established" tuberculosis, and she was forced to go for a year (September 1913 to August 1914) for treatment in a private nursing home at Saranac Lake, New York.

Thirty-two letters written by Adelaide Crapsey to Esther Lowenthal between July 1913 and May 1914 provide a rare opportunity to study a person always reticent and elusive, although never reclusive or withdrawn until her health had been seriously impaired. In these letters Crapsey displays resolute courage and humor despite "ghastly fatigue" and painful medical treatments, which included the unsuccessful attempts to collapse a lung described in her letter to Esther Lowenthal postmarked 4 February 1914:

> I had hoped to have the "notes" ready by this time but my mild prosodic fit was interrupted by the pneumo-thorax treatment. Yes its the treatment you speak of—the lung is collapsed—therefore gets an absolute rest—therefore heals more rapidly. It succeeds in 60% of the cases where its used. Well, we've tried it once— It was rather funny. 1st Much beating of rugs + general clearing of room. 2d—Me fresh from the tub and all scrubbed + clean— Miss Lucy in spick + span uniform—all this in honor of the "surgical" character of the event. 3d—Arrival of Dr Baldwin and Dr Price with gas + things. Most businesslike 4th Jamming of hollow [explanatory note in lower margin: 'Why I dont know whether its hollow or not anyway there is a needle to make a puncture and then the gas goes through—maybe just the hole in you'] needle through which the gas goes (or is supposed to go) into me— then ought to come 5th entrance of gas and collapse of lung but what as a matter of fact happened was—nothing! Dr Baldwin tried 3 places and struck each time in [an] adhesion (inner and outer lining or something stuck together) so that the gas wouldnt go in. They worked a little over an hour and by that time we were all tired so we gave it up and now we'll try again. It isn't awfuly bad you know though not what one would choose for a diversion. I had a hypodermic injection of morphine and atropine and Dr Baldwin used cocaine for each of the places. The only (slightly) trying thing was doing it all over again 3 times + still getting no where—and I admit that no one cares less for this sort of thing than I do. Somehow when a competent finger goes tapping along my side and a placid meditative voice says—"Now, Price, do you think we can get in here?"— and "in here" is between my own most precious ribs I do feel a bit of qualm. However everyone was very gay—my "pne[u]mo

> thorax party" it got called—and chatted most sociably—the patient occassionally lapsing into silence (after her usual fashion)— I report one nice retort— It was getting to be pretty clear that the 3d try was not going to be successful—and I heard Dr Price say gaily— "Well, you know, with one man we tried 57 times" and placidly Dr Baldwin's voice remarking—"Oh, Price is thinking of pickles"

In several letters she apologizes for her handwriting, explaining that she wears mittens because she has been instructed to sit outdoors in the winter sunshine. Medical theory at the time also encouraged sleigh rides in November and December, and she dutifully complied with the directions of her doctor. Little had been learned in the almost one hundred years since Dr. Clark advised the dying Keats to ride horseback in Rome.

Adelaide Crapsey often writes to Esther Lowenthal of her determination to continue work on "the favorite literature." When she was forbidden to continue with her metrical studies she turned to poetry, but she does not discuss the poetry in letters although she was apparently enclosing poems in letters to both Esther Lowenthal and Jean Webster or giving them copies when they came to visit. She refers to a poem only once in the entire group of letters. This poem is the grimly humorous "To My Left Lung" enclosed with a letter written between 16 February and 21 February 1914. She writes enthusiastically of *The Idiot* and Henry James, indulges in "3.75 worth of Willy Yeats," and looks forward to Wilfred Meynell's edition of Francis Thompson. Her judgment of contemporary English poetry is flavored with humorous self-awareness. She had received an English *Poetry Review* edited by Stephen Phillips and found its contents disappointing: "The Poetry Review like the others—thin and stodgy but a degree more provincial more amateurish—(whats happening to intellectual life in England!) Not much good for fav. Lit., I fear— You'll notice the delightful implication that my intellectual life is neither thin, stodgy, provincial nor amateurish!" (25 November 1913).

In an undated letter apparently from late in 1913 or early in 1914, Jean Webster writes to Glenn Ford McKinney from New York:

> Yesterday morning I mailed your tokimento to Adelaide—she has it by now. I told her last week that she was going to get a nice surprise within the next ten days, and a few days ago I casually mailed a new variety of French soap. It is my custom to pepper her with small offerings so that she will always have an abundance of mail to open. This morning comes a letter thanking me for the nice surprise. She admires its pleasant smell and likes its lathering

> qualities. She *will* have a nice surprise when Today's mail comes! It was sweet of you to do it. *Grazie tanto.* . . .

Although still unwilling to admit the serious nature of her illness—"*if* its chronic tuberculosis" (21 April 1914)—Crapsey was forced to recognize that she would not be able to return to teaching and resolved to find a sanitarium "less expensive more livable and less arctic" (21 April 1914). She had friends and family investigating alternatives to Saranac Lake. In an undated letter to Glenn Ford McKinney from Tyringham in late August 1914 Jean Webster writes:

> The more I think of a house for Adelaide the more dubious I become. Pipes might freeze—roof might leak—walks need shovelling[—]butcher forget meat—all very trying to a sick person. Adelaide leaves Saranac Saturday for a week or so in Rochester before moving on to a new place. I've just written to Dr. J. Alexander Miller in New York to see if he won't be able to suggest a place where he could take charge of the case. He has a wide variety of non-charity patients and he must know some nice places for them to live. . . .

After the poet's return to Rochester, she grew suddenly worse. (A long train ride in very hot August weather must have been ill-advised.) On 19 September 1914, ten days after her thirty-sixth birthday, she wrote to Jean Webster that her brother was investigating another possible sanitarium; on 8 October she died of chronic pulmonary tuberculosis.

Mrs. Arthur H. Crapsey, Sr., the widow of the poet's youngest brother, Arthur H. Crapsey (1896–1955), was one of Adelaide Crapsey's nurses for the final ten days of her life. As the night nurse she often held the tiny Adelaide over her shoulder as if she were a child, so difficult was it for her to breathe. Mrs. Crapsey's short acquaintance with Adelaide made a lasting impression. She remembers Adelaide as having had great consideration for the feelings of others, sick as she was. Indeed, Mrs. Crapsey felt that Adelaide was perhaps "the most considerate person she had ever known."[21] She remembers Esther Lowenthal, Jean Webster, and Claude Bragdon among the visitors in these final weeks.

Jean Webster left the beginning of the Broadway run of her play, *Daddy Long-Legs,* to come to Rochester and her friend's bedside. After her last visit she wrote from the Hotel Seneca to her fiancé. (The letter was postmarked in Rochester at 2 A.M. on 8 October, the day of the poet's death.)

8 P.M. Wednesday

Dear Glenn

Adelaide is terribly weak. I doubt if she can live through the night—and the most horrible thing is that I don't want her to. She hasn't slept for four nights. She isn't able to lie down, but sits huddled in the nurse's arms gasping for breath. She is wasted away till she is just like a little child. It's the most pitiful thing I have ever seen. She recognized me and talked a little in whispers. I staid all day at the house and went in and sat with her three times when she asked for me. There isn't anything to do to help. They have four nurses, and two doctors but no one can help her. If they gave her enough morphine to relieve the pain, it would kill her. Her pulse was very weak at seven when I left the house. I didn't wait any longer because I couldn't see her again tonight anyway. Poor Mrs. Crapsey is worn out with nervous strain. All of the children have been called home—and there they sit listening to her moaning and waiting for her to die. It is the most ghastly thing I have ever seen!

I didn't mean to write such a dreadfully depressing letter—I just meant to talk with you a little while before going to bed and get poor Adelaide out of my mind— But you see!

I meant to go to the theatre tonight and take your Father back to the star's dressing room and give him a real sensation!

Good night my dear
Yours always
Jean

A two-line poem by Crapsey entitled "On Seeing Weather-Beaten Trees" asks "Is it as plainly in our living shown,/ By slant and twist, which way the wind hath blown?" For the poet herself the answer is, "No." Family and friends watched a hard-working yet fun-loving young woman stricken by disease, but could only guess at her inner struggle. The reticence and firm control characteristic of her finest poetry marked her own conduct. The "moment of exasperation" that provoked her to cry out "I'll not be patient! I will not lie still!" in the poem "To The Dead In The Grave-Yard Under My Window" was rare, and even this poetic cry of anguish was revealed to her parents only after her death. Self-control, great consideration for others, and her belief in "the right of every individual . . . to unexplained acts and motives" explain something of the slant and twist of Adelaide Crapsey. This very strength of character, however, ensures that biographical facts can provide only hints of the inner life. The reader can only guess at the struggle of a strong character fighting bravely and even humorously what she herself knew to be a losing battle, anticipating the "grim casual comment on rebellion's end," and avoiding the indulgence of self-pity by exercising immense self-control.

Although hardly the breezy juvenile heroine of a Jean Webster story, Crapsey kept her vigorous sense of humor to the end of a long illness. The deaths of two sisters and a brother, her own ill-health, and the prospect of an early death provoked acute poetic probings, not withdrawal from life, morbidity, or self-pity. Her absences from society resulted from her efforts to conserve her physical strength and her determination to continue her work on the study of English metrics. Though a good many of her poems must have followed the unwilling suspension of her metrical studies at Saranac Lake, she had long been experimenting with poetic forms.

Adelaide Crapsey is buried in the Crapsey family plot in Mount Hope Cemetery, Rochester, her ashes in an urn given by her college classmates. John Rothwell Slater (1872–1965), former chairman of the University of Rochester's Department of English, wrote these "lines for Adelaide Crapsey's grave in Mount Hope":

Here she rests
  Who never rested,
Waits for time
  That never came.
Here she speaks
  For all the silent;

Hers the ashes,
  Theirs the flame.
Here lies beauty
  Still untold.
Here the young
  Never grows old.[22]

Neither Crapsey's story nor that of her poetry would be complete without noting that she wasn't allowed to "rest" immediately. In a city that had given birth to America's native variety of "spirits" and boasted a monument to the Fox sisters, rappings began again. The first edition of Crapsey's poems, entitled *Verse,* was published by the Manas Press in Rochester in 1915. The publisher, Claude Fayette Bragdon (1866–1946), had been Crapsey's friend. She is said to have kept house for Bragdon, then between wives, and her brother Paul while the rest of the family were away for the summer of 1911. An architect and later a noted stage designer, Bragdon wrote and published on a wide variety of subjects throughout his long life: his last book, *Yoga for You,* was published in 1943. Chiefly because of his interest in the occult, Bragdon had established the Manas Press in 1911, and it published books and pamphlets on theosophy by Bragdon and others.

Claude Bragdon's later accounts of the first edition of *Verse* picture a most unusual author-editor-publisher relationship. Bragdon regularly described his second wife, Eugénie, as a "Delphic Woman," in constant communication with the spirit world and, accordingly, in his autobiography, *More Lives Than One,* he gives the following account of the circumstances that eventually resulted in the publication of *Verse:* "One morning in the summer of 1915 I was awakened by my wife Eugénie, who asked me if I knew anyone by the name of Adelaide. I told her that Mrs. Algernon Crapsey's name was Adelaide, and it had also been that of her daughter, who had died a short time before. 'Take me to see Mrs. Crapsey,' said Eugénie, 'because I was awakened by the sound of her name, repeated over and over: Adelaide! Adelaide!' "[23] Bragdon's home at this time was 3 Castle Park, across Mt. Hope Avenue from the cemetery in which Adelaide Crapsey was buried, and geographical contiguity may have increased his willingness to believe in messages from another world. Many examples of Eugénie Bragdon's automatic writings, concerning *Verse* and domestic matters such as the education of her stepsons, are now among the Bragdon Papers at the University of Rochester Library. Among these messages in Eugénie's automatic writing, "in the first person singular, as though from Adelaide herself," says Bragdon,[24] are the following uncharacteristic effusions:

> Know that I am grateful. It is full of terror that I came, but I am glad I doffed the body. Life has been so full here, and I have known things impossible to the flesh. I am going now.
>
> Great grief purifies and the terror of coming brought us together. It is not remorse, but love for her and for him [her parents]. My father needs faith.

None of the automatic writings concerns the practical problems of printing or publication, although a final message from the "oracle" offered this comment when the book was almost ready for publication:

> It is well, I am pleased, accept my gratitude. You have done me a

great service; I thank you from the country of the free in thought; so good bye, Adelaide Crapsey.

Whatever one makes of Eugénie's spirit messages, some of Bragdon's other statements certainly agree with the evidence offered by the author's holographs and lists of poems. In his foreword to the 1915 edition he says that "this collection of her verse is of her own choosing, arranged and prepared by her own hand."

There are, however, some discrepancies between Claude Bragdon's statements in 1915 and 1938 and another account, published in *Merely Players*: "Adelaide Crapsey was my friend. It was my privilege to edit, introduce and publish her poems, the existence of which were [*sic*] not known until after her death. . . . Shortly after all this [Eugénie's communications with her "oracle"] happened [between 18 and 20 July 1915] Doctor and Mrs. Crapsey came to me for advice about the publication of Adelaide's verse, which had been found, carefully prepared and arranged, among her effects. They had submitted it to one or two publishers without success."[25] His account in *More Lives Than One* differs: "So we called on the Crapseys, and in the course of the conversation it developed that after their daughter's death they had found a sheaf of poems left by her with the request that they be printed. Not having succeeded in finding anyone who would undertake their publication, Doctor Crapsey asked me if I would read the manuscript and advise him how to proceed."[26] Although Bragdon's statements do not agree about who went where, they insist firmly that a group of poems was prepared by the author for publication.

Adelaide Crapsey, who did not herself believe in an afterlife, would have been amused by Bragdon's accounts. Writing to Esther Lowenthal from Saranac Lake in November 1913, she had smiled and recalled his good intentions when he bombarded her with his own writings on the occult: "Letter from Claude Bragdon and book—wait till I've opened them—another Man the Cube [her title for his pamphlet on the fourth dimension]? Next door to it *A Primer of Higher Space* 'hot from the press.' "

Esther Lowenthal offers a more prosaic picture of the relationship between the author and her prospective publisher. In an interview on 8 October 1969 she said that Adelaide Crapsey had shown her the poems when Esther Lowenthal visited Saranac Lake about 10 February 1914. Esther Lowenthal had taken charge of having the poems typed by the same person who had been typing the metrical studies. Adelaide Crapsey, said Miss Lowenthal, "had arranged the poems as she wanted them to be printed. She seemed to assume that Claude Bragdon would print them." Miss Lowenthal was not certain whether Adelaide Crapsey had corresponded with Claude Bragdon or spoken to him about printing the poems before her death.

Whatever Claude Bragdon's sources of inspiration and information, he proved a faithful editor, reproducing the poet's unusual punctuation, and having the binding and the geometrically patterned endpapers, which he drew himself, executed in the poet's favorite gray.

Previous Criticism of the Poems

Criticism of Crapsey's poetry suffers from the fondness some admirers have for examining the poems as "human documents," which substitutes inaccurate and sentimental thoughts about her life for any consideration of her work. These critics have been influenced by the well-meant but florid prose of Claude Bragdon's foreword to the first edition: "The keen and shining blade of her spirit too greatly scorned its scabbard the body, and for this she paid the uttermost penalty."[1] The disposition to cluck over a poet too soon cut off pervades Harriet Monroe's effusions on Crapsey as one of the "song-impassioned women of this century":

> Adelaide Crapsey, dying at thirty-five in 1914 used her art like a sword to defend herself bitterly against the threatening enemy. Frail and aloof, she wrote of the fullness and glory of life, of *Birth Moment* and *The Mother Exultant.* From her deathbed she uttered, to "the dead in the graveyard" under her window, a fierce protest against their thwarted lives. . . . And so, "mistily radiant," she was led off by the conqueror—but not to utter silence and darkness, for the shadowed fire of her spirit burns on with singular intensity in her small book of tragic but exultant song.[2]

Harriet Monroe's associate editor, Alice Corbin Henderson, writes a more sensible, if rambling and inaccurate, review for *Poetry,* saying truthfully that it was "hard to separate Adelaide Crapsey's poems from the circumstances of her death, as recorded in the brief preface by a friend."[3] Mrs. Henderson had moved to New Mexico in 1916 as part of her treatment for tuberculosis, and her review was prompted by some letters from her fellow Chicago poet, Carl Sandburg: "From Adelaide Crapsey's book I get much of the repression, the reticences, and the quivering color points of your work. Have you seen the book?"[4] "Your New Mexico songs are hauntingly beautiful. Your groups in back numbers of Poetry have for me the same irreducible glimmer that there is to Adelaide Crapsey's work and when you cash in if I don't write a better obituary for you than I did for Adelaide I'm guessing wrong."[5] Sandburg's disappointing lyric tribute, entitled "Adelaide Crapsey," included in the "Persons Half Known" section of *Cornhuskers,* endows the poet with "a mouth of blue pansy,"[6] but his sense of reticences and repression seems right.

An interesting appreciation of the first edition of *Verse,* with only a glancing reference to the poet's early death, survives in a letter from John Livingston Lowes to an unidentified Mr. Abbott, dated 24 October 1919 (now among the Rochester papers): "I think it is one of the most poignantly beautiful things that I have seen for many a day. It makes me think of what Pater says somewhere of the blending of the *askesis* of stone with evanescent flowering and fading of a rose. The 'Cinquains' are as austere as marble in their restraint and as vibrant as a tense lute string."

Many misunderstandings about Crapsey and her work have originated with the widely read anthologies and criticism of Louis Untermeyer. For fifty years (1919–1969) he published inaccurate information on her places of birth and death and gave wide circulation to a distorted definition of the cinquain as a strictly syllabic form, a notion that the cinquain was somehow based on Japanese verse forms, and the idea of Crapsey as an "unconscious imagist."[7] Untermeyer and his fellow-anthologist Burton E. Stevenson (editor of the often reprinted *Home Book of Verse)* may be the compilers Yvor Winters has in mind when, with characteristic tartness, he blames Crapsey's obscurity on anthologists "who have an infallible taste for the weakest work of any poet they consider."[8]

Misconceptions about what the cinquain is and about how the form Crapsey invented relates to Japanese verse forms have long prevailed. The standard definition of the cinquain, as old as Untermeyer's first essay and perhaps older, and repeated again in the *Encyclopedia of Poetry and Poetics* in 1965, is merely a description: "a precise five-line stanza . . . employing lines of, respectively, 2, 4, 6, 8, and 2 syllables."[9] Although adequate as a description, because Crapsey almost always uses a dissyllabic foot, it does nothing to elucidate the principle of the form. The cinquain is not strictly syllabic; its structural principle is its pattern of stresses. Louise Townsend Nicholl in 1923 accurately defined the five-line form as "one-stress, two-stress, three-stress, four-stress, and then caught back suddenly again to one-stress."[10] Sister M. Edwardine O'Connor also made this clear in 1930: "Her [Crapsey's] own stanza is built on stresses, one for the first line, two for the second, three for the third, four for the fourth, with a drop back to one for the fifth line. In the poet's opinion this made the most condensed metrical form in English that would hold together as a complete unit."[11] Such explanations of the cinquain's form have failed, however, to gain attention, and the superficial syllabic description persists. A Scottish poet, William Soutar

(1898–1943), wrote almost one hundred poems in what he believed to be this form, always confining himself to the strictly syllabic construction.[12]

The relation of the cinquain to Japanese forms, especially to the tanka, a five-line poem of thirty-one syllables, grouped in lines of 5, 7, 5, 7, 7, has long been disputed. Louis Untermeyer early stated and long repeated (in successive editions of his *Modern American Poetry*) that the cinquain had been influenced by Japanese forms. Mary Elizabeth Osborn reports the declaration of Crapsey's friends (Esther Lowenthal and Mary Delia Lewis) "that the cinquain is an independent form, and that any talk of Oriental influences is pure myth."[13] Sister M. Edwardine O'Connor states flatly: "This verse form grew out of a deliberate effort on her part to find the shortest form of English verse. At the time she evolved this form she knew little or nothing of the Japanese *tanka* which many consider to have been her inspiration."[14]

Investigating Crapsey's library on a visit to Rochester, Mary Elizabeth Osborn found a copy of William N. Porter's 1909 translation of the *Hyaku-nin-isshiu* or "Single Verses by a Hundred People," a collection of tanka made in 1235 by Sadaiye Fujiwara. She concluded that these translations might have suggested the form of the cinquain.[15] Earl Miner says that Mary Elizabeth Osborn is "no doubt right" in believing that Crapsey was inspired to write the five-line cinquain by her reading of Porter's translations.[16] Examination of Porter's versions makes it obvious, however, that they could have inspired a poet only with a desire to do better. In his attempt to retain some resemblance to the original form, he uses a five-line stanza with the second, fourth, and fifth lines rhyming, and produces an awkward jingle whose only resemblance to the unrhymed cinquain is its five lines:

> All through the never-ending night
> I lie awake and think;
> In vain I look to try and see
> The daybreak's feeble blink
> Peep through the shutter's chink.[17]

The first valid link between Crapsey and Japanese verse was established by Hideo Kawanami after examination of manuscripts in the Adelaide Crapsey Papers.[18] Three holograph leaves of French and English poems, which had been placed among Crapsey's own poems, prove to be her copies of poems found in Michel Revon's *Anthologie de la Littérature Japonaise des Origines au XXe Siècle* and in *From the Eastern Sea,* a book of original verse and translations from the Japanese by Yone Noguchi. The majority of Noguchi's poetic translations do not seem successful as poems in English; however Crapsey copied down his translation of a poem by Basho:

I have cast the world
   And think me as nothing,
Yet I feel cold at snow-falling day,
And happy on flower-day.[19]

She copies Revon's translations of eleven tanka and eight haiku, including the tanka "Comment ai-je pu penser / Que la rosée"[20] which becomes the cinquain "Why have / I thought the dew." She copies another tanka translated by Revon from the ninth-century poet Korenori:

Au point du jour,
Paraissant aux yeux presque
Comme la lune de l'aube,
La neige blanche tombe
Sur la village de Yoshino.[21]

On another leaf Crapsey gives her own translation of the tanka:

At daybreak,
Seeming to my eyes almost
Like the moon of dawn,
The white snow falls
On the village of Yoshino.

Much of the value of Revon's work lies in the excellent explanatory notes and historical surveys accompanying his translations. His note on the tanka by Korenori, for example, explains much that would otherwise be lost in the translation from one culture to another: "Yoshino est un village des montagnes dont les poètes chantent surtout les cerisiers; en nous le montrant enveloppé dans un brouillard lumineux de neige tombante, Korénori nous donne une note plus originale; c'est une impression fugitive très délicatement fixée."[22] The Japanese original thus implies a fusion of images reversing Housman's "cherry hung with snow," but this richness is lost if translation provides no explanation of the village's fame.

In his note on the famous haiku by Moritake (1473–1549), which Crapsey also copies into her notes, Revon again provides information necessary to the Western reader's complete comprehension of the conceit:

> Une fleur tombée, à sa branche
> Comme je la vois revenir:
> C'est un papillon!
>
> Un proverbe japonais dit que "la fleur tombée ne revient pas à sa branche"; le poète a eu, un instant, l'illusion contraire.[23]

(Ezra Pound translates this famous haiku: "The fallen blossom flies back to its branch:/ A butterfly."[24])

Dr. Kawanami seems to have discovered the true source of the Japanese influence on Crapsey's poetry. Crapsey's notes on Revon provide a more valid indication of her indebtedness to Japanese literature than her supposed familiarity with and admiration for Porter's anthology. Miner says of the cinquain "Anguish":

> Keep thou
> Thy tearless watch
> All night but when blue-dawn
> Breathes on the silver moon, then weep!
> Then weep!

that it "echoes Porter's translation of a poem by Mibu no Tadamine":

> I hate the cold unfriendly moon
> That shines at early morn
> And nothing seems so sad and gray
> When I am left forlorn
> At day's returning dawn.[25]

Crapsey seems to echo even more closely the tanka by Satô Yoshikiyo (Le Bonze Saïghyô) found in her manuscript notes on Revon:

> Tandis que je pense
> A des choses tristes, est-ce la lune
> Qui m'a dit: "Pleure!"
> Sur mon visage inquiet,
> Hélas! mes larmes![26]

Revon adds this explanatory note to his translation: "Le clair de lune, considéré comme éveillant les vieux souvenirs, s'associe par là même aux émotions tristes."[27]

Miner also suggests a comparison between the cinquain "Trapped" and Chamberlain's translation of Issa's famous haiku "A Dew Drop World":

Well and
If day on day
Follows, and weary year
On year . . and ever days and years . .
Well?

Granted this dewdrop world is but
A dewdrop world—this granted, yet. . . .[28]

Keene translates the same haiku and supplies some of the explanations so necessary for a Western reader: "Certainly no modern poet has managed to suggest more with so few words than did Issa (1763–1828) after the death of his only surviving child. We may imagine that his friends attempted to console him with the usual remarks on the evanescence of this existence as compared to the eternal life in Buddha's Western Paradise. Issa wrote:

The world of dew
Is a world of dew and yet,
And yet."[29]

This haiku, however, is not among Revon's translations from Issa, and Crapsey's "Trapped" seems to owe more to Revon's translation of a haiku by Bouçon she copies into her notes:

Ah, le passé!
Le temps où se sont accumulés
Les jours lents![30]

A related critical problem concerns the designation of Crapsey's poetry as "imagist" and the question of her relation, if any, to the Imagist movement. Louis Untermeyer early calls her an "unconscious Imagist," and the label is often applied tentatively, for want of a better. Four cinquains appear in William Pratt's excellent short anthology, *The Imagist Poem*.[31] Babette Deutsch recognizes the confusion associated with the term "imagism," but links her with the movement: "a number of poets of widely different backgrounds, who made no special plea for it, were illustrating the principles of imagism. Among these was Adelaide Crapsey, inventing a form as strict as the haiku: a five-line poem of twenty-two syllables."[32] Given the continuing debate about the nature of the Imagist movement, its members, and their ideas, it seems wisest to avoid the too-easy adoption of this label. Winters's "loose but usable" classification of Crapsey as a member of the "Experimental Generation" with

Pound, Stevens, Williams, Eliot, H. D., and others, sidesteps many a squabble.[33]

Winters praises Crapsey as a "minor poet of great distinction" who "achieves more effectively than did most of the Imagists the aims of Imagism."[34] In *The Anatomy of Nonsense,* Winters rebukes historians of American literature for their failure to mention Crapsey, "who died in 1914, who antedates many of the writers discussed, who is certainly an immortal poet, and who has long been one of the most famous poets of our century."[35] All of Winters's scolding and earnest advocacy could not make such wishful assertions as this last come true: "Fame is no plant that grows on mortal soil." Although six of her poems are included in the 1969 Winters-Field anthology, *Quest for Reality,*[36] recent criticism of Crapsey—by Dr. Kawanami in Japan and by several contributors to a special number of the international review ADAM—has been too little and too widely scattered to gain her poetry many new readers.[37]

Toward a Critical Revaluation

Crapsey's newly discovered poems or forms of poems, her letters, and more facts about her life should aid in critical revaluation of her work. What is her distinctive tone; what images and gestures recur? Can we guess at the psychological impulses of her "slant and twist"? Crapsey's poems also show some of the ways in which her seemingly isolated poetic development relates to several aspects of the work of her contemporaries and to Japanese poetry. The biographical and textual materials for this edition, hitherto unused or unknown, correct some inaccurate impressions about the relation of Crapsey's art to her life and reveal something of her artistic process.

While this understanding of the true nature and extent of Crapsey's poetic career provides little new evidence that she knew or was directly influenced by any of her contemporaries, it enables us to place her strangely parallel development along some lines and her sensitivity to contemporary movements in proper perspective. Long interested in and writing poetry—the poems here may have been as much as twenty years apart in composition—she had devoted many hours to the study of metrics and to teaching poetry at the secondary and college levels. In an era of poetic circles and groups, she seems to have been aware of her position as an outsider. She copies a passage from the letters of Keats onto the left back endpaper of her Everyman edition of Keats's poems (London: J. M. Dent, 1906), that seems to indicate her interest in and sympathy for the idea of poetic development in isolation:

> And also when I feel I am right, no external praise can give me such a glow as my own solitary *re*perception and ratification of what is fine—I will write independently, I have written independently *without judgement* (Sic) [the 'Sic' is Crapsey's], I may write independently and *with judgment* hereafter. The genius of poetry must work out its own salvation in a man. It cannot be matured by law and precept, but by sensation and *watchfulness in itself.*

Crapsey was receptive to, if amused by, the experiments of her contemporaries. In one of her final letters to Esther Lowenthal, postmarked 16 May 1914, she encloses a typically strident advertisement for "*BLAST*, A NEW ILLUSTRATED QUARTERLY. EDITED BY WYNDHAM LEWIS" "TO BE READY ON THURSDAY, JUNE 18th":

THE MANIFESTO OF THE VORTICISTS. THE ENGLISH PARALLEL MOVEMENT TO CUBISM AND EXPRESSIONISM. IMAGISM IN POETRY. DEATH BLOW TO IMPRESSIONISM AND FUTURISM AND ALL THE REFUSE OF NAIF SCIENCE. WITH ARTISTIC (TWENTY) AND LITERARY CONTRIBUTIONS BY LAURENCE ATKINSON, GAUDIER-BRZESKA, JACOB EPSTEIN, FREDERICK ETCHELLS, CUTHBERT HAMILTON, FORD MADDOX HUEFFER, EZRA POUND, WILLIAM ROBERTS, EDWARD WADSWORTH, REBECCA WEST, WYNDHAM LEWIS.

THE SPIRIT AND PURPOSE OF THE ARTS AND LITERATURE OF TO-DAY EXPRESSED IN *BLAST.* NO PERIODICAL SINCE *THE FAMOUS YELLOW BOOK* HAS SO COMPREHENDED THE ARTISTIC MOVEMENT OF ITS DECADE. THE ARTISTIC SPIRIT OF THE EIGHTEEN-NINETIES WAS THE *YELLOW BOOK*, THE ARTISTIC SPIRIT OF TO-DAY IS *BLAST.*

At the bottom of the cutting, Crapsey writes, "Rather delightful, dont you think so—We must have it! I'll order it & have it for your entertainment." Crapsey found the squabbles of the literary and artistic cliques, in this heyday of movements and manifestoes, as amusing as the academic feuds and conspiracies of the Smith faculty described for her by Esther Lowenthal. Although too sick to know anything of Pound's later pronouncements,[1] Crapsey would probably have regarded his "Don't's" and "Do's" with the same kindly humor. The quotation from Keats suggests that she would have regarded these laws and precepts for poetry with the tolerance she accorded Bragdon's earnest communications on the fourth dimension, higher space, and theosophy.

Though her knowledge of the Imagists and their movement was limited and indirect—T. E. Hulme prowled periodically through the British Museum, but was not in search of American schoolteachers—Crapsey follows, by accident or intent, many of Pound's "tenets of the Imagiste faith" and his "forty cautions to beginners."[2] In poems such as "Amaze," "Roma Aeterna," and "Snow" she achieves what Pound would call "direct" presentation of "an intellectual and emotional complex in an instant of time."[3]

Crapsey shared with the Imagists, of course, an interest in Japanese poetry. She probably made her notes on Michel Revon and Yone Noguchi before Pound began his work on the manuscripts of Ernest Fenollosa in 1912. Her encounter with the Japanese tradition seems to have resulted in the development of something very much like Pound's idea of "super-position."[4] The Japanese influence upon Crapsey is a fundamental one of perception and expression, involving the juxtaposition of images rather than the superficial ornamental trappings present in many poets since the nineties. Revon's sensitive translations, with their careful explanations of the multiple meanings present for the Japanese reader, had probably led the way to this consciousness of converging ideas or images. Her own love of "a few fine things" and avoidance of any excess may have attracted her to the Japanese suggestion of the large in the small, as the tiny Japanese sand garden suggests the immense sweep of land and sea.

Although the source of the Japanese influence upon Crapsey now seems firmly identified in Revon's excellent, "authoritative" translations in his 1910 *Anthologie de la Littérature Japonaise*, the effect of this influence on her poetry is still far from clear. As Donald Keene points out, many Western poets, enthusiastic imitators of Japanese forms, have written what they called haiku without understanding the essence of the "seventeen-syllable nature poem":

> The *haiku*, for all its extreme brevity, must contain two elements, usually divided by a break marked by what the Japanese call a "cutting word" *(kireji)*. One of the elements may be the general condition—the end of autumn, the stillness of the temple grounds, the darkening sea—and the other the momentary perception. The nature of the elements varies, but there should be the two electric poles between which the spark [the sudden perception of a truth which leads to enlightenment] will leap for the *haiku* to be effective. Otherwise it is no more than a brief statement. That is the point which has been missed by such Western imitators of the *haiku* form as Amy Lowell, who saw in the *haiku* its brevity and suggestion, but did not understand the methods by which the effects were achieved.[5]

Pound was one of the few Western poets to grasp this idea of "superposition" or "one idea set on top of another."[6]

Did Crapsey have any such grasp of the essential haiku technique, and did the superposition of images become an essential part of her poetry? In the absence of any statement or explanation from the author, the only answers must come from her manuscript notes and from her poems. Crapsey's notes on Revon's translations show that she was interested in other Japanese verse forms besides the epigrammatic haiku: she copies seven haiku and seven tanka, and one of the tanka is the closing stanza of a long poem by the eighth-century poet Okura, entitled "La Misère":

Bien qu'on pense
Que ce monde

Est mauvais et détestable,
On ne peut s'envoler,
N'étant pas oiseau, hélas![7]

The longer tanka has the same "break" or jump between ideas so important in the haiku. Examination of the cinquains seems to show that some indeed involve a superposition of ideas or intersection between the eternal and the momentary, the motionless and the moving. These cinquains include those entitled "Niagara," "Amaze," "Roma Aeterna," "Snow," "Saying of Il Haboul," and "Blue Hyacinths."

The cinquain "Roma Aeterna" contrasts the evanescent perceptions of the moment—the warmth of sunlight and the sound of birdsongs—with the timeless, changeless presence of Rome's site and its mythical founder:

The sun
Is warm to-day,
O Romulus, and on
Thine olden Palatine the birds
Still sing.

The cinquain entitled "Blue Hyacinths" summons up another contrast between the transitory and the permanent:

In your
Curled petals what ghosts
Of blue headlands and seas,
What perfumed immortal breath sighing
Of Greece.

In this cinquain visual and olfactory images work toward the same end as the aural and kinesthetic images of "Roma Aeterna": the color and scent of the living flowers is linked in imagery to the permanence of seas, headlands, and the idea of all that is Greek.

Although they employ different worlds as the settings and stuff of their transcience and permanence, such cinquains as "Roma Aeterna" and "Blue Hyacinths" could hardly be closer in structure and spirit to a famous haiku of Bashō (1644–94) as it is explained by Keene:

> For Bashō both change and permanence had to be present in his *haiku*. In some of his greatest poems we find these elements present, not only in the sense just given but also, if we may state the terms geometrically, as an expression of the point where the momentary

> intersects the constant and eternal. We find it, for example, in what was perhaps his most famous *haiku:*
>
> The ancient pond
> A frog leaps in
> The sound of the water.
>
> In the first line, Bashō gives us the eternal component of the poem, the timeless, motionless waters of the pond. The next line gives us the momentary, personified by the movement of the frog. Their intersection is the splash of water. Formally interpreted, the eternal component is the perception of truth, the subject of countless Japanese poems; the fresh contribution of Bashō is the use of the frog for its movement, instead of its pleasing cries, the hackneyed poetical image of his predecessors.[8]

In subject and structure, rather than in numbers of syllables or lines, consists the true identity between the cinquain and such Japanese forms as the tanka and haiku.

Another cinquain has for its theme change and changelessness, yet serves to illustrate the great variety possible within what some would consider a limited range of subject:

Saying of Il Haboul

Guardian Of The Treasure Of Solomon
And Keeper Of The Prophet's Armour

My tent
A vapour that
The wind dispels and but
As dust before the wind am I
Myself.

Although the form of a poem in English does not allow for a break or cut at any one word, the same juxtaposition or superposition forms the poem's heart: the vulnerability and impermanence of the speaker and his tent (body) are set against the eternal force of the wind and the dust whirled before it. The title of the cinquain adds a further ironic contrast: the evanescent speaker, only a little more permanent than his flimsy dwelling, announces himself as a symbol of security, an officially recognized bulwark protecting the precious and perishable against change, "Guardian Of The Treasure Of Solomon / And Keeper Of The Prophet's Armour."

In these cinquains, an underlying psychological tension seems to contribute to a "break" or "jump" even sharper than that of the haiku or tanka. Crapsey considers the contrast of change and permanence, the momentary and the eternal, not in detached disinterest, but from a hospital bed that did indeed, at Saranac Lake, look out upon a graveyard. Her body changes, wastes, and dies—a "vapour" and "as dust before the wind." Birdsongs or the perfumes of flowers—her memories or evocations of Rome or Greece—will cease when she ceases. Compressing and repressing the tensions of her awareness into the cinquains gives them much of their force.

An even more restrained and subtle variation on the theme of change and permanence sparks the perception of truth in the cinquain "Snow":

> Look up. . .
> From bleakening hills
> Blows down the light, first breath
> Of wintry wind. . .look up, and scent
> The snow!

Here, one term in the equation of time and timelessness is hardly mentioned: the unchanging hills are caught as they appear to change, "bleakening" in the changing light of a shortening day. The preponderance of the words of change—"blows," "breath," "wind," and "scent"—gives to airy nothing an incongruous force, and this uncanny power is heightened by the acute perception that responds to the scent of imminent snow, capturing the sensations of an entire season in a single sharp detail. Such suggestiveness linked with brevity is also highly characteristic of Japanese literature: "What Japanese poets have most often sought is to create with a few words, usually with a few sharp images, the outline of a work whose details must be supplied by the reader, as in a Japanese painting a few strokes of the brush must suggest a whole world."[9] Another instance of an acutely perceived natural detail whose tiny truth suggests an immensity may be observed in "November Night":

> Listen. .
> With faint dry sound,
> Like steps of passing ghosts,
> The leaves, frost-crisp'd, break from the trees
> And fall.

The almost imperceptible sound of the many leaves being detached and drifting downward (not the more often noted sound of their landing) reinforced by the onomatopoeia of repeated sibilants, suggests the innumerable changes, the innumerable tiny deaths that make up the great changelessness and life of the seasonal cycle.

"Look up . . ." and "Listen . . .": these imperatives command or announce expectancy or waiting, an attitude or gesture common to many Crapsey poems. What are we waiting for? The answer is implied in "The Warning" or "Triad," explicit in "Moon-shadows," "As I Went," "Expenses," "The Lonely Death," "Song," "To The Dead In The Grave-Yard Under My Window," and many other poems: "Death . . it is death." Sometimes the poetic response is one of hope; pain may literally be the "door of life," if the needle of the pneumo-thorax treatment succeeds. Sometimes the response is a yielding, as in "Languor After Pain" or a weary stoicism, as in "Lo, All The Way." And in such lines as "I will not be patient, I will not lie still," the impatient patient vows to "flash an unquenched defiance to the stars." "Moon-shadows" employs a structure of superposition and a single, sharply focused natural detail; the poem also exemplifies a third characteristic many cinquains share with Japanese poetry, restraint:

> Still as
> On windless nights
> The moon-cast shadows are,
> So still will be my heart when I
> Am dead.

The visual image of the starkly etched moon-cast shadows becomes the metaphoric equal of the speaker's heart, but the deliberate statement of the fact suggests reflection or meditative observation rather than a covert appeal for pity. Such restraint also typifies Japanese poetry, and Donald Keene describes the effect of these poems on the Western reader: "Many of these poems seem curiously passive to us, for the writer does not specify the truth taught him by an experience, nor even in what way it affected him."[10] As Keene points out, this aspect of Japanese literature appealed strongly to the "imagist school," whose "main thesis" was that "poetic ideas are best expressed by the rendering of concrete images rather than by comments."[11] The cinquain "Amaze" demonstrates the completeness with which Crapsey's poetry exemplifies this ideal of concreteness and restraint:

I know
Not these my hands
And yet I think there was
A woman like me once had hands
Like these.

The poem deals, as Winters says, with "a sudden and almost hallucinatory realization that she is leaving life":[12] the contrasting elements might be formulated as being suddenly confronted with the comprehension of what it is not to be, yet there is contrast at the same time and in the same spare images between the changing, physical hands of now and the unchanging hands of memory. One must look closely at a photograph of Crapsey taken a few days before her death even to see her hands, wasted to an almost transparent thinness.

Can the psychology of Crapsey's poems be related directly to the physiological changes of her disease? The nineteenth century held many strange and now discounted theories about the relation between consumption and creative power. More sensible later scientists have pointed out that the "white Plague," which caused 25 percent of the deaths in the nineteenth century, would inevitably kill off poets, painters, and composers, along with millions of more commonplace people, but they have concluded that

> There may be, nevertheless, some basis for the statement that consumption fosters and nourishes genius. Within certain limits fever from any source can heighten emotion, sharpen perception and render intellectual processes more lucid and rapid. "Six weeks with fever is an eternity," wrote Balzac. "Hours are like days . . . then the nights are not lost."
>
> Since consumptives often experience mild fever without gross toxemia and without physical prostration, they may crave a full life and exhibit eagerness to seize the fleeting moments for creative efforts. Furthermore, the decreased physical vigor of the tuberculosis patient limits his ability to fulfill natural urges and thereby increases his tendency to sublimate them into those forms of mental activity that are most natural to him.[13]

The body lies still and the mind races—to the leaves falling from trees on a November night, to moon-shadows and one's own heartbeat, to the hands on the counterpane. The poem's restraint makes it noncommittal: the poem "must be completed by the reader," and, like the best Japanese poems, may suggest, indeed, should suggest, more than one experience of the truth.[14]

Although many of the best cinquains show the contrast of elements, the suggestiveness, and the restraint of Japanese forms, some cinquains, often the weaker as poems, might be described—as are Amy Lowell's "haiku"—as mere brief statements, devoid of haiku structure and spirit. Such cinquains include "Release," "Laurel in the Berkshires," "The Grand Canyon," "Fate Defied," and "Languor After Pain." It is worth noting that several of these poems, different in structure, also differ by being more "poetic" or melodramatic than the most successful and more restrained examples of the form. "Fate Defied," for example, suggests conscious bravery as "Amaze" does not:

As it
Were tissue of silver
I'll wear, O Fate, thy grey,
And go mistily radiant, clad
Like the moon.

This is not to suggest that Crapsey succeeded as a poet only when she was most influenced by the ideas or ideals of Japanese literature. It seems likely, however, that certain qualities exemplified in the Japanese poetry she knew in translation—brevity, suggestiveness, restraint, the contrast of elements, and the blending of images—appealed strongly to her and confirmed or strengthened her own inclination to write a poetry of reticence, even repression. In her best poems she is truest to her own character, as this is suggested by her biography, and this truth happens also to be the truth of Japanese poetry.

One final aspect of the cinquain may indicate a possible Japanese influence. The reader's appreciation of the very short poems of Pound, Hulme, and other Imagists is heightened by his seeing the poem upon the page and appreciating its spareness, suppleness, and brevity. The cinquain shares this quality and is, in this respect, an "eye poem," with its meaning linked to the line lengths as well as to the increasing and decreasing numbers of stresses.

When the various drafts, worksheets, copies made for Esther Lowenthal, Jean Webster, and copies made in the course of metrical analyses have all been taken into account, many of Crapsey's fair copies of single poems seem to have been made because of her pleasure in the shape of a poem as it appears in her tiny but precise and decorative handwriting. The holograph copy of the cinquain "Niagara" artfully balances the title, the descriptive subtitle, "Seen on a Night in November," and the poem itself. Part of the fascination of this poem, even in printed form, seems to lie in the discrepancy between the largeness of its subject—the noise and motion of the moonlit cataract and the stillness of the poised satellite—and the extreme compression of the poem surrounded by the empty space of a page. A related characteristic of the cinquain, the variation in the length of its lines and the number of their stresses, functions to make this compression work: four lines of increasing length present a mysterious something "Above the bulk / Of crashing water," with the longest a group of adjectives as yet unattached to any noun, "Autumnal, evanescent, wan." The fifth line, abruptly decreasing in number of stresses and length, also abruptly presents and fixes the second element in the scene, and the picture is all the more striking for the speed and restraint with which it has been created. A companion cinquain with many of the same potential poetic virtues, "The Grand Canyon," fails where "Niagara" succeeds. It fails not only because it appeals for attention with strident and heightened mechanical exclamations—"By Zeus!"—but also because there is no clear relationship between the increasing and decreasing stresses and the poem's meaning. Line divisions seem arbitrarily imposed upon a message rather than integral parts of the whole.

Although her consciousness of contemporary poetic and artistic developments is important, it is also important to recognize the role of Crapsey's own informed craftsmanship and studies in metrics in shaping her poetry. Her poetry shows affinities with Georgian and Imagist movements, and her *Verse* was later praised by adherents of both, yet the form of her poems, particularly the development of the cinquain, seems to have been influenced chiefly by the metrical theories of Robert Bridges. In the course of her readings on Milton's metrics, especially on the metrics of *Samson Agonistes,* at the British Museum in 1910 and 1911, she may have encountered for the first time Bridges's theory of patterns of stress as the bases of poetic forms. Her reader's slips show that, besides editions of his verse—*Now In Wintry Delights* (called for on three days), *Demeter: A Mask,* and *The Shorter Poems of Robert Bridges*—she read his work on Milton's prosody. In his "Appendix F: On Metrical Equivalence" in the 1893 edition, Bridges acknowledges his indebtedness to his friend "the late Father Gerard Hopkins"[15] and it has never been determined who was indebted to whom in the development of these closely related theories or "metrical re-discoveries" of stresses and sprung rhythm.[16] Bridges emphasizes the importance of stress as the shaping factor in English poetry: "Immediately English verse is written free from a numeration of syllables, it falls back on the number of stresses as its determining law: that is its governing power, and constitutes its form; and this is a perfectly different system from that which counts the syllables."[17] In this discussion, Bridges uses the unusual symbol for a stressed syllable, â,[18] which Crapsey employs so consistently in metrical analyses of her own poetry and the poems of others copied into her commonplace book, the Academy notebook. A substantial group of holographs is marked with this symbol. A few poems have been marked with the more conventional symbols ă and ā. Perhaps because she was familiar with the complexities of English prosody, Adelaide Crapsey was not a dogmatic advocate of any one theory or any one system of notation. She indicates her preference for the form of notation she employs most frequently in the course of an explanation of her own metrical theories (now in the Adelaide Crapsey papers):

> For verse in duple metre (rising cadence), having as its metric norm the two syllable construction model _ _̂ [Footnote: I have used Mr Omond's terms (duple metre, triple metre) because I follow his primary metrical classification of poems by their time. I do not give the more usual symbol ˘̲ ¯̲ because it does not seem to me to be accurate but I think it clear that the symbol _ _̂ stands for the same fact and in the present connection the identity of the fact is of greater immediate importance than the question of its more or less accurate description.] the problem can be at least indicated at a central point in this way. As soon as the vocabulary contains words over two syllables in length the question of secondary speech-accent will arise except in connection with mid-stress trisyllables (phonetic type _ _ _). In keeping to the norm in his metrical arrangement the artist must use each one of the secondary speech-accent syllables in a verse-accent place. If he does not so use them conditions arise which the prosodist is bound to note, and finally, to explain.

Her continuing interest in these metrical problems helps to explain the prosodic analysis to which she subjected her own poems: the several different sets of symbols for the indication of stressed and unstressed syllables (_ _̂ and ˘̲ ¯̲) used extensively on her holographs and the vertical lines with which feet or groups of syllables are often divided. For some poems she made a line-by-line syllable count and totals of stressed and unstressed syllables. She often seems to have used an existing rough draft of a poem for this investigation of stresses.

Examination of the holographs, particularly of the rough drafts, reveals the crucial importance of stress patterns in shaping Crapsey's forms. In the case of an apparently unfinished poem, "Thou art not friendly sleep," what began as a quatrain (abab) is being revised into a shorter poem, something more like a cinquain. Here the distinctive stress marks are carefully added to the first version (listed as C), but omitted from a later version (B). Rough drafts of such cinquains as "Snow" and "Fresher / Than spring's new scents" show her consistent use of stress marks in the earliest stages of poetic composition. Drafts of "Nor moon, / Nor stars" show a six-line poem, rather like an overgrown cinquain, which starts to be revised into a shorter poem. The poet marks some of the stressed syllables, experiments with line lengths, and eliminates adjectives. The building up and falling away of stresses seems intended, here as elsewhere, to have a definite relation to the poem's meaning. Certainly the most successful cinquains seem to be those where there is a firm relation between the increase and sharp drop in the number of stresses and the meaning of the poem. Such cinquains as "Niagara" and "Amaze" succeed, as we have seen, not only because they superimpose images and use the haiku technique of break and contrast, but also because the final drop in stresses coincides with a dramatic, emotional development in the poem. A cinquain that lacks either or both of these qualities, which is more a brief statement than a juxtaposition and has no real correlation between its stresses and its meaning, falls flat. "Shadow" seems relatively weak for both of these reasons:

A-sway,
On red rose,
A golden butterfly. .
And on my heart a butterfly
Night-wing'd.

The fifth line, with its single stress, reveals something, but with such understatement that the effect of the revelation is almost lost. Is this black butterfly death? The lack of contrast can be shown by comparing the cinquain with one of the Japanese poems it superficially resembles, such as this haiku by Buson (1716–84):

On the temple bell
Resting, asleep
A butterfly.[19]

The Japanese poem juxtaposes the evanescent and the eternal as the cinquain does not.

Crapsey's experiments were not confined to work with stress-patterns or to the development of the tight, spare form of the cinquain. One group of holographs indicates that she followed the lead of French poets in experiments with *vers libre* and "prose poetry," as did contemporary Imagists Amy Lowell and Richard Aldington. Of three draft versions of "What news comrade" one is written out as a paragraph and then divided.

Earl Miner sums up the enthusiasms and interests of the Imagists, as these were expressed at various times by T. E. Hulme, F. S. Flint, and Ezra Pound:

> Biblical, Symbolist, Japanese poetry, and *vers libre* were what they set up as examples or goals; and all are represented, usually in interminglings, in their poetry and in the poetry of the Imagists who succeeded them. The "sacred Hebrew form" turns out to be chiefly the poetry of the Canticles, which the Imagists imitated in most of their love poems, borrowing (from the King James Version) diction, images, and to a lesser degree, balanced syntax.[20]

Although she wrote as an outsider, relying on her " 'own solitary reperception and ratification of what is fine,' " Adelaide Crapsey proves very much a poet of her time, for she shares most of these interests with the avowed Imagists. Her experiments in other areas were far less successful than the cinquains. Her longer free verse poems, such as "Birth-Moment," "The Mother Exultant," and "The Song of Choice," employ an unfortunate pseudo-Biblical diction and tired similes and tend to mechanical exclamation and exhortation. In spite of the free verse form we feel that the speakers and actors, whether lovers, or mothers, or nubile maidens, are posing stiffly in musty costumes and hefting well-worn stage properties. "The Song of Choice," for example, presents a standardized poetic maiden, equipped with long golden hair, a mouth like "wine-stains," and white breasts, who has a choice between two lovers. One lover "saith" three times:

> I bring you white poppies:
> They are white as the still white thought of holiness
> That stirred in your soul when you awoke alone at dawn.
>
> (ll. 13–15, 24–26, 35–37)

The maiden stretches out her hands for the poppies that are "red as blood": "Whenas she felt as it were a great rending within her" (l. 46). It must be noted that Crapsey did not include "The Song of Choice" or such love poems as "Aubade," "I offer my self to you as cool water in cup of crystal," or "Cry of the Nymph to Eros" in her final selection for "Verse." Crapsey's longest and most famous free verse poem, "To The Dead In The Grave-Yard Under My Window," is also absent from "Verse." Whether the poet omitted it because she felt its subject too personal and painful, or because she had doubts about its quality we do not know.

Although the impossibility of dating many of Crapsey's poems makes generalizations about her poetic development difficult, some changes are evident. A great part of her verse, especially her earlier poems, is eclectic and literary in inspiration. The poets of the nineties, particularly those she copied into her commonplace book (including Oscar Wilde and Lionel Johnson) influenced her, as the surprising and glitteringly lurid poem "Evil" shows. The poem "La Morte," beginning "Vision of vice grown old," celebrates the jewel-like phosphorescence of decay—"beauty mysteriously / Present in scum blurred thin on stagnant ill-odoured pond"—with a *fin de siècle* decadence that recalls Ernest Dowson, Lionel Johnson, and the irony and morbidity of the French Symbolists by whom these poets were inspired.

The nineties influence evident in the poem "Pierrot," subtitled "For Aubrey Beardsley's picture 'Pierrot is dying,' " may also be linked to her readings in the British Museum: she called for Beardsley's *Under the Hill and Other Essays in Prose and Verse,* the *Last Letters of Aubrey Beardsley,* and *The Later Work of Aubrey Beardsley.* An influence less easily specified, but still more important may have been exerted by her study of A. E. Gallatin's *Whistler's Art Dicta.* Whistler's influence, as a prophet of Impressionism and also as the popularizer and explicator of "Japonisme," can hardly be overestimated.

The strongest influences upon Crapsey do not seem to have been the literary and artistic figures of the nineties, however, but two earlier nineteenth century English poets: Keats and Landor. The extensive notations in Crapsey's Everyman edition of Keats give evidence of an enduring interest in Keats's life and work. The only souvenir photographs from Europe pasted in the blue album are of the Keats house and grave, although Crapsey writes her parents that she only went along to the Protestant Cemetery because someone else wanted to go. Among the many, many editions and studies of Milton's work, and such titles as "Intensives and Down-Toners: A Study in English Adverbs," *Secondary Accent in Modern English Verse: Chaucer to Dryden,* and "Syllabification and

Accent in *Paradise Lost,*" her British Museum reader's slips call for a wide variety of editions and studies of Keats and his poetry. In addition to the long free verse poem on the death of Keats, Crapsey wrote other poems on Keatsian subjects: "Endymion," "The Elgin Marbles," and "Autumn." Direct experiences, such as her visits to Keats's house and grave, become poetry only after having been worked through a literary source: Severn's letter describing Keats's final days and hours. (Life was to imitate art: in Crapsey's own last hours she, too, experienced many of Keats's torments as these had been described in her poem.)

Landor's name, like that of Keats, appears in Crapsey's poetry in part because she visited a place associated with him, Fiesole. His epigrammatic style seems also to have exerted an influence upon her and Landor's influence supplements or perhaps vies with that of Keats. Crapsey copied three of Landor's poems, "Dirce," "Mother, I Cannot Mind My Wheel," and "On His Seventy-fifth Birthday," into her commonplace book. Her own poems include a group of quatrains—"To Walter Savage Landor," "The Pledge," "Expenses," "Adventure," "To Man Who Goes Seeking Immortality Bidding Him Look Nearer Home," "Safe," and "The Immortal Residue: Inscription for My Verse,"—several of which—"The Immortal Residue," "Expenses," and "To Man Who Goes Seeking Immortality,"—are close to Landor in spirit as well as in form. The contrasts between Crapsey's favorite poets, between one with fears that he "may cease to be" and one who has "warmed his hands before the fire of life," seem to indicate again the tensions within her own character revealed in the poetry.

Other poems, influenced by no one poet or period, are experiments in different forms. "On Seeing Weather-Beaten Trees" may have been inspired by a collection of famous epigrams she made for use in teaching; among the holographs now in the miscellaneous notes at Rochester are copies of Pope's "I am his Highness' dog at Kew; / Pray tell me, sir, whose dog are you?" and Henry Patmore's "The truth is male, and females shy / Come near it with a careful lie." "Milking Time" makes use of "Cushy Cow, Bonny," a "charm used by milkmaids to induce refractory or bewitched cows to give up their milk,"[21] and other poems imitate ballad refrains and folk lyrics: "Chimes," "As I Went," "The Fiddler." In many forms, she displays inventiveness and a facility for fruitful experiment.

Her most successful experiment, of course, led to her development of the cinquain. In this shorter form her interest in metrics and stress-shaped forms combines with the juxtaposition of images—visual, aural, tactile, and kinesthetic—and a sensitivity to impressions drawn directly from life and less preoccupied with literary or artistic allusions. Two unattributed quotations Crapsey copies into her commonplace book, the Academy notebook, make clear her concern with poetic forms and a personal reality: "A certain type of mind [is] not content in a vague sense of unity and is impelled by the desire to find out what in fact is the structure that determines it"; "Artists give us not conclusions but evidence."

Readers fortunate enough to know more than a few of Crapsey's poems may well feel, as Winters does, that the poems have worn well, that many of them remain "in their way honest and acutely perceptive."[22] The distinctive compression of her best work offers striking proof that "less is more" and seems particularly attractive to those surfeited with the aesthetic sprawl of the space age: she calls the poems in her "Verse" her "funeral urn," and her best poems have the edge a well-wrought urn always enjoys over a half-acre tomb.

A Note on the Present Text of the Poems

Although all of Crapsey's mature poetry was published posthumously, she had prepared a substantial group of her poems for publication. In two almost identical holograph letters to "Messrs G. P. Putnam's Sons" and "The F. A. Stokes Company," each in envelopes addressed by Crapsey and both apparently enclosed in a letter to Jean Webster as late as September 1914, the poet offers "a manuscript" for publication:

> Gentlemen
>
> May I submit to you for publication the enclosed poems? The volumn is, you will see, divided into two parts. The poems in the first part are all in blank verse; those in the second are, with some few exceptions, in rhymed verse.
>
> If you do not find it available will you please return the manuscript to me by express?
>
> Sincerely yours
> Adelaide Crapsey

The address given in both letters is "128 West 59th Street, New York—, c/o Mrs Webster" and a parcel post label from the Macmillan Company to the poet at this return address seems to indicate that one publisher had not "found it available."

The "volumn" making the rounds of the publishers at the time of the poet's death seems to have been the "Presentation" copy,[1] or a typed copy identical with this. Many of Crapsey's final intentions for her completed poems are represented by the Presentation copy. It preserves the author's final plan for the arrangement of the poems and punctuation and capitalization of which she approved or in which she acquiesced. This is also true of additional groups of author-corrected typewritten copies. Consideration of each of these groups, especially the groups of typewritten copies not fastened together, involves the assumption that if notes in the hand of the author appear on one or several of the leaves of that group, the entire group represents the author's intentions.

To preserve the integrity and completeness of Crapsey's "Verse" as she planned it, the poems given in the table of contents in the Presentation copy are presented in the divisions and subdivisions devised by the author: "Part I," "Cinquains," and "Part II." The author-corrected Presentation copy has furnished the copy-text of its poems as they appear in this edition. Poems missing from the Presentation copy have been supplied from the other groups of author-corrected typewritten copies or from holographs.

The two groups of "Additional Poems" not included in Adelaide Crapsey's selection for "Verse" both mirror her general arrangement in "Verse": blank verse poems, including cinquains, are followed by rhymed verse. The two groupings result entirely from editorial preferences. The editor can indulge her whims—elevate some poems to the elite group and banish others (some abominable) to the second group—because "complete" and "incomplete" have no necessary relation here to "better" or "worse," and fair copy does not mean a fine poem. Several groups among the extant poems may be regarded as having been completed by the author. Some poems she apparently prepared for publication, but decided against including in her selection (her decision seems wise): "The Song of Choice" and "Aubade" are listed in ink and deleted in pencil on a preliminary table of contents. The poet seems to have made fair copies of many poems as part of her selection process. Her fondness for making fair copies, sometimes destroying earlier copies, makes dating most poems impossible and precludes chronological arrangement. This leaves her admirers free to imagine "Non Solo" as a "bad example" devised for a poetry class at Smith, or "Traces of the Rustic in Amos" as something left over from a school, college, or family skit.

Another group of the "Additional Poems" may have been prepared for publication: poems apparently either submitted or prepared for submission to periodicals. Holographs and typewritten copies of various poems have pencil notes by Crapsey: "Century" on "Susanna And The Elders," and "McClures" on "Ah Me. . Alas."

A smaller group of poems must be regarded as having been left uncompleted by the author. For poems offering one or more rough draft or semifinal versions, the problem is analogous to that presented by the poems of Emily Dickinson. As R. W. Franklin says of editing unfinished writing: "the principle of editing that a text exactly represent the author's final intention is inadequate, since finality cannot be established."[2] The copy-text selected for an unfinished poem may or may not be the author's latest version, because no extant text can be said to represent her final intention. A study of the holographs of "Thou art not friendly sleep" indicates that what began as a quatrain was being revised into something resembling a cinquain. In this instance, the latest revised version is the copy-text. The three holographs on one leaf of "Nor moon,/ Nor stars" show a six-line poem, rather like a sprawling cinquain, being revised into a tighter and shorter poem. The earliest version is the copy-text because its relative completeness makes it intelligible as a poem.

The varying nature of the copy-texts—typed copies corrected by the author, holograph fair copies and drafts, and a copy by Esther Lowenthal (whether this is a transcription or an attempt to recall the poem from memory)—results in texts given with differing punctuation and capitalization. Crapsey often places a period after the title in holographs. The poem titles in the Presentation copy and in the other author-corrected typewritten copies sometimes have a period following the title, and the first letter of almost every word in the titles is capitalized. The present text does not attempt to regularize or minimize these differences.

Crapsey's punctuation is preserved unless it obviously obscures the meaning. Her unusual two-period ellipsis, found in many holographs and author-corrected typed copies, is retained. She seems to have felt that if two periods would convey the idea it was unnecessary to use three. This economy seems to accord well with the spareness of her preferred verse forms. Although Crapsey prefers two- (or three-) period ellipsis to the three- (or four-) period ellipsis, her usage is hardly consistent: she uses different forms in analogous situations in the course of the same poem and changes from one form to another in different versions of the same line (see ll. 61, 13, 58, 59, 61, 76 in "Birth Moment.") Neither the number of periods nor their spacing conforms to any logical rule, but they are preserved in preference to any attempt to standardize her highly personal forms.

Only one change in punctuation is made silently. Crapsey's holograph dash is so short that it consistently appears to be a hyphen, and it is sometimes typed as a hyphen in the author-corrected typewritten copies. In the present text it is silently extended, so that it will be understood immediately as a dash. Typist's errors in spacing, such as the typing of "dark-hidden" in l. 9 of "Birth-Moment " as "dark- hidden" in the Presentation copy, and typing errors corrected merely by erasing an extra letter, as in the first line of "To Man Who Goes Seeking Immortality Bidding Him Look Nearer Home," where "far" is typed "afar" in the Presentation copy and the *a* is erased, are not reported in the notes.

Misspellings or inadvertent omissions of letters are corrected; possibly substantive spelling changes are noted in the textual apparatus. Crapsey consistently uses the English spelling for such words as "grey," "colour," "enamoured," and "travelling." These spellings are retained. Her occasional use of "its" for "it's" or "it's" for "its" may result from inadvertence or haste, but may also result from a genuine confusion about the forms. Although she often seems to have little regard for standard spelling and punctuation (her letters are punctuated largely with dashes), her errors are most frequently associated with the formation of the possessive and the use of the possessive form: "heaven's" for "heavens" in "My Birds That Fly No Longer" (l. 2) and "her's" for "hers" in "Arbutus" (l. 2).

Emendations of positive errors, such as the substitution of "cries" for "Crys" in "Truthful Love" (1. 6), are also noted. Conjectural readings for undeciphered words, as in "What news, comrade," are bracketed in the text.

Adelaide Crapsey
Vassar Yearbook Photo (1901)

Algernon Sidney Crapsey (1847-1928)

Adelaide Trowbridge Crapsey (1855-1950)

Adelaide Crapsey and Siblings

Adelaide Crapsey with Jean Webster and Sam Webster on the Webster Front Porch in Fredonia, New York (1901 or 1902)

Adelaide Crapsey as the Manager of the Vassar College Class of 1901 Basketball Team (Vassarion 1900)

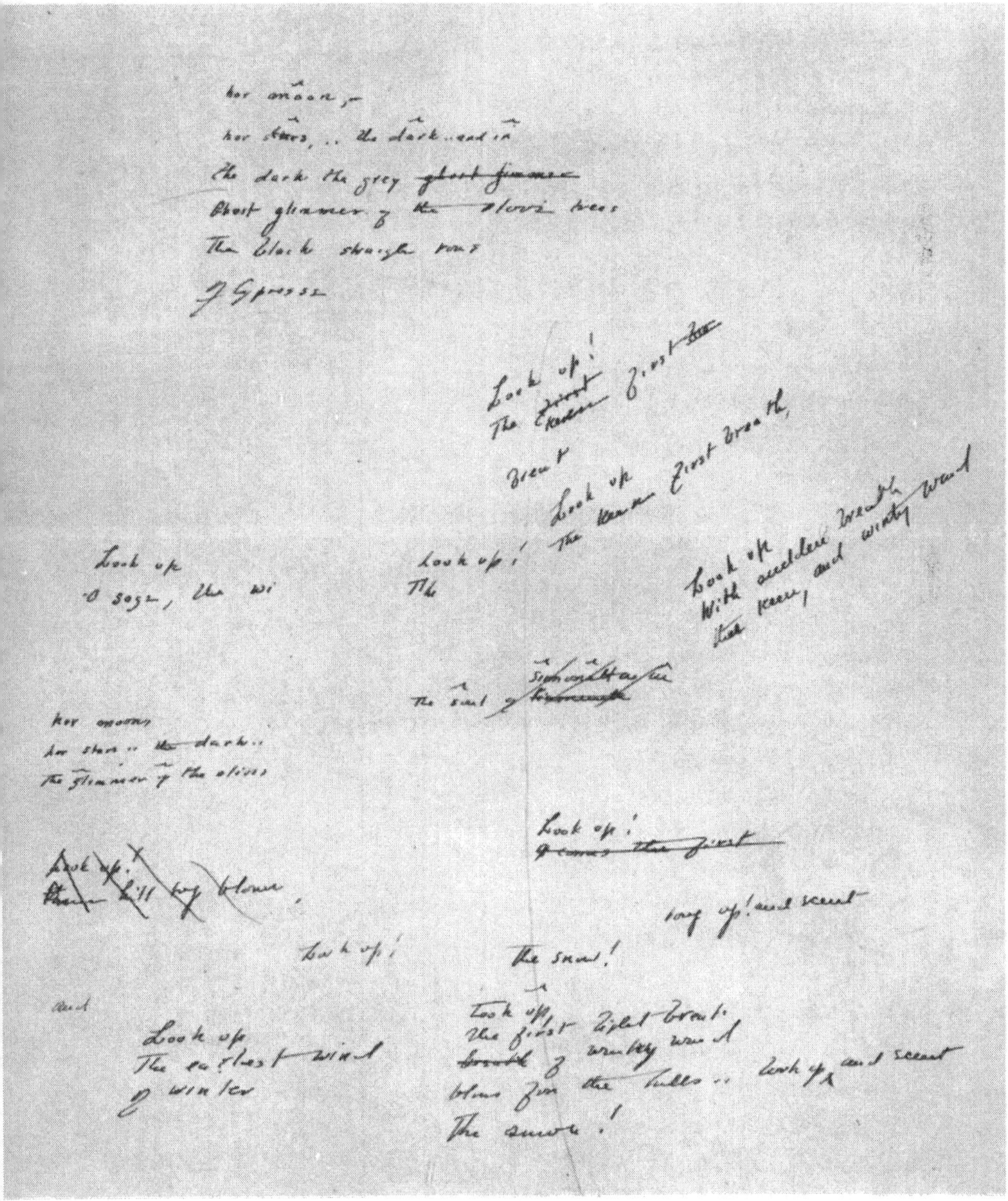

"Nor moon, —/Nor stars" and Several Starts of "Snow"

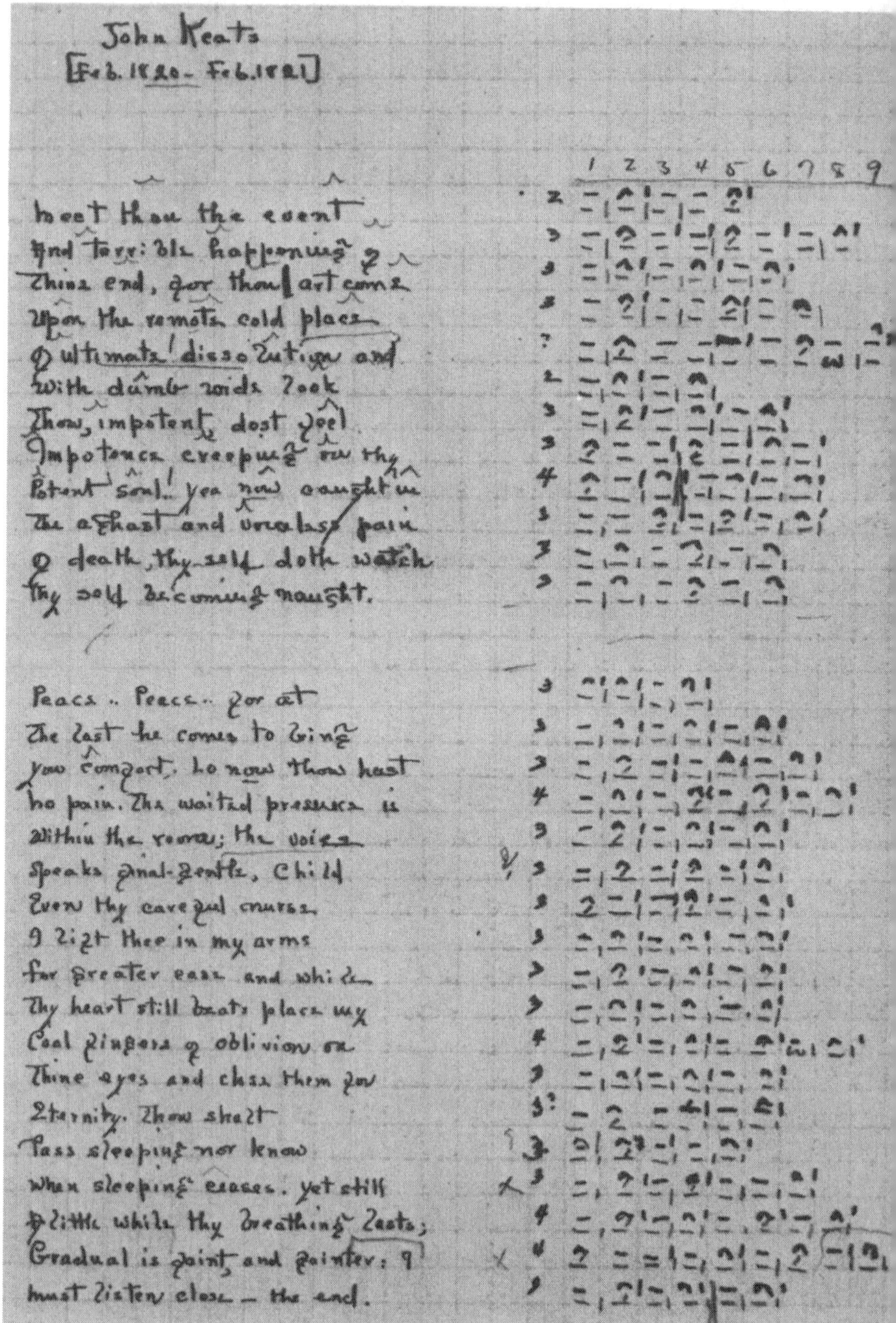

John Keats
[Feb. 1820 – Feb. 1821]

Meet thou the event
And terrible happening of
Thine end, for thou art come
Upon the remote cold place
Of ultimate dissolution and
With dumb voids look
Thou, impotent, dost feel
Impotence creeping on thy
Potent soul. Yea now caught in
The aghast and voiceless pain
Of death, thyself doth watch
Thy self becoming naught.

Peace .. Peace .. for at
The last he comes to give
You comfort. Lo now thou hast
No pain. The waited presence is
Within the room; the voice
Speaks final-gentle, Child
Even thy careful nurse
I lift thee in my arms
For greater ease and while
Thy heart still beats place my
Cool fingers of oblivion on
Thine eyes and close them for
Eternity. Thou shalt
Pass sleeping nor know
When sleeping ceases. Yet still
A little while thy breathing lasts;
Gradual is faint, and fainter: I
must listen close – the end.

"John Keats" with Stress Analysis

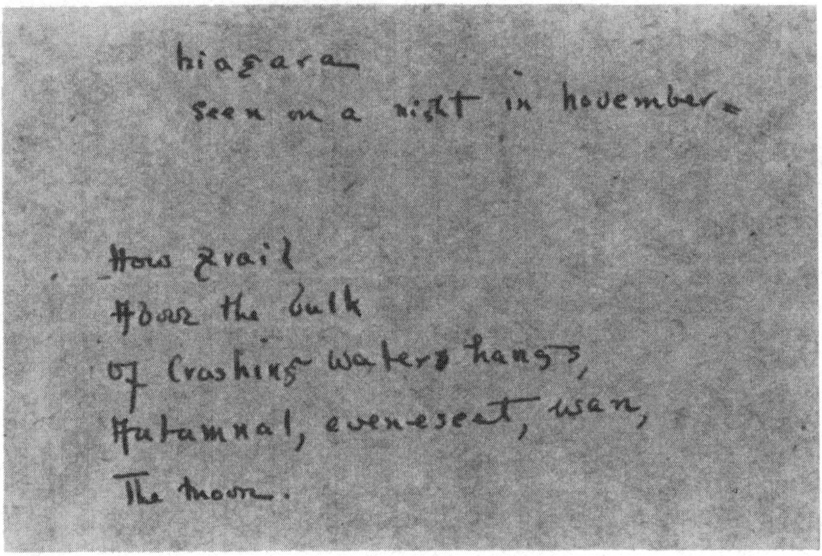

Niagara
Seen on a night in November

How frail
Above the bulk
Of crashing waters hangs,
Autumnal, evanescent, wan,
The moon.

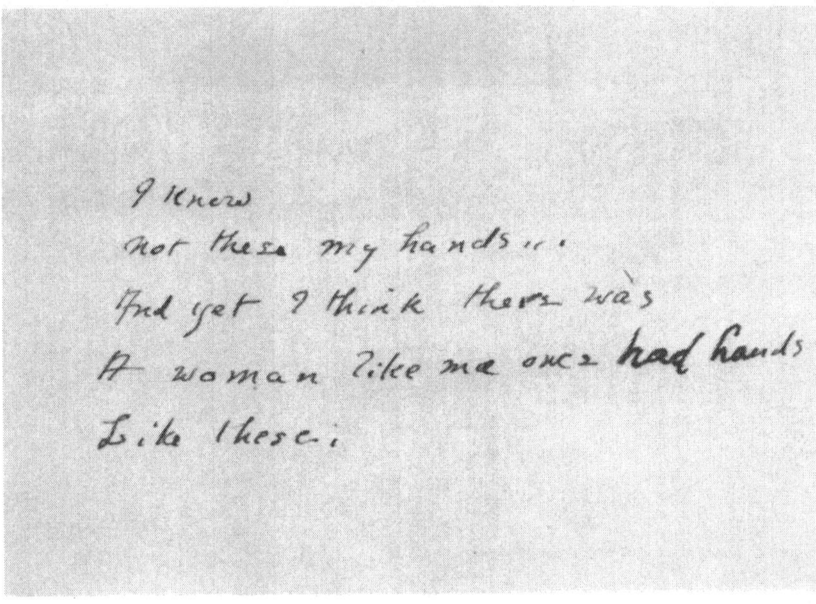

I know
Not these my hands . . .
And yet I think there was
A woman like me once had hands
Like these.

"Niagara" and "Amaze"

Adelaide Crapsey a Few Days Before her Death (1914)

Poems

"VERSE"

Poems Selected and Arranged by

Adelaide Crapsey

Part I

Birth-Moment

Behold her,
Running through the waves,
Eager to reach the land;
The water laps her,
Sun and wind are on her,
Healthy, brine-drenched and young,
Behold Desire new-born;—
Desire on first fulfillment's radiant edge,
Love at miraculous moment of emergence,
This is she,
Who running,
Hastens, hastens to the land.

Look. . Look. .
Her blown gold hair and lucent eyes of youth,
Her body rose and ivory in the sun. .
Look,
How she hastens,
Running, running to the land.

Her hands are yearning and her feet are swift
To reach and hold
She knows not what
Yet knows that it is life;
Need urges her,
Self, uncomprehended but most deep divined,
Unwilled but all-compelling, drives her on.
Life runs to life.
She who longs,
But hath not yet accepted or bestowed,
All virginal dear and bright,
Runs, runs to reach the land.

And she who runs shall be
Married to blue of summer skies at noon,
Companion to green fields,
Held bride of subtle fragrance and of all sweet sound,
Belovèd of the stars,
And wanton mistress to the veering winds.

Oh breathless space between:
Womb-time just passed,
Dark-hidden, chaotic-formative, unpersonal,
And individual life of fresh-created force
Not yet begun:
One moment more
Before desire shall meet desire
And new creation start.
Oh breathless space,
While she,
Just risen from the waves,
Runs, runs to reach the land.

(Ah, keenest personal moment
When mouth unkissed turns eager-slow and tremulous
Towards lover's mouth,
That tremulous and eager-slow
Droops down to it:
But breathless space of breath or two
Lies in between
Before the mouth upturned and mouth down-drooped
Shall meet and make the kiss.)

Look. . Look. .
She runs. .
Love fresh-emerged,
Desire new-born. .
Blown on by wind,
And shone on by the sun,
She rises from the waves
And running,
Hastens, hastens to the land.

Belovèd and Belovèd and Belovèd,
Even so right
And beautiful and undenied
Is my desire;
Even so longing-swift
I run to your receiving arms.

O Aphrodite!
O Aphrodite, hear!
Hear my wrung cry flame upward poignant-glad. . .
This is my time for me.
I too am young;
I too am all of love!

1905.

The Mother Exultant

Joy! Joy! Joy!
The hills are glad,
The valleys re-echo with merriment,
In my heart is the sound of laughter,
And my feet dance to the time of it;
Oh, little son, carried light on my shoulder,
Let us go laughing and dancing through the live days,
For this is the hour of the vintage,
When man gathereth for himself the fruits of the vineyard.

Look, little son, look:
The grapes are translucent and ripe,
They are heavy and fragrant with juice,
They wait for the hands of the vintagers;
For a long time the grapes were not,
And were in the womb of the earth,
Then out of the heavens came the rain,
The sun sent down his warmth from the sky,

At the touch of life, life stirred,
And the earth brought forth her fruits in due season.

I was a maid and alone,
When, behold, there came to me a vision;
My heart cried out within me,
And the voice was the voice of God.
Yea, a virgin I dreamed of love,
And I was troubled and sore afraid,
I wept and was glad,
For the word of my heart named me blessèd,
My soul exalted the might of creation.

I was a maid and alone,
When, behold, my lover came to me,
My belovèd held me in his arms.

Joy! Joy! Joy!
Now is the vision fulfilled;
I have conceived,
I have carried in my womb,
I have brought forth
The life of the world;
Out of my joy and my pain,
Out of the fulness of my living
Hath my son gained his life.

Look, little son, look:
The grapes are ripe for the gathering;
The fresh, deep earth is in them,
And clean water from the clouds.
And golden, golden sun is in the heart of the grapes.
Look, little son, look:
The earth, your mother,
And the touch of life who is your father,
They have provided food for you
That you also may live.

The vineyards are planted on the hillside,
They are the vineyards of my belovèd,

He chose a favorable spot,
His hands prepared the soil for the planting;
He set out the young vines
And cared for them till the time of their bearing.
Now is his labour fulfilled who worked with God.
The fruit of the vineyard is ripe,
The vintagers laugh in the sun,
They sing while they gather the grapes,
For the vintage is a good one,
The wine vats are pressed down and running over.

Joy! Joy! Joy!
Now is the wonder accomplished;
Out of the heart of the living grape
Hath the hand of my belovèd
Wrung the wine of the dream of life.

Belovèd,
My little son's father,
Together we have given life,
And the vision of life;
Shall we not rejoice
Who have made eternal
The days of our living.

Look, little son, look:
The grapes glow with rich juice;
The juice of the grape hath in it
The substance of the earth,
And the air's breath;
It hath in it the soul of the vintage.
Put forth your hand, little son,
And take for yourself the life
That your father and your mother
Have provided for you.

Joy! Joy! Joy!
The hills are glad,
The valleys re-echo with merriment,
In my heart is the sound of laughter,

And my feet dance to the time of it;
Oh, little son, carried light on my shoulder,
Let us go laughing and dancing through the live days,
For this is the hour of the vintage,
When man gathereth for himself the fruits of the vineyard.

1905.

John Keats

(February 1820–February 1821)

Meet thou the event
And terrible happening of
Thine end: for thou art come
Upon the remote, cold place
Of ultimate dissolution and
With dumb, wide look
Thou, impotent, dost feel
Impotence creeping on
Thy potent soul. Yea, now, caught in
The aghast and voiceless pain
Of death, thyself doth watch
Thyself becoming naught.

Peace. . Peace. . for at
The last is comfort. Lo, now
Thou hast no pain. Lo, now
The waited presence is
Within the room; the voice
Speaks final-gentle: "Child,
Even thy careful nurse,
I lift thee in my arms
For greater ease and while
Thy heart still beats, place my
Cool fingers of oblivion on
Thine eyes and close them for

Eternity. Thou shalt
Pass sleeping, nor know
When sleeping ceases. Yet still
A little while thy breathing lasts,
Gradual is faint and fainter; I
Must listen close—the end."

Rest. And you others. . All.
Grave-fellows in
Green place. Here grows
Memorial every spring's
Fresh grass and here
Your marking monument
Was built for you long, long
Ago when Caius Cestius died.

Rome 1909.

Cinquains

1911–1913

November Night

Listen. .
With faint dry sound,
Like steps of passing ghosts,
The leaves, frost-crisp'd, break from the trees
And fall.

Release

With swift
Great sweep of her
Magnificent arm my pain
Clanged back the doors that shut my soul
From life.

Triad

These be
Three silent things:
The falling snow. . the hour
Before the dawn. . the mouth of one
Just dead.

Snow

Look up. . .
From bleakening hills
Blows down the light, first breath
Of wintry wind. . .look up, and scent
The snow!

Anguish

Keep thou
Thy tearless watch
All night but when blue dawn
Breathes on the silver moon, then weep!
Then weep!

Trapped

Well and
If day on day
Follows, and weary year
On year. . and ever days and years. .
Well?

Moon-shadows

Still as
On windless nights
The moon-cast shadows are,
So still will be my heart when I
Am dead.

Susanna And The Elders

"Why do
You thus devise
Evil against her?" "For that
She is beautiful, delicate:
Therefore."

Youth

But me
They cannot touch,
Old age and death. . the strange
And ignominious end of old
Dead folk!

Languor After Pain

Pain ebbs,
And like cool balm,
An opiate weariness
Settles on eye-lids, on relaxed
Pale wrists.

The Guarded Wound

If it
Were lighter touch
Than petal of flower resting
On grass oh still too heavy it were,
Too heavy!

Winter

The cold
With steely clutch
Grips all the land. . alack,
The little people in the hills
Will die!

Night Winds

The old
Old winds that blew
When chaos was, what do
They tell the clattered trees that I
Should weep?

Arbutus

Not spring's
Thou art, but hers,
Most cool, most virginal,
Winter's, with thy faint breath, thy snows
Rose-tinged.

Roma Aeterna

The sun
Is warm to-day,
O Romulus, and on
Thine olden Palatine the birds
Still sing.

"He's killed the may and he's laid her by To bear the red rose company."

Not thou,
White rose, but thy
Ensanguined sister is
The dear companion of my heart's
Shed blood.

Amaze

I know
Not these my hands
And yet I think there was
A woman like me once had hands
Like these.

Shadow

A-sway,
On red rose,
A golden butterfly. .
And on my heart a butterfly
Night-wing'd.

Fate Defied

As it
Were tissue of silver
I'll wear, O Fate, thy grey,
And go mistily radiant, clad
Like the moon.

Madness

Burdock,
Blue aconite,
And thistle and thorn. . of these,
Singing I wreathe my pretty wreath
O'death.

The Warning

Just now,
Out of the strange
Still dusk. . as strange, as still. .
A white moth flew. Why am I grown
So cold?

Saying of Il Haboul Guardian Of The Treasure Of Solomon And Keeper Of The Prophet's Armour

My tent
A vapour that
The wind dispels and but
As dust before the wind am I
Myself.

The Death Of Holofernes

Israel!
Wake! Be gay!
Thine enemy is brought low—
Thy foe slain—by the hand, by the hand
Of a woman!

Laurel In The Berkshires

Sea-foam
And coral! Oh, I'll
Climb the great pasture rocks
And dream me mermaid in the sun's
Gold flood.

Niagara
Seen on a night in November

How frail
Above the bulk
Of crashing water hangs,
Autumnal, evanescent, wan,
The moon.

The Grand Canyon

By Zeus!
Shout word of this
To the eldest dead! Titans,
Gods, Heroes, come who have once more
A home!

Now Barabbas Was A Robber

No guile?
Nay, but so strangely
He moves among us. . Not this
Man but Barabbas! Release to us
Barabbas!

Refuge In Darkness

With night's
Dim veil and blue
I will cover my eyes,
I will bind close my eyes that are
So weary.

Part II

To Walter Savage Landor

Ah, Walter, where you lived I rue
    These days come all too late for me;
What matter if her eyes are blue
    Whose rival is Persephone?

Fiesole, 1909.[1]

The Pledge

White doves of Cytherea, by your quest
    Across the blue Heaven's bluest highest air,
And by your certain homing to Love's breast,
    Still to be true and ever true—I swear.

Hypnos, God of Sleep

The shadowy boy of night
    Crosses the dusking land;
He sows his poppy-seeds
    With steady, gentle hand.

The shadowy boy of night
    Young husbandman of dreams,
Garners his gracious blooms
    By far and moonlit streams.

Expenses

Little my lacking fortunes show
For this to eat and that to wear;
Yet laughing, Soul, and gaily go!
An obol pays the Stygian fare.

London, 1910

Adventure

Sun and wind and beat of sea,
Great lands stretching endlessly. . .
Where be bonds to bind the free?
All the world was made for me!

On Seeing Weather-Beaten Trees

Is it as plainly in our living shown,
By slant and twist, which way the wind hath blown?

Warning To The Mighty

Ere the hornèd owl hoot
Once and twice and thrice there shall
Go among the blind brown worms
News of thy great burial;
When the pomp is passed away,
"Here's a King," the worms shall say.

Oh, Lady, Let The Sad Tears Fall

Oh, Lady, let the sad tears fall
To speak thy pain,
Gently as through the silver dusk
The silver rain.

Oh, let thy bosom breathe its grief
In such soft sigh
As hath the wind in gardens where
Pale roses die.

Dirge

Never the nightingale,
Oh, my dear,
Never again the lark
Thou wilt hear;
Though dusk and the morning still
Tap at thy window-sill,
Though ever love call and call
Thou wilt not hear at all,
My dear, my dear.

The Sun-Dial

Every day,
Every day,
Tell the hours
By their shadows,
By their shadows.

The Entombment

In a cave born,
(Mary said)
In a cave is
My Son buried.

Autumn

Fugitive, wistful,
Pausing at edge of her going,
Autumn, the maiden, turns,
Leans to the earth with ineffable
Gesture. Ah, more than
Spring's skies her skies shine
Tender and frailer
Bloom than plum-bloom or almond
Lies on her hillsides, her fields,
Misted, faint-flushing. Ah, lovelier
Is her refusal than
Yielding who pauses with grave
Backward smiling, with light
Unforgettable touch of
Fingers withdrawn. . . Pauses, lo
Vanishes. . fugitive, wistful. . .

Ah me. . Alas. .
(He)

Ah me, my love's heart,
Like some frail flower, apart,
High, on the cliff's edge growing,
Touched by unhindered sun to sweeter showing,

Swung by each faint wind's faintest blowing,
But so, on the cliff's edge growing,
From man's reach aloof, apart:
Ah me, my love's heart!

(She)

Alack, alas, my lover,
As one who would discover
At world's end his path,
Nor knows at all what faëry way he hath
Who turneth dreaming into faith
And followeth that near path
His own heart dareth to discover:
Alack, alas, my lover!

Perfume of Youth
(Girl's Song)

In Babylon, in Nineveh,
  And long ago, and far away,
The lilies and the lotus blew
  That are my sweet of youth to-day.

From those high gardens of the Gods
  That eyes of men may never see,
The amaranth and asphodel
  Immortal odours shed on me.

In vial of my early years,
  As in a crystal vial held,
What precious fragrance treasured up
  Of age and agelessness distill'd.

Thine but to give. Give straightway all.
  Yea, straight, mine hands, the ointment rare

In great libation joyous pour!
  Oh, look of youth. . . Oh, golden hair. . .

Rapunzel

All day, all day I brush
  My golden strands of hair;
All day I wait and wait. .
  Ah, who is there?

Who calls? Who calls? The gold
  Ladder of my long hair
I loose and wait. . and wait. .
  Ah, who is there?

She left at dawn. . I am blind
  In the tangle of my long hair. .
Is it she? the witch? the witch?
  Ah, who is there?

Narcissus

"Boy, lying
Where the long grass
Edges the pool's brim,
What do you watch
There in the water? the blue
Colour of Heaven
Mirrored, repeated? the brown
Tree-trunks and branches
Waveringly imaged? These,
Boy, do you watch?"

"Nay but mine eyes;
Nay but the trouble
Deep in mine eyes."

Vendor's Song

My songs to sell, good sir!
  I pray you buy.
Here's one will win a lady's tears,
  Here's one will make her gay,
Here's one will charm your true love true
  Forever and a day;
Good sir, I pray you buy!

Oh, no, he will not buy.

My songs to sell, sweet maid!
  I pray you buy.
This one will teach you Lilith's lore,
  And this what Helen knew,
And this will keep your gold hair gold,
  And this your blue eyes blue;
Sweet maid, I pray you buy!

Oh, no, she will not buy.

If I'd as much money as I could tell,
I never would cry my songs to sell,
I never would cry my songs to sell.

AVIS

Avis, the fair, at dawn
Rose lightly from her bed,
Herself arrayed,
Avis, the fair, the maid,
In vestiment of lawn;
Across the fields she sped,
Five flowerets there she found,
In fragrant garland wound,
Avis, the fair, at dawn,
Five roses red.

Go thou from thence of thy pity!
Thou lov'st not me.

Doom

Peter stands by the gate,
And Michael by the throne.
"Peter, I would pass the gate
And come before the throne."
"Whose spirit prayed never at the gate
In life nor at the throne,
In death he may not pass the gate
To come before the throne:"
Peter said from the gate;
Said Michael from the throne.

Grain Field

Scarlet the poppies
Blue the corn-flowers,
Golden the wheat.

Gold for The Eternal:
Blue for Our Lady:
Red for the five
Wounds of her Son.

Song

I make my shroud but no one knows,
So shimmering fine it is and fair,
With stitches set in even rows.
I make my shroud but no one knows.

In door-way where the lilac blows,
Humming a little wandering air,
I make my shroud and no one knows,
So shimmering fine it is and fair.

Pierrot
For Aubrey Beardsley's picture "Pierrot is dying."

Pierrot is dying;
  Tiptoe in,
Finger touched to lip,
  Harlequin,
Columbine and Clown.

Hush! how still he lies
  In his bed,
White slipped hand and white
  Sunken head.
Oh, poor Pierrot.

There's his dressing-gown
   Across the chair,
Slippers on the floor. . .
   Can he hear
Us who tiptoe in?

Pillowed high he lies
   In his bed;
Listen, Columbine.
   "He is dead."
Oh, poor Pierrot.

The Monk In The Garden
He comes from Mass early in the morning

The sky's the very blue Madonna wears;
   The air's alive with gold! Mark you the way
The birds sing and the dusted shimmer of dew
   On leaf and fruit? . . Per Bacco, what a day!

The Mourner

I have no heart for noon-tide and the sun,
But I will take me where more tender night
Shakes, fold on fold, her dewy darkness down,
And shelters me that I may weep in peace,
And feel no pitying eyes, and hear no voice
Attempt my grief in comfort's alien tongue.

Where cypresses, more black than night is black,
Border straight paths, or where, on hillside slopes,
The dim grey glimmer of the olive trees
Lies like a breath, a ghost, upon the dark,

There will I wander when the nightingale
Ceases, and even the veilèd stars withdraw
Their tremulous light, there find myself at rest,
A silence and a shadow in the gloom.

But all the dead of all the world shall know
The pacing of my sable-sandall'd feet,
And know my tear-drenched veil along the grass,
And think them less forsaken in their graves,
Saying: There's one remembers, one still mourns;
For the forgotten dead are dead indeed.

Night

I have minded me
Of the noon-day brightness,
And the crickets' drowsy
Singing in the sunshine. .

I have minded me
Of the slim marsh-grasses
That the winds at twilight,
Dying, scarcely ripple. .

And I cannot sleep.

I have minded me
Of a lily-pond,
Where the waters sway
All the moonlit leaves
And the curled long stems. .

And I cannot sleep.

Harvesters' Song

Reap, reap the grain and gather
The sweet grapes from the vine;
Our Lord's mother is weeping,
She hath nor bread nor wine;
She is weeping, The Queen of Heaven,
She hath nor bread nor wine.

ROSE-MARY OF THE ANGELS

Little Sister Rose-Marie,
Will thy feet as willing-light
Run through Paradise, I wonder,
As they run the blue skies under,
Willing feet, so airy-light?

Little Sister Rose-Marie,
Will thy voice as bird-note clear
Lift and ripple over Heaven
As its mortal sound is given,
Swift bird-voice, so young and clear?

How God will be glad of thee,
Little Sister Rose-Marie!

Angélique

Have you seen Angélique,
What way she went?
A white robe she wore;
A flickering light near spent
Her pale hand bore.

Have you seen Angélique?
Will she know the place
Dead feet must find,
The grave-cloth on her face
To make her blind?

Have you seen Angélique. .
At night I hear her moan,
And I shiver in my bed;
She wanders all alone,
She cannot find the dead.

Chimes

(1)

The rose new-opening saith,
And the dew of the morning saith,
(Fallen leaves and vanished dew)
Remember death.

Ding dong bell
Ding dong bell

(2)

May-moon thin and young
 In the sky,
Ere you wax and wane
 I shall die;
So my faltering breath,
So my tired heart saith,
That foretell me death.

Ding-dong
Ding-dong
Ding-dong ding-dong bell

(3)

"Thy gold hair likes me well
  And thy blue eyes," he saith,
Who chooses where he will
  And none may hinder—Death.

At head and feet for candles
  Roses burning red,
The valley lilies tolling
  For the early dead:
Ding-dong ding-dong
Ding-dong ding-dong
Ding-dong ding-dong bell

Ding dong bell

Mad-Song

Grey gaolers are my griefs
  That will not let me free;
The bitterness of tears
  Is warder unto me.

I may not leap or run;
  I may nor laugh nor sing.
"Thy cell is small," they say,
  "Be still thou captived thing."

But in the dusk of the night,
  Too sudden-swift to see,
Closing and ivory gates
  Are refuge unto me.

My griefs, my tears must watch,
  And cold the watch they keep;

They whisper, whisper there—
  I hear them in my sleep.

They know that I must come,
  And patient watch they keep,
Whispering, shivering there,
  Till I come back from sleep.

But in the dark of a night,
  Too dark for them to see,
The refuge of black gates
  Will open unto me.

Whisper up there in the dark. .
  Shiver by bleak winds stung. .
My dead lips laugh to hear
  How long you wait. . . how long!

Grey gaolers are my griefs
  That will not let me free;
The bitterness of tears
  Is warder unto me.

The Witch

When I was girl by Nilus stream
  I watched the desert stars arise;
My lover, he who dreamed the Sphinx,
  Learned all his dreaming from my eyes.

I bore in Greece a burning name,
  And I have been in Italy
Madonna to a painter-lad,
  And mistress to a Medici.

And have you heard (and I have heard)
  Of puzzled men with decorous mien,

Who judged—The wench knows far too much—
   And burnt her on the Salem green?[2]

Cry Of The Nymph To Eros

Hear thou my lamentation,
Eros, Aphrodite's son!
My heart is broken and my days are done.

Where the woods are dark and the stream runs clear in the dark,
Eros!

I prayed to thy mother and planted the seeds of her flowers,
And smiled at the planting and wept at the planting. Oh, violets,
Ye are dead and your whiteness, your sweetness, availed not. Thy
   mother
Is cruel. Her flowers lie dead at the steps of her altar,
Eros! Eros!

With a shining like silver they cut through the blue of the sky
Eros!
The dove's wings, the white doves I brought to thy mother in worship;
And I said, she will laugh for joy of my doves. Oh, stillness
Of dead wings. She laughed not nor looked. My doves are dead,
Are dead at the steps of her altar. Thy mother is cruel,
Eros, Eros!

Hear thou my lamentation,
Eros, Aphrodite's son!
My heart is broken and my days are done.

Cradle-Song

Madonna, Madonnina
Sat by the grey road-side,
Saint Joseph her beside,
And Our Lord at her breast;
Oh they were fain to rest,
Mary and Joseph and Jesus,
All by the grey road-side.

She said, Madonna Mary,
"I am thirsty, Joseph, and weary,
All in the desert wide."
Then bent a tall palm-tree
Its branches low to her knee;
"Behold," the palm-tree said,
"My fruit that is drink and bread."
So were they satisfied,
Mary and Joseph and Jesus,
All by the grey road-side.

From Herod they were fled
Over the desert wide,
Mary and Joseph and Jesus,
In Egypt to abide:
Mary and Joseph and Jesus,
In Egypt to abide.

The blessèd Queen of Heaven
Her own dear Son hath given
For my son's sake; his sleep
Is safe and sweet and deep.

Lully. . Lulley. .
So may you sleep alway,
My baby, my dear son:
Amen, Amen, Amen.

My baby, my dear son.

To Man Who Goes Seeking Immortality Bidding Him Look Nearer Home.

Too far afield thy search. Nay, turn. Nay, turn.
  At thine own elbow potent Memory stands,
Thy double, and eternity is cupped
  In the pale hollow of those ghostly hands.

The Lonely Death

In the cold I will rise, I will bathe
In waters of ice; myself
Will shiver, and shrive myself,
Alone in the dawn, and anoint
Forehead and feet and hands;
I will shutter the windows from light,
I will place in their sockets the four
Tall candles and set them a-flame
In the grey of the dawn; and myself
Will lay myself straight in my bed,
And draw the sheet under my chin.

Lo, All The Way

  Lo, all the way,
Look you, I said, the clouds will break, the sky
  Grow clear, the road
Be easier for my travelling, the fields,
  So sodden and dead,
Will shimmer with new green and starry bloom,
  And there will be,
There will be then, with all serene and fair,
  Some little while

For some light laughter in the sun; and lo,
  The journey's end,
Grey road, grey fields, wind and a bitter rain.

The Crucifixion

And the centurion who stood by said:
  Truly this was a son of God.[3]

Not long ago but everywhere I go
  There is a hill and a black windy sky.
Portent of hill, sky, day's eclipse I know;
  Hill, sky, the shuddering darkness, these am I.

The dying at His right hand, at His left,
  I am—the thief redeemed and the lost thief;
I am the careless folk; I those bereft,
  The Well-Belov'd, the women bowed in grief.

The gathering Presence that in terror cried,
  In earth's shock, in the Temple's veil rent through,
I; and a watcher, ignorant, curious-eyed,
  I the centurion who heard and knew.

The Immortal Residue
Inscription for my verse

Wouldst thou find my ashes? Look
In the pages of my book;
And as these thy hand doth turn,
Know here is my funeral urn.

ADDITIONAL POEMS I

To The Dead In The Grave-Yard Under My Window:—Written in A Moment of Exasperation

How can you lie so still? All day I watch
And never a blade of all the green sod moves
To show where restlessly you toss and turn,
And fling a desperate arm or draw up knees
Stiffened and aching from their long disuse;
I watch all night and not one ghost comes forth
To take its freedom of the midnight hour.
Oh, have you no rebellion in your bones?
The very worms must scorn you where you lie,
A pallid mouldering acquiescent folk,
Meek habitants of unresented graves.
Why are you there in your straight row on row
Where I must ever see you from my bed
That in your mere dumb presence iterate
The text so weary in my ears: "Lie still
And rest; be patient and lie still and rest."
I'll not be patient! I will not lie still!
There is a brown road runs between the pines,
And further on the purple woodlands lie,
And still beyond blue mountains lift and loom;
And I would walk the road and I would be
Deep in the wooded shade and I would reach
The windy mountain tops that touch the clouds.
My eyes may follow but my feet are held.
Recumbent as you others must I too
Submit? Be mimic of your movelessness
With pillow and counterpane for stone and sod?
And if the many sayings of the wise
Teach of submission I will not submit
But with a spirit all unreconciled
Flash an unquenched defiance to the stars.
Better it is to walk, to run, to dance,
Better it is to laugh and leap and sing,
To know the open skies of dawn and night,
To move untrammel'd down the flaming noon,

And I will clamour it through weary days
Keeping the edge of deprivation sharp,
Nor with the pliant speaking on my lips
Of resignation, sister to defeat.
I'll not be patient. I will not lie still.

And in ironic quietude who is
The despot of our days and lord of dust
Needs but, scarce heeding, wait to drop
Grim casual comment on rebellion's end:
"Yes; yes ... Wilful and petulant but now
As dead and quiet as the others are."
And this each body and ghost of you hath heard
That in your graves do therefore lie so still.

Saranac Lake—
November—1913

To an Unfaithful Lover

What words
Are left thee then
Who hast squandered on thy
Forgetfulness eternity's
I love?

To A Hermit Thrush

Art thou
Not kin to him
Who loved Mark's wife and both
  Died for it? O, thou harper in
  Green woods?

The Source

Thou hast
Drawn laughter from
A well of secret tears
And thence so elvish it rings,—mocking
And sweet.

For Lucas Cranach's *Eve*

Oh me,
Was there a time
When Paradise knew Eve
In this sweet guise, so placid and
So young?

Blue Hyacinths.

In your
Curled petals what ghosts
Of blue headlands and seas,
What perfumed immortal breath sighing
Of Greece.

Fresher
Than spring's new scents
The winter's earliest wind
Blows from the hills the first faint breath
Of Snow.

Why have
I thought the dew
Ephemeral when I
Shall rest so short a time, myself,
On earth?

Lunatick.

Dost thou
Not feel them slip,
How cold! how cold! the moon's
Thin wavering finger-tips, along
Thy throat?

Thou art not friendly sleep that hath delayed
The long night through and still at dawn doth keep
Estranged from eyes that very weariness
Makes blind to dawn.

Nor moon,
Nor stars . . the dark . . and in
The dark the grey
Ghost glimmer of the olive trees
The black straight rows
Of Cypresses.

Old Love

More dim than waning moon
Thy face, more faint
Than is the falling wind
Thy voice, yet do
Thine eyes most strangely glow,
Thou ghost. . thou ghost.

My Birds That Fly No Longer

Have ye forgot, sweet birds,
How near the heavens lie?
Drooping, sick-pinion'd, oh
Have ye forgot the sky?

The air that once I knew
  Whispered celestial things;
I weep who hear no more
  Upward and rushing wings.

The Elgin Marbles

The clustered Gods, the marching lads,
  The mighty-limbed, deep-bosomed Three,
The shimmering grey-gold London fog . . .
  I wish that Phidias could see!

Safe.

Force and bluster? Mighty threatenings?
  Scorn I lightly,—Not for these.
Tell me when shall great Orion
  Catch the flying Pleiades?

Sad of Heart.

Thou beautiful and ivory gates
  That shut my tears away from me—
Even, at last, such refuge yield
  The great, safe doors of Ebony.

The Event.

Lo, how they weave—the imperturbable three—
   Those threads that are my destiny:
Steadily at the eternal task they're bent
   Industrious . . . indifferent . . .

Weave, Fates! And what your spinstry weaves I'll forthwith wear
And if it clothe me for the day or death's no air.

The Companions

Three grey women walk with me
Fate and Grief and Memory.

My fate brought grief; my grief must be
With me through Eternity,
Such thy power, memory.

Three grey women walk with me.

Epigram

If illness' end be health regained then I
Will pay you, Asculapeus, when I die.

You Nor I Nor Nobody Knows

You nor I nor nobody knows
Where our daily-taken breath
Vanisheth and vanisheth:
Where our lost breath's flying goes
You nor I nor nobody knows.

The Proud Poet

Great Kings were dust and all their deeds forgot
  Did my harp's taut and burnished strings stand mute;
The fragrance of dead ladies' lovely names
  Blew never down the wind but for my lute.

The Plaint

Musicians O Musicians: Heartsease
Heartsease; an you will have me live play heartsease.

Light wind in the small green leaves
Play, oh play, my sad heart ease;

Birds, shake from your wilding throats
Tunèd charm of happy notes;

Shepherd, shepherd, pipe a shrill
A jocound pipe o'er vale and hill;

For from too much weeping I,
Maid forlorn, am like to die.

Endymion.

"Let me be young," the Latmian shepherd prayed,
"And let me have on night-time hills long sleep;"
Whom she of Cynthus saw, Heaven's crownéd maid,
And gave his youth and dreams her love to keep.

What news comrade upon the mountain top
From the courts of the sun? What news from the skies
When great Orion strides the open night,
Heaven's Hunter: hath he told you of Heaven's
Forests and the quarry of the Gods? They do
Not spare their prey I warrant you. Skillful
And merciless. . Saw you young Cynthia threading her
Silver way among the stars and when she yearned o'er him,
The sleeping shepherd on the hills, caught you
Her breath of love? The winds have passed
You in the night, what have they told you of the
Illimitable?—Hath your soul followed thence and gone
beyond the [two undeciphered words] of their journey
envisaged the Ultimate—

Now doth blue kirtled night relume the stars
Bidding them light my dear love on his way,
And for his coming takes all tender cares
That he shall find the night more sweet than day.

Tears.

The immemorial grief of all years
Burdens my heart sorely, and the tears
Of slow eternal crying stain my cheeks.
Forever and forever my soul speaks
Saying: I am thy self: Look on me—
And weep. Never and never shalt thou be
As I. Weep; for weeping and hard pain
Of loss measure joy of last visioned gain.

John-a-dreams—[4]

A laggard in the rear of time's swift feet,
And one who loiters on an aimless way
Through lands he knows not; lured by birds to stray
In secret paths where silence holds the beat
And rustle of ascending wings. Roads meet;
He turns by hazard of some far-glimpsed spray
Of blossoming tree. Shall condemnation say,
Unprofitable! Empty thy days as fleet?

Nay, if perchance he wanders Paradise,
And in unhurried immortality,
Treads child-like wise and ignorant the thrice
Blessed, ultimate regions of the throne of God?
Then needs he not to fear who walks the sod
Of Heaven in angels' radiant company.

Incantation.

O mia Luna! Porta mi fortuna!
(You must say it nine times, curtseying, and then wish.)

In rose-pale, fading blue of twilight sky,
See, the new moon's thin crescent shining clear;
Nine times I'll curtsey murmuring mystic words,—
And wish good fortune to our love, my dear.

Milking Time

Heard ye the maidens
Went through the meadows,
Early, O, early,
While yet the dew was
Wet on the grass?
Heard ye the milk-maids
Singing and singing?

"Cushy cow[5] bonny let down your milk,
And I will give you a gown of silk,
A gown of silk and a silver tee,[6]
If you will let down your milk to me."

Hear ye the maidens,
Over the meadows,
Where the dew gathers,
Where shadows lengthen,
Hear ye the milk-maids'
Aery, hushed voices
Singing, ah, singing?

"Cushy cow bonny let down your milk,
And I will give you a gown of silk,
A gown of silk and a silver tee,
If you will let down your milk to me."

Morning and evening,
In the green meadows
Hear ye the milk-maids
And their sweet singing?

The Fiddler

"There'll be no roof to shelter you;
  You'll have no where to lay your head.
And who will get your food for you?
  Star-dust pays for no man's bread.
    So, Jacky, come give me your fiddle
    If ever you mean to thrive."

"I'll have the skies to shelter me,
  The green grass it shall be my bed,
And happen I'll find some where for me
  A sup of drink, a bite of bread;
    And I'll not give my fiddle
    To any man alive."

And it's out he went across the wold,
  His fiddle tucked beneath his chin,
And (golden bow on silver strings)
  Smiling he fiddled the twilight in;

And fiddled in the frosty moon,
  And all the stars of the Milky Way,
And fiddled low through the dark o' dawn,
  And laughed and fiddled in the day.

But oh, he had nor bite nor sup,
  And oh, the winds blew stark and cold,
And when he dropped on his grass-green bed
  It's long he slept on the open wold.

They digged his grave and "There," they said,
  "He's got more land than ever he had,
And well it will keep him held and housed,
  The feckless bit of a fiddling lad."

And it's out he's stepped across the wold
  His fiddle tucked beneath his chin—
A wavering shape in the wavering light,
  Smiling he fiddles the twilight in,

And fiddles in the frosty moon,
  And all the stars of the Milky Way,
And fiddles low through the dark o' dawn,
  And laughs and fiddles in the day.

He needeth not or bite or sup,
  The winds of night he need not fear,
And (bow of gold on silver strings)
  It's all the people turn to hear.

"Oh, never," it's all the people cry,
  "Came such sweet sounds from mortal hand;"
And "Listen," they say, "It's some ghostly boy
  That goes a-fiddling through the land.

Heark you! It's night comes slipping in,—
  The moon and the stars that tread the sky;
And there's the breath o' the world that stops;
  And now with a shout the sun comes by!"

Who heareth him he heedeth not
  But smiles content, the fiddling-lad;
"It's many and many a happy day,"
  He says, "My fiddle and I have had;
And I'll not give my fiddle
  To any man alive."

Aubade.

The morning is new and the skies are fresh washed with light,
The day cometh in with the sun and I awake laughing.

Hasten, belovèd!
For see, while you were yet sleeping
The cool and virgin feet of dawn went soundless over grey meadows,
And the earth is requickened under her touch.
The vision that came with gradual steps departeth in an instant;
Hasten, lest it be unbeheld of your eyes.

The Parting.

Was it love breathed on us as on the skies
Dawn breathes for a short space and then is fled;
Or loved we never at all who but misread
With too dim vision the guarded mysteries?

Were we unfaithful or were we unwise,
Knew we not love, or if our love is dead,
If such were true, for grace of what is sped,
Could we not part with unaverted eyes?

But whence these looks askance as at strange fears?
And whence the far and muffled cryings that beat
Across the moment of our dire farewell?

Is here of sentience the dread burial?
Is it a still quick love that hear, oh hears,
The last earth fall, the sound of vanishing feet?

As I Went

As I went, as I went,
  Over the mountains,
I heard, I heard,
  Through cloud-wreath and mist,
  A hound that was baying—
Death . . it was death.

As I went, as I went
  Over the meadows,
I heard, I heard,
  From thicket, from shadow,
  A hidden bird fluting—
Death . . it was death.

As I went, as I went
  By rocks and by sand-dunes,
I heard, I heard,
  At the sea's bottom
  A silver fish swimming—
Death . . it was death.

As I went, as I went
  In my house, in my house,
I heard, I heard,
  A footfall, a footfall
  Closely behind me—
Death . . it is death . .

ADDITIONAL POEMS II

Lines Addressed To My Left Lung Inconveniently Enamoured Of Plant-Life

It was, my lung, most strange of you,
  A freak I cannot pardon,
Thus to transform yourself into
  A vegetable-garden.

Though laking William set erewhile
  His seal on rural fashions,
I must deplore, bewail, revile
  Your horticultural passions.

And as your ways I thus lament
  (Which, plainly, I call crazy)
For all I know, serene, content,
  You think yourself a daisy!

Lament

Oh dear me, a maid unlucky,
Though I've searched the green fields over,
Peering, peeping, I have never
Found a single four-leaf clover.
Oh dear me, it's *most* unlucky.

Grave Digger Catch

The new moon
  And a red rose
The old moon
  And a dead rose
Wield the pick
  And wield the spade

Dig . . dig . . dig
  And a grave is made:
Who danced in the light
In dark he'll sleep
Dig his bed for him
Deep . . deep . . deep.

The Song of Choice.

The maiden sat enthroned on the throne of her maidenhood:
There were two lovers that came to her to win her,
And one lover brought gift of red poppies,
And the other carried a sheaf of white poppies in his arms.

And one lover said:
  I bring you gift of red poppies:
  Your hair is golden and long,
  Your hair is soft as cast shadows,
  Your hair is as the path of the sun's light on the sea.
  Make for yourself a wreath of red poppies
  For the adorning of your golden hair.
And the other saith:
  I bring you white poppies:
  They are white as the still white thought of holiness
  That stirred in your soul when you awoke alone at dawn.

And the maiden rejoiced in her hair that was golden.

And one lover said:
  Your eyes are as wells of darkling light
  And your mouth is as wine-stains:
  Let the red of my poppies gladden your eyes,
  Take my red poppies in your hands
  And lift them up for the kisses of your red, red mouth.
And the other saith:
  I bring you white poppies:

They are white as the still white thought of holiness
That stirred in your soul when you awoke alone at dawn.

And the maiden rejoiced that her eyes were as wells of light and her mouth as crimson wine-stains.

And one lover said:
Hold my red poppies between your breasts.
Your breasts are lovely and white
And colour against colour it shall be as blood upon snow;
Your breasts shall be rosily overcast
With the light of the poppies between them.
And the other saith:
I bring you white poppies:
They are white as the still white thought of holiness
That stirred in your soul when you awoke alone at dawn.
And the maiden rejoiced in her breasts that were lovely and white;
She longed for the red poppies to hold them between her breasts.

And one lover said:
Your blood is red and your heart is red
And the poppies of my offering are a fine, keen scarlet.

The maiden arose and stepped down from her throne.
She reached forth her hands to take the heart-red poppies,
She stretched out her hands for the poppies that were red as blood;
Whenas she felt as it were a great rending within her
And faltering she stood in trouble between her lovers.

And one lover said:
It is your pleasure that cries out in you to be accomplish'd.
And the other saith:
Oh, sweet, I know your pain.

Behold the maiden hath chosen a lover:
She hath stepped down from her throne,
She hath found her a dwelling in the heart of her lover:
He holds her in his arms:
He stoops to kiss the sleeve of her garment that is white as the wings of white doves.

Behond the maiden hath chosen a lover:
She hath woven for herself a bride-wreath of white poppies,
She hath given herself into the arms of him that knows her,
And the maiden and her love are content.

The Two Mothers

The evening before the serpent came,
Just at the hour of the Angelus,
"Body o'me what thing is this,"
Said Eve, sighed Eve,
"That if I be merry and glad,
Or if I be sorry and sad,
I cannot tell;"—and a strange sweet name,
The evening before the serpent came,
Whispered and cried in the heart of Eve.

All alone in Eden's bowers,
Eve went gathering Mary's flowers.

The evening before the serpent came,
Just at the first hour of the night,
She reached a flagon of crystal bright,
Sweet Eve, Young Eve,

Snow-white, rose-red, a twi-forked flame,
The evening before the serpent came,
Kindled and burnt in the heart of Eve.

"Where have you been, my bride, my bride?"
"Through the garden's dusk to the sealèd well
'Neath the green hillside."

"What did you see, my wife, my wife?"
"A little white dove in the silvern leaves
Of the Tree of Life."

Oh dew! Oh tears! in Eden's bowers
Fell sweet, fell bitter on Mary's flowers.

The Expulsion

Adam, thou banished man,
Who may not come again,
From thy lost Eden,
Thy loved Garden,
What wilt thou take,
What wilt thou take with thee?

These will I take
These will I take with me:
Odours of cinnamon
Of spikenard of saffron

Dooms-Day

With terror and delight
I meditate Thine eyes
That must, all-seeing, just,
My doings scrutinize

I offer my self to you as cool water in cup of crystal,
So, sweetly fulfilling the needs of thy body
For thou must drink water or die.

I offer myself as wine graciously held in golden goblet
A subtle drink of fire—
Thy soul hath need of this to live.

Between us two no thanks save knowledge that the gift is life to both:
Were it not sin and bitter waste that thou should die thirsty—
Or poured wine and water lie undrunk?

Evil.

In place secluded from the skies
A silent woman with strange eyes
Hiddenly waiting sits alone
Upon a royal-massive throne
Of smoothly polished malachite;
An emeraldine curious light
Fills all the place and through its chill
Sapphired pale glow, arrested still,
Unpalpitant as heart of death,
I watch her soft-drawn patient breath. . .

I will go creeping softly in
Her eyes are promises of sin.

La Morte

Vision of vice grown old,
Harlot with wisped grey hair
Streaked drab and green
Where once was false gold's sheen,
Slack chin, rough wrinkled cheeks, lips bloodless cold,
Going at mid-day through the city streets
In hideous slattern guise;
She whose whole business was to show her body's sweets
Alluringly, indifferent leaves her ugliness unobscured.

And yet look long and secretly. .
Doth there not emanate from where

She is a strange concentrate glow?
Doth not the air about her show
A dove-throat iridescence copper-blue? . . beauty mysteriously
Present in scum blurred thin on stagnant ill-odoured pond?
Corpse-light of lust. . desire's fixed death-filmed eyes.
Still ghost of touch once live and eager-fond. .
Who kissed her pale stale lips would kiss ten thousand thousand kisses
  sepulchered.

Girl Fleeing Love

Bridget! Saint Bride!
Whither shall I go
Lest my red cheeks show,
Lest my cheeks sudden-pale
Cry aloud, a tale
I am fain to hide;
That my heart not know
Its own secret oh!
Whither shall I go?
Bridget! Saint Bride!

It's oh, my dear, the sun shines clear,
  And the white road's fair to see;
And it's will you follow by hill and hollow
  The long white road with me?

It's love, my dear; it's joy, my dear,
  Oh it's life calls, sweet and free:—
By hill and hollow, oh will you follow
  The long white road with me?

What is to fear when skies are clear
  And lover and lass are we?

Then, dear, ah follow, by hill and hollow
The long white road with me!

Clotilda Sings

What is the bitter song that young
Clotilda sings and works all day,
And will not go where lad and lass
Are met in joyous village play?

Oh, young Clotilda sings, how clear
How high and sweet for all to hear,—

Blossoming plum and cherry,
Flowering apple and quince,
In springtime I was merry,
I've learned weeping since,
Bitter weeping since.

Her baby at her woeful breast,
Clotilda sings who hath no rest.

Journey's End.

The sea swings out, the sea swings in,
The grey gulls fly afar,
Each sun-beam catches a crested wave
Like the gleam of a separate star.

She looks to East, she looks to West,
She laughs in the wind and sun;
"He sailed for a year and a day," she saith,
"And this time is almost done;"

"He has found the gold and the shining gems,
He is bringing them home to me.
Oh long-winged gulls, have you seen his ship?
Where is he, oh swaying sea?"

The gulls fly grey across the clouds,
Sunless the grey waves beat. .
Look down, look down, oh doomed woman,
Your love lies at your feet.

There's a gay girl laughing.

There's a gay girl laughing
For pleasure of the sky,
Oh, laughing low and tenderly
In love of soft-breathed sigh
Of wind and greying shadows,
That incorporeal lie
Across sun-ardent grasses
Where bird wings poise and fly.

There's a woman very sorrowful
As empty days go by,
Uncounted hours watched hopelessly
By heart too hurt to cry;
There's a gay girl laughing
For joy of earth and sky,
And a woman dumbly sorrowful,
Who am I . . . Who am I . .

Champagne.

Yellow-pale and bubbling-bright,
Effervescence of delight,

Froth of laughter, foam of song,
Rain of rose leaves blown along;
Pretty women dressed in pink,
Kisses swift as glasses' clink:—
Over brim of lifted light,
Yellow-pale and bubbling-bright,
Life, a laugh's length old is he,
Tips alluring wink at me!

The Black-mailing Ruffian.

But let him try, the Sinner with the Key,
  To block my way; I'll make him let me through!
A tip-toe stand, (ha! ha! now do you see?)
  Flap crooked-up arms . . Cry *Cock-a-doodle-doo!*

Bob White.

Bob White! Bob White!
On brink of night,
On edge of day,
While dawn is grey
In eastern sky,
I hear your cry
Bob White! Bob White!

And what do you say
Bob White? Bob White?
That the sun is up,
That it's light, light, light!
That it's time to be out,
Out, out and away,
The day is here,
The glorious day!

That's what you say
Bob White! Bob White!
In sweet of day
While dawn grows bright.

An Early Christian Hymn
"How doth the Heathen rage"

How doth the ramping Roman rage
  These peaceful vales among;
How wide the swathe his comment cuts,
  How fatal is his tongue.

We may not smoke, we may not drink,
  Our work he holds in scorn;
Of joy bereft, of use despoiled,
  He leaves us all forlorn.

A cultured bunch, we hang our heads
  While he our faults reveals;
And yet, O Lord, we often write
  Our Lectures for ourselves.

Protect, O Lord, thy simple sheep,
  These peaceful vales among;
Protect them from the Roman ramp,
  The raging Roman tongue!

Non Solo.

The stars are up there in the sky,
I cannot tell the reason why,

Nor call a single one by name—
And yet I love them just the same.

The grass is cool and green and sweet,
I like its feel beneath my feet;
But why it's green and how it grows
I don't think anybody knows.

That human beings all should be
Is not a thing that troubles me,
I let the simple facts suffice,
We are—and most of us are nice.

The way a person's mind can change
From day to day is very strange,
Yet, though I only see it's true,
I like variety—don't you?

Oh, many things I do not know;
It's rather nice to have it so.
The Universe is heaps of fun
If I can't say how it is run.

To Anacreon.
On his Age.

What thoughtless, silly nymph was she,
The Lesbian, whose divinity
Of darling charm set worshiping
The heart to love's enrapturing
Sweet service ever dedicate;
But briefest moment would she wait
For the immortal golden ode
To hers and love's dear beauties vow'd,
Then, careless-mocking, took her flight
Because for-sooth the snow of white

Advancing age lay on the brow
Of him who sang. Ah, let her go,
Belov'd Anacreon, nor grieve
To think that therefore he will leave,
Venus' wing'd and laughing boy,
His votary bereft of Joy.
Beguiling girls there many be,
As fair, and wiser far, than she.
They welcome time whose coming brings
The art that deep enlighten'd sings
More perfectly their blandishments.
The fine-discerning eye resents
Not signs of wisdom throned secure,
For youth was never connoisseur
And added years do but improve
The heart that's warmed by wine and love.

Bewail not then the coronal
Of snowy age and venerable
That binds your brow with shining band.
For him whose song-inspired hand
Strikes tunefully the eternal lyre
Of vibrant flaming-stringed desire,
The day of bliss is never over;
He is forever ardent lover.

Traces of the Rustic in Amos.

Tis sad but true that Amos he
Was less polite than ought to be
A prophet though he is but minor;
If he were bidden out to dine or
Sup with colleagues then who knew
What Amos would or wouldn't do!
When he was urged a fork to try
"A knife is good enough for I,"
The rural Prophet would return,

And, careless, smash the coffee-urn.
Polish he lacked and eke repose,
And now in Paradise he goes.
Are his rough ways still with him there?
For all his colleagues what a care!
How, burdened with a social sinner,
Must they lament his lack of manner!
How, blushing, bitterly regret
His rudimentary etiquette!
Saying, What will the Seraphim
And all the angels think of him!
Crying, Alas how grieve, how shame us
These rustic traces in our Amos!

Truthful Love.

Oh smiling-eyes and darling-heart;
  I'm sitting at your feet;
Who ever thought to find on earth
  One so beguiling-sweet?
I long to kiss your pretty hands,
  My heart cries out aglow,
I love you, love you, smiling-eyes—
  And goodness knows, it's so.

Oh darling-heart and smiling-eyes
  You're so bewitching-dear,
I'd like to spend enchanted days
  Just sitting by you here;
My voice implore, ah, may I stay
  And never, never go?
You are so sweet, dear darling-heart,
  I'm sure you will say no.

The Golden Princess.

Under the lemon trees and orange trees,
 Where the birds sing and airy fountains play,
She laughs to feel the laughing breeze,
 She laughs to feel the shining of the day.

The fair corn's silken colour is her hair,
 A broidered aureate shimmering is her gown,
Amber and topaz are her chosen wear,
 Crowned is she with her royalty's bright crown;

Sing, birds, for her whose heart sings radiantly
 Fountains and breezes laugh as laughs her heart,
Day's glories, lighten on her lovingly,
 Who glorious-loving takes love's glorious part.

Oh, gallant princess, soul and self sun's hue,
As heaven tender are thine eyes of blue.

The changed request
O que m'importe que tu sois sage
Sois belle et sois triste

"Be sad, be beautiful, my love,"
 He prayed, oh ardent lad;
"Be never a lesser thing, sweet love;
 Than beautiful and sad."

But now what while the coffee steams,
 And he grows wise the while,
His ardour prays—"The coffee steams,
 Good Lord, my dear—please smile!"

UNDERGRADUATE POEMS

Loneliness.

The earth's all wrapped in gray shroud-mist,
  Dull gray are sea and sky,
And where the water laps the land
  On gray sand-dunes stand I.
Oh, if God there be, his face from me
  The rolling gray mists hide;
And if God there be, his voice from me
  Is kept by the moan of the tide.

Time Flies.

Yesterday in the garden-close
Budded and blossomed and blew a rose,
Faded and fallen its petals gay;
The rose lies dead in the garden to-day.
But, sweet, I pray you do not sorrow,
As fair a rose will bloom to-morrow.

Yesterday, dearest, you and I,
Swore that our love would never die.
Our vows were frail as all vows be.
To-day love's fled from you and me.
But, sweet, I pray you do not sorrow,
New love will come to us to-morrow.

Thus the hours swiftly by us go;
Well, I e'en wist it must be so.
Do not weep now for what is past,
Love and roses will never last.
Then gaily speed past what is over,
And gladly greet new rose and lover.

The Heart of a Maid.

"Petals of the marguerite,
Tell me, pray,
Doth he love me?—Answer
'Yea' or 'nay.' "

"Loveth?" laughs she gaily,
"Let him sigh!
For all the love he offers,
What care I?"

"Petals of the marguerite,
Tell me, pray,
Doth he love me?—Answer
'Yea' or 'nay.' "

"Loves not?" weeps she sorely,
"Let me die!
For life without his love,
What care I?"

Repentance.

(From the old French.)

In very truth, I've been a sinner
And spent my life in foolish manner;
Too much I've used my youthful days
In lightsome, vain and sinful ways.
Aye, oft I've visited the court,
Made love to ladies—idle sport!
To them I've written triolets,
Rondeaux, sonnets and chansonettes.
With naughty lords I've often dined,
Gamed, fought and all too often wined.
Aye, much I've walked in paths of evil;

My boon companion's been the devil.
But now, alack! gay youth is spent;
I'm getting old—I'd best repent!

Hail Mary!

In loveliness and purity,
In faith and grace and piety,
In love and in humility,
God give me grace to be like thee,
That in my poor and low degree
I, like thyself, may blessed be.
Hail, Mary!

CHEROKEE INDIAN CHARMS

The 'Charms (Cherokee Indians)' are Adelaide Crapsey's rearrangements and revisions of prose translations provided by James Mooney in a monograph, "Sacred Formulas of the Cherokees," found in the *Seventh Annual Report of the Bureau of Ethnology to the Secretary of the Smithsonian Institution 1885–1886* by J. W. Powell, Director (Washington: Government Printing Office, 1891). "The sacred formulas here given," writes Mooney, "are selected from a collection of about six hundred, obtained on the Cherokee reservation in North Carolina in 1887 and 1888. . . . The original manuscripts, now in the possession of the Bureau of Ethnology, were written by the shamans of the tribe, for their own use, in the Cherokee characters invented by Sikwâ̆ya (Sequoyah) in 1821, and were obtained, with the explanations, either from the writers themselves or from their surviving relatives." (p. 307) The relevant translations and explanations from Mooney are given below, before Crapsey's poetic versions.

Concerning Living Humanity (Love).

Kû! Listen! In Alahĭ́yĭ you repose, O Terrible Woman, O you have drawn near to hearken. There in Elahiyĭ you are at rest, O White Woman. No one is ever lonely when with you. You are most beautiful. Instantly and at once you have rendered me a white man. No one is ever lonely when with me. Now you have made the path white for me. It shall never be dreary. Now you have put me into it. It shall never become blue. You have brought down to me from above the white road. There in mid-earth (mid-surface) you have placed me. I shall stand erect upon the earth. No one is ever lonely when with me. I am very handsome. You have put me into the white house. I shall be in it as it moves about and no one with me shall ever be lonely. Verily, I shall never become blue. Instantly you have caused it to be so with me.

And now there in Elahiyĭ you have rendered the woman blue. Now you have made the path blue for her. Let her be completely veiled in loneliness. Put her into the blue road. And now bring her down. Place her standing upon the earth. Where her feet are now and wherever she may go, let loneliness leave its mark upon her. Let her be marked out for loneliness where she stands.

Ha! I belong to the (Wolf) (+   +) clan, that one alone which was allotted for you. No one is ever lonely with me. I am handsome. Let her put her soul into the very center of my soul, never to turn away. Grant that in the midst of men she shall never think of them. I belong to the one clan alone which was alloted for you when the seven clans were established.

Where (other) men live it is lonely. They are very loathsome. The common polecat has made them so like himself that they are fit only for his company. They have become mere refuse. They are very loathsome. The common oppossum has made them so like himself that they are fit only to be with him. They are very loathsome. Even the crow has made them so like himself that they are fit only for his company. They are very loathsome. The miserable rain-crow has made them so like himself that they are fit only to be with him.

The seven clans all alike make one feel very lonely in their company. They are not even good looking. They go about clothed with mere refuse. They even go about covered with dung. But I—I was ordained to be a white man. I stand with my face toward the Sun Land. No one is ever lonely with me. I am very handsome. I shall certainly never become blue. I am covered by the everlasting white house wherever I go. No one is ever lonely with me. Your soul has come into the very center of my soul, never to turn away. I—(Gatigwanasti,) (O O)—I take your soul. Sgĕ!

Explanation.

This unique formula is from one of the loose manuscript sheets of Gatigwanasti, now dead, and belongs to the class known as Yù wĕhí or love charms (literally, concerning "living humanity"), including all those referring in any way to the marital or sexual relation. No explanation accompanies the formula, which must therefore be interpreted from analogy. It appears to be recited by the lover himself—not by a hired shaman—perhaps while painting and adorning himself for the dance. . . .

The formula contains several obscure expressions which require further investigation. Elahiyĭ or Alahiyĭ, for it is written both ways in the manuscript, does not occur in any other formula met with thus far, and could not be explained by any of the shamans to whom it was submitted. The nominative form may be Elahĭ, perhaps from *ela*, "the earth," and it may be connected with Wáhilĭ, the formulistic name for the south. The spirit invoked is the White Woman, white being the color denoting the south.

Uhisá'tĭ, rendered here "lonely," is a very expressive word to a Cherokee and is of constant recurrence in the love formulas. It refers to that intangible something characteristic of certain persons which inevitably chills and depresses the spirits of all who may be so unfortunate as to come within its influence. Agisá'tĭ nigésû na, "I never render any one lonely," is an intensified equivalent for, "I am the best company in the world," and to tell a girl that a rival lover is uhisátĭ is to hold out to her the sum of all dreary prospects should she cast in her lot with him.

The speaker, who evidently has an exalted opinion of himself, invokes the aid of the White Woman, who is most beautiful and is never uhisá'tĭ. She at once responds by making him white—that is, a happy—man, and placing him in the white road of happiness, which shall never become blue with grief or despondency. She then places him standing in the middle of the earth, that he may be admired by the whole world, especially by the female portion. She finally puts him into the white house, where happiness abides forever. The verb implies that the house shelters him like a cloak and goes about with him wherever he may go.

There is something comical in the extreme self-complacency with which he asserts that he is very handsome and will never become blue and no one with him is ever lonely. As before stated, white signifies peace and happiness, while blue is the emblem of sorrow and disappointment.

Having thus rendered himself attractive to womankind, he turns his attention to the girl whom he particularly desires to win. He begins by filling her soul with a sense of desolation and loneliness. In the beautiful language of the formula, her path becomes blue and she is veiled in loneliness. He then asserts, and reiterates, that he is the one of the only clan which was alloted for her when the seven clans were established.

He next pays his respects to his rivals and advances some very forcible arguments to show that she could never be happy with any of them. He says that they are all "lonesome" and utterly loathsome—the word implies that they are mutually loathsome—and that they are the veriest trash and refuse. He compares them to so many polecats, oppossums, and crows, and finally likens them to the raincrow (cuckoo; *Coccygnus),* which is regarded with disfavor on account of its disagreeable note. He grows more bitter in his denunciations as he proceeds and finally disposes of the matter by saying that all the seven clans alike are uhisá'tĭ and are covered with filth. Then follows another glowing panegyric of himself, closing with the beautiful expression, "your soul has come into the very center of mine, never to turn away," which reminds one forcibly of the sentiment in the German love song, "Du liegst mir im Herzen." The final expression, "I take your soul," implies that the formula has now accomplished its purpose in fixing her thoughts upon himself.

When successful, a ceremony of this kind has the effect of rendering the victim so "blue" or lovesick that her life is in danger until another formula is repeated to make her soul "white" or happy again. Where the name of the individual or clan is mentioned in these formulas the blank is indicated in the manuscript by crosses + + or ciphers 0 0 or by the word iyústĭ, "like."

(pp. 376–378)

This is to Treat Them If They Are Bitten by a Snake.

1. Dûnúwa, dûnúwa, dûnúwa, dûnúwa, dûnúwa, dûnúwa.
   [*song*]

Listen! Ha! It is only a common frog which has
   passed by and put it (the intruder) into you.

2. Dayuhá, dayuhá, dayuhá, dayuhá, dayuhá.
   Listen! Ha! It is only an *Usú'gĭ* which has
   passed by and put it into you.

(Prescription.)—Now this at the beginning is a song. One should say it twice and also say the second line twice. Rub tobacco (juice) on the bite for some time, or if there be no tobacco just rub on saliva once. In rubbing it on, one must go around four times. Go around toward the left and blow four times in a circle. This is because in lying down the snake always coils to the right and this is just the same (*lit.* "means like") as uncoiling it.

Explanation.

This is also from the manuscript book of Gahuni, deceased, so that no explanation could be obtained from the writer.

(p. 351)

CHARMS (CHEROKEE INDIANS)—

(1) Love Charm—

Ku! Listen! In Alahiyi you repose, O Terrible Woman,
O you have drawn near to hearken.
There in Elayihi you rest, O White Woman.
When with you no one ever is lonely.
Most beautiful are you.
At once you have made me a white man.
When with me no one ever is lonely.
Now you have made the path white for me.
Never shall it be dreary.
Now you have put me into it.
Never shall it become blue.
The white road you have brought down to me.
There in mid-earth you have placed me.
Upon the earth shall I stand erect.
When with me no one ever is lonely.
Into the white house you have led me.

There in Elayihi you have made the woman blue.
Now you have made the path blue for her.
Let her be wholly veiled in loneliness.
Where her feet are now and where ever she goes
Let loneliness leave its mark upon her.

Ha! I belong to the Wolf clan,
That one alone which was destined for you.
No one is ever lonely with me.
In the midst of men may she never think of them.
I belong to the one clan destined for you
When the seven clans were established.

For I was ordained to be a white man.
I stand with my face towards the sun.
No one is ever lonely with me.
Every where I am shadowed by the white house everlasting.

No one is ever lonely with me.
Your soul has come
Into the very core of my soul
Never to turn away.
I—I take your soul. Sge!

(2) Charm to cure the bite of a snake.

Dunuwa, dunuwa, dunuwa, dunuwa, dunuwa, dunuwa.
Listen! Ha! It is only a common frog which
Has passed by and put it into you.

Dayuha, dayuha, dayuha, dayuha, dayuha, dayuha.
Listen! Ha! It is only an Usugi which
Has passed by and put it into you.

Letters

The extant letters of Adelaide Crapsey comprise two main groups, for the most part found in the University of Rochester's Adelaide Crapsey papers: letters to her family in a blue scrapbook and a group of letters written to Esther Lowenthal in 1913 and 1914.

The letters in the scrapbook prepared by Adelaide T. Crapsey after her daughter's death date from two distinct periods. The first group, written while Adelaide Crapsey was a student at the Kemper Hall preparatory school in Kenosha, Wisconsin (from the fall of 1893 to June 1897), consists of fifteen letters. The second group comprises sixteen letters written to her mother, father, and family during her third trip to Europe (1908–1911). In addition to the two larger groups there are: two letters to her family in Rochester written from Plainfield, New Jersey in 1911; a letter from Tyringham, Massachusetts to a Miss Van Horn in Northampton; a card to Marie Louise Crapsey, her youngest sister; two letters to Jean Webster written from Rochester within weeks of her death. (The letters to Jean Webster are from the Connor collection.) Adelaide T. Crapsey labels the card as from Smith College and assigns it a date in 1912, but passages in the Crapsey letters to Esther Lowenthal make it more probable that the card was written from Saranac Lake.

The dating and ordering of the scrapbook letters presents problems. No envelopes are included and Crapsey almost never dates her letters (she remarks upon one of the rare occasions when she does so) so that any attempt to place the letters in chronological order must be guided by evidence within the letters or, to a limited extent, by Mrs. Crapsey's assigned labels and sequence in the scrapbook. Mrs. Crapsey's order may be mistaken and does not follow chronological order: one leaf has fastened to it letters from London dated by Mrs. Crapsey as 1909 and 1910, while an earlier leaf holds a letter assigned a 1910 date, and the laced looseleaf pages of the book themselves may at some time have been reordered. The typewritten "Extracts from her Mother's Journal," two leaves fastened into the same scrapbook, offer some clues about dates and a list of "Addresses during two years" (1909-1911): "Piazza Venezia, Rome, Italy; 56 Haymarket, London, England; Herne Bay, Kent, England; 116 Ebury St. Eaton Sq., London; 86 Oakley St. Chelsea, London S.W. England."

If Mrs. Crapsey's identifications of the letters are accepted as accurate, the scrapbook contains no letters from Adelaide during her four years at Vassar College (1897–1901), no letters from her years as a teacher at Kemper Hall (1902–1904), no letters from her year in Rome (1904–1905), no letters from her years as a teacher at Miss Lowe's school in Stamford,

Connecticut (1906–1908), or from her trip with her father to the Hague Peace conference in the summer of 1907, no letters from her year and a half as a teacher at Smith College (1911–1913), or her year at Saranac Lake (1913–1914) except for the card, although it does contain one letter from her brother Paul Crapsey describing her arrival in Saranac Lake in September 1913. The scrapbook, indeed, preserves a mysteriously selective and tantalizingly small group of letters, all carefully, if sometimes inaccurately, labeled by Mrs. Crapsey. The principle of selection, perhaps simple availability, remains a mystery.

The Crapsey-Lowenthal letters, preserved with their envelopes in almost every case, seem to present the complete correspondence of a specific, clearly defined period: a period critical both for Crapsey's life and her poetry. The interest of the Lowenthal letters and of most surviving Crapsey letters as human documents makes the apparently certain destruction of all but two of the poet's letters to her friend Jean Webster a great loss. Mrs. Connor says that Crapsey's letters to her mother were probably cleaned out of Mrs. McKinney's New York apartment soon after her death in 1916.

Within the three groups of Crapsey letters the arrangement is by chronological order or probable chronological order. The heading provides the name of the addressee, the date or probable date, the place from which the letter is written, and the number of leaves. In the Lowenthal letters the addressee is always the same, so the first line of the heading is omitted. If any element in the heading is uncertain, it is placed in square brackets. When an envelope survives, the address and the postmark follow the text of the letter. All of the letters are Crapsey holographs, except as noted.

The editor's aim has been to present a text faithful to the wild originality of Crapsey's prose and reflecting her processes of composition, which yet was easy and enjoyable to read. Crapsey's spelling and punctuation have been preserved as they stand in the manuscripts with minimum interference, and with more standard spellings or punctuation supplied in square brackets only where confusion might arise. Her characteristic use or omission of apostrophes in possessives and contractions has not been normalized. She punctuates largely with dashes, and dashes of varying lengths have been represented by the standard dash. Where a dash seems to be intended as a dash, no space precedes or follows. Where a dash seems to signify a full stop, space is left as it would be after a period or semicolon. Quotation marks, dashes, and parentheses missing from intended pairs have been silently supplied. Crapsey's double, triple, and quadruple underlinings have been interpreted by italics. Omitted silently are slips of the pen, false starts at words, and careless repetitions of a single word.

A

To Family

1893–1895

1

Adelaide T. Crapsey
[1893]
Kemper Hall, Kenosha, Wisconsin
6 fols.

My dearest Mamma

At last we know when vacation begins. We leave here on the 21st of Dec and come back the 6th of January. That is I reach home one week from next Sunday. I have to travel on Sunday both coming and going but I guess I can stand that. Does it seem possible that the vacation is so nearly here? Emily is going to write you today about Mays invitation. As there are not going to be any other girls here this Xmas I think it would be nice for her to go and of courese it would not be any more expensive which is the chief thing to consider. She has not said anything about [it] to me lately so I don't know what she thinks about it.

Mr Burton Holmes lectured here the other night on Spain. He is becomming [undeciphered word ends in 'ly'] monotonous. He started to show us pictures of the bullfights but Sister wouldn't let him. Said it was not "proper." Mary Draper is back. I went over there to her on Thursday which is the reason why I did not write. We have a lecture on Art this week and an Exhibition in gyms. Next week are Exams. How I hate them. But we never think much of Exams when a holliday comes right after them. In the way of work everything is the same as usual. I've got two themes to write and not an idea what to write about which is a delightful situation. I wrote one about Algy the other day which Miss Ramsey [?] said was "very good indeed". French is out of sight. I enjoy it more than anything else. There are only two of us in the class you know and we are simply flying. We are reading "The Black July", one of Dumas you know, now. I expect to finish that some time this week and start another one. You must have had a fine time thanksgiving with all the cream at home. I am so sorry Phil is not getting on at Catskill. I wish he could go somewhere where there is more life.

Did you get the Kodacs [the Kemper Hall *Kodak,* the school newspaper]—What did you think of Emilys "Told by the Roadside." Wasn't it out of sight? Miss Adams farely raved over it and a thing has to be pretty good for that. We are beginning now to work over the December number. Thank fortune I have not the editorials to write this year but it will be my turn next. Our class gave a sleigh ride last Tuesday night. We had a fine time.

Has Rachel seen about my "Diana of The Crossways". Tell her she will be an angel if she will.

I suppose it is about time to talk about the money for my ticket. Papa knows how much that is doesn't he? O dear! I feel as if it were awfully selfish to take all that money for traveling expensis. If you think I had better I will stay here this vacation too. Doesn't Papa know some railroad man he can get a pass from?

Love to all + especiall[y] you + P.A.
Ever affectioeatly
Adelaide

2

Adelaide T. Crapsey
[1893]
Kemper Hall, Kenosha, Wisconsin
5 fols.

My dearest Mamma
Emily and I were no end glad to get your letter today. I am so glad you have had your picture taken but I'm sorry they did not turn out better. When will we get them. Soon I hope for we are awfully anxious to see them. Harrys pictures are very good don't you think.

I am glad you like the pictures I sent, every one here does too. It is very good of all of us that is as good as a group can be. They are the girls I go with most and like the best. The first girl (Grace Chapman) + the third Louisa Cary (beginning with the tallest) I like about as well as any girls in school. They are *mighty* nice. The sixth one is my roommate Ada Ferry [?]. Don't you think she looks awfully nice and jolly. She is I can tell you and we get on beautifully. We say with pride that we haven't had even the beginning of a scrap since we roomed together. We have already decided to room together next year and are going to ask for Emily's room.

Charlie sent me a dear box of Huylers the other day and a letter. I must write + thank him. Its too bad isn't it that he is not in Rochester. He seems to think there is no hope of his going their [there] again either. Got a letter from Hawley yesterday which was of course foot-ball from beginning to end. They are jubilant at Princeton + are going to do Yale up if it takes a neck.

I am so glad you have a cook and if she only will turn out as well as Annie did wont it be smooth— And you've engaged a nurse for Charly allready! If Charily isn't a boy I wont speak to her. Emily has only mentioned her "plan" to me once—you know I see very little of her—and then she seemed to think it would be the best thing to do. I cant bear either to think of you all alone when you are ill and wish we could both be there—but if only one of us can be I suppose Emily would be lots more help than I. You know by sad experience that I'm pretty much of a good for nothing. However we needn't decide yet.

Love to everybody and lots for yourself "Adelaide" dear

lovingly
Adelaide

3

Adelaide T. Crapsey
[1894]
Kemper Hall, Kenosha, Wisconsin
2 fols.

My dearest Mamma

The box arrived yesterday afternoon. Thank you so much for sending the things. It was awfully good of you to bother about it when you are so tired and busy. The black skirt is not at all to [too] short and goes finely with my silk waist. I found the belt in a box on the top shelf of my wardrobe. The stockings and underwaists fit too. Emily has that silk scarf on her beaureau and it looks "too sweet for any good use". Tell Phil he was a duck to send the nuts. Douglas is not to be crushed. Yesterday Emily received a "Princeton Bric a Brac." But really it was very sweetly done; Emily will tell you about it so I guess I won't. Poor little Monamie! I hope she is ever and ever so much better by this time. When is everybody going to be well? Won't you be glad when they are. We have visitors day tomorrow. A lot of the town people come up and we preform in the Gymnasium there will be vaulting and swinging and barbell excercises. Those (the barbells) are awfully pretty. Sister was'ent going to let us vault but Miss Wilder got her to change her mind. Mable Horlick is the best vaulter in the school. She went home Saturday; I do hope she will be back in time. She goes over the bar so easily and grasefully. Emily hurt her foot the other day and has been limping round in a bright pink knitted slipper. She has a shoe on this morning. We both went to early service this morning. Harriet Woodward went too and fainted or had a fit or something of the sort. She is allright now I guess. Fifteen weeks to the

June vacation. O dear if we only were going home Easter. These letters will reach you on your birthday, wont they. Suppose we could be home that day. Phil will be eighteen won't he? Dear me! with a brother eighteen and a sister seventeen I feel more than young. I will be glad when September comes and I shall be sixteen. Have you begun to make plans for the summer after the usual custom of the Crapseys. Emily had a letter from Marjorie the other day suggesting that we take their cottage. Even if we stay in Rochester we will have an out of sight time. As long as we are at home we will not ask for any thing else. With many many happy returns of the day

very lovingly Adelaide

4

Adelaide T. Crapsey
1894
Kemper Hall, Kenosha, Wisconsin
3 fols.

My dearest Mamma

Everything here is about settled and going on in the same old way. I feel as though I had been here weeks instead of days. Our chair [?] came today and Sister Carolyn is going to have it unpacked for us. After school we are going to fix our room. It is simply splendid having that room. It is on the fourth floor and in the new part so that we are just as private as if we were at home. There is just one thing more we want and that is a clock. You see we are so out of the way that we hardly ever hear the bells and so have to rely on our selves. This morning we made a mistake and got up long before the risingbell rang much to our disgust. The first morning we were here we slept till the breakfast bell rang you know.

Could Papa make any sence out of the letter I wrote him Thursday? I wrote it in such a hurry that I did'ent know whether he could or not. You see Emily and I are taking College Prep. and as Emily wants to graduate next year we have got to do a lot of extra work. Will you ask Papa to write soon as we want to start as soon as possible It will be awfully hard work and will take no end of time but Emily and I are both willing to do it.

Last night we did not have lectures. We are hoping that we are going to get out of it alltogether but I am afraid that no such good luck is in store for us.

I think of you today as triming the church for Harvest home. I hope you won't get very tired.

School is over so I must close my letter. Give my love to Papa, Phil and all the "Kidlets".

Most lovingly
Adelaide—

Will you please send us a Bible *immediatly*—

5

Adelaide T. Crapsey
October 15, 1894
Kemper Hall, Kenosha, Wisconsin
4 fols.

Oct 15–1894

My dearest Mamma

Have Emily and I got to be vaccinated again? Please write soon and say we havee'nt got to be. You know Dr Carr said last year that it wasent necessary. I think it is a crazy idea anyhow don't you?

I suppose Annie has left by this time and you are struggling with A[u]gusta the superior. Do you think you will keep her? Is Mire better? I hope no one is going to be very ill this winter

I have just been writing the date of my last vaccination. I wrote it in a hurry and first put down that I was vaccinated in 1789 and then changed that to 1897. Finally I managed to get it 1879 the correct date.

Absolutely nothing has happened here lately except that we went on a moonlight walk the other night and that the new part of the house was blessed yesterday. That reminds me that we havent a bible yet. Will you send us one please.

Has Papa written to Sister M. C. [Margaret Clare]? Fraulein is getting very impatient and I don't know what she will do if we don't hear this week. You see we have lost three weeks already and that is quite a good deal. Will you ask him if he wont write *soon.*

What do you think I have done, Mamma? It will please you and Papa I guess. I have stopped curling my hair and wear it parted in the middle just as straight as yours. Marjorie says I look exactly like you. Everyone

here likes it much better straight than curled. It is rather a nusance now for I have to pin all the short locks down and the hairpins *will* not stay in. I drop them where ever I go.
Is everything at the Rectory going along smothly so that you can go to Mrs Allen's? How is Charles? Is he going to be in Rochester long?

Emily is going to Brassville so she says to give you her love and she will write Thursday as she has'ent time now.

We expect to have a feast tonight in our room in honor of its being blessed. Love to all and a great deal for yourself

very affectionately
Adelaide.

6

Adelaide T. Crapsey
[1894]
559 Marshall Street, Milwaukee, Wisconsin
2 fols. [letterhead '559 Marshall Street.']

My dearest Mamma

I suppose you have received my two K.H. [Kemper Hall] scrawls and here is one from Milwaukee. I am having a no end good time here. It is perfectly delightful not to have school and no[t] to have to hustle every minute. Miss Miller is lovely and a charming hostess. Does'nt make you feel as if you were "company" you know. She gave a luncheon for me yesterday. It was just as pretty as it could be. There were ten or eleven girls at it and as I knew most of them is [it] was not at all stiff. In the evening we went to a candy pull and had a good time too. This afternoon there was to have been a tea but the brother of the girl who was to have given it has come down with typhoid and so it is "off" On Saturday there is a tea at Miss Julia Mullers so I shall stay till Monday and not go tomorrow (Friday) as I had expected. We have breakfast at eight o'clock, drive downtown at half past nine or ten, get back at twelve or half past and read and talk till lunch at one. After dinner we either lie around and read, which you know I am not averse to doing, or go out to see one of the girls. We have been out two or three times in the evening and the rest we have been at home reading or talking. Miss Miller is engaged. Her fiancé, an awfully nice jolly fellow is here every night till about ten. We go to bed at half past ten or eleven. Altogether it is quite out of sight.

Of course you have heard of Mother Hariett's death. I saw in the paper the other morning and was very much surprised as I did not even know she was ill. Do you suppose Sister Margaret Clare will be Mother Superior. That is what I am afraid of and what would K.H. [Kemper Hall] be without Sister M.C. Mary Draper writes that the sisters are very much broken up over it.

How are you and the baby and the cook getting on. Those are the only three members of the family that I worry about. Do you know that there are only about nine weeks after vacation before we go home. School closes on the elevent[h] but I have to stay a week later to get out that wretched Kodak. I would give anything to get out of that. I suppose you have heard from Emily. I forgot to give her my adress so I haven't. I am going to write her this afternoon if I have time. Just now I am going to pay up the letter I have owed my reverend uncle for some time past   With lots of love to every one and especially you and "de Kid"

I remain
your affectonat
and
loving daughter
Adelaide Jr.

7

Adelaide T. Crapsey
[1895]
Kemper Hall, Kenosha, Wisconsin
3 fols.

My dearest Mamma

I sent you a line the other day to let you know that I passed through the great and wicked city of Chicago without being sandbagged, kidnapped or having any adventures of any sort. I write now to let you know that I have not yet joined the Housboat on the Styx nor have I developped any symptoms of chickenpox though Sister expects them momentairaly. When I arrived I found that I was to room in the big infirmary with Mary Draper (!!) so that there would be no danger of infection but before night Sister Flo. sent for me and said that she did not think it was necessary so I went right into my own room with Ada. And I can tell you we were mighty glad. Almost all the girls are back and there are now—with the new girls who came in this term—an even 90 on the roll book. So you see we are quite full.

I unpacked my trunk yesterday and we had a feast in Grace Chapmans room on the grub that I brought. The crackers and wafers that were left we put in our closet where the[y] were unfortunately discovered by Miss Edwards and confiscated together with one of Balzac's novels that I brought with me. I expect to be invited to the office in a day or tow [two]. I would like to send regrets but I am afraid that would hurt Sisters feelings.

Emily is looking very well and is not at all tired. That "ill" story certainly looks rather fishy. Of course I have gone right into the same old round of work. Tuesday I started studying at 5 P.M and studied from then till ten minutes of ten with a short interval for supper and the Epifhany [Epiphany] cake. What do you think of that for a beginning? As usual I've a wretched theme on my hands. Wish I'd written it when I was home!

I went to the dressmakers today and she is going to rebind and mend my skirt. By the way I left my dearly beloved slippers under my bed. Do you think you could send them on by mail.

How is Tom and when is Maggie coming back. Can you have Mrs Rolf in often.

Emily says to give you her best. She is writing to Mrs Valentine.

Love to all the Kids and lots for yourself.

Ever Affectionately
Adelaide.

8

Adelaide T. Crapsey
[1895]
Kemper Hall, Kenosha, Wisconsin
1 fol. [letterhead in blue 'Kemper Hall,/Kenosha, Wisconsin.']

My dearest Mamma

I know you think I am a perfect brute about writing but if you could see me hustling you would excuse the lack of letters, I know. What do you think of your lazy daughter having to get up at half past four in the morning? I shall be no end glad when vacation and rest come. I had a jolly good time in Chicago. It was all right for me to go wasn't it. Of course it did not cost anything as I was Flodis's [?] guest. Don't you think we were idiots. We had letters of introduction to Maude Adams and never went to call on her— We have been kicking ourselves ever since. We are having a lovely time with money aren't we. Do you think we will ever get out. I am no end sorry but I'm afraid I'll have to ask for some. I haven't had any since before Easter you know and I'm dead broke. I have some class expenses which I shall have to meets [meet]. I think that with a 5 [?] I can get throug[h] till June

Isnt it fine that Papa is coming? Only I *do wish* you were. You'll come next year wont you?

Lots of love to ev[er]yone

Your loving but hustled daughter
Adelaide

9

Adelaide T. Crapsey
[1895]
Kemper Hall, Kenosha, Wisconsin
3 fols.

My dearest Mamma

I received a note from Billy this morning containing your ad[d]ress and telling us when the mail steamer sailed. We are very anxious to know what kind of a voyage you had, wheather you were ill or not, how you like the Bermudas and everything else. O Dear! I wish we were with you. What fun we could have. I had a letter from Harry the other day he says things at the rectory are getting along beautifully. Charlotte is there for one or two days now. But I suppose you know all this. Emily and I are still in existance and are manageing to get a little more fun out of it than we did when we first came. But the summer still seems in the very very dim and distant future. I shall not be surprised to hear that Papa is charmed with the Bermudas and intends to build our "palace" there instead on [of] on the shores of Canandaigua. Everything here is as beastly stupid as ever. Emily is writing you a long letter I can't imagine what she finds to say: she wants me to bustle with this so we can get it off soon. We have the mild excitement of a lecture on Japan tonight.

Tomorrow is Tuesday and lessons begin again. Emily has of course told you about her letter from Douglas. I don't believe I ever laughed so much about anything in my life. It was the funniest thing I ever read. Not that it was intended to be so. O Dear no! But it was its seriousness that killed us. Douglas is saved. I wonder wheather he intends to be any "gooder" than he was before. Emily says I must stop or this letter will not

get to New York in time. My letter is awfully short but you know what I said when I left home. Love to Papa and a very great deal for yourself
very affectionately
Adelaide

10

Adelaide T. Crapsey
[1895]
Kemper Hall, Kenosha, Wisconsin
1 fol. [letterhead in gray 'Kemper Hall,/Kenosha, Wis.']

My dearest Mamma
How you will laugh when I tell you what Emily received the other day. Nothing more or less than Douglas'es picture! We more than howeled over it. Talk about perseverence! I wrote a letter to you in Study hour this evening but it was so mixed that I tore it up. I wrote it just after I had finished a lot of German and I was rather rattled I guess. I guess this won't be much better though for Emily will not keep still. She says she has nervous prostration and I guess she has—not that or something else. She is talking a blue streak and scribling all over my paper. I will explain that remark on the margin some other time. [A pencil note along the right side of the leaf reads: 'tell Phil Adelaide is coming out Green all over.'] It is very amusing now but it was'ent so much so at the time. How is everything at the Rectory? In two weeks we will be there, houpla!!! Wont it be gorgeous. Emily and I are both very well now but we don't expect to survive the exams. They are going to be something to dream off. Writing hour is almost over and I must close. Will write a longer letter Monday very lovingly Adelaide

11

Adelaide T. Crapsey
March 1, 1895
Kemper Hall, Kenosha, Wisconsin
1 fol.

My dearest Mamma
I have spent almost all writing hour waiting for my turn at book press, the result is I have only about twenty minutes left for letter writing.

Rachel wrote me the other day that you would be downstairs soon. We were awfully glad to hear that, you have been having an awfully hard time ever since you came back, hav'ent you? I hope everybody will get well and stay well. All the girls are beginning to count the days to the Easter hollidays. O if we were only going to go to be home for the hollidays! Ev[e]rything here is the same as usual. Indeed it always is the "same as usual."

My letter will be even shorter than Emilys I am afraid. I wish we had more time. Miss Wilder makes me tired, she send[s] me out almost every afternoon. I had a letter from Hawley the other day directed to Mrs. Adelaide Crapsey. Guess he was thinking of you. Tell Phil I wrote to him but can't find the letter. O I will be glad when we are home again. How is Grandma? Love to all

very lovingly
Adelaide

March 1st.

12

Adelaide T. Crapsey
[1895]
Kemper Hall, Kenosha, Wisconsin
2 fols.

My dearest Mamma

Emily has just received your letter and we were awfully glad to hear from you. I had a letter from Charles yesterday in which he told me of the nice long talk you and he had on Sunday. How you must have enjoyed it and how we envied you.(?) I was very much surprised when the letter came and could not for a moment think who it was from. Emily and I have been out walking this afternoon; we went alone!! During the Easter vacation we can go *down town* alone the girls say. Did you ever hear of anything so shocking? Our alcoves are very pretty and Emily and I have decided not to have curtains. We never could make them and get them up. We just managed to survive the table; the curta[i]ns would kill us. It is almost like summer here. Just as warm as it can be. It seems so strange to think that it is only march; 13 weeks till the June vacation. O dear! Visitors Day was quite a success. Although it was a beastly night quite a good many people were out. Ruth Ray won the prize. She is the girl who sings so beautifully. Did I ever tell you about her? She has a magnificent alto voice. I wish you could hear her sing. We havent ma[n]y good voices here. Ruth's is far and away the best in school. Belle Bailly had an very sweet voice but she did not come back this term. The bell for Study hour has rung and I have about a million lessons to get. (that is four).

Love to all
very affectionately
Adelaide

13

Adelaide T. Crapsey
[1895]
Kemper Hall, Kenosha, Wisconsin
2 fols.

My dearest Mamma

I am afraid you think that I have given up letter writing for the rest of the term but I haven't only it is rather hard for me to find time for it. I think your pictures are lovely. I like the one you sent first the better I think. We are *so* glad to have them. What do Paul and Phil think of them? Now Papa ought to have one taken to go with it and then we would have the whole Crapsey family out here.

How I envy Paul going home for Thanksgiving. But Xmas will be here in no time now. Wont it be odd for me to go home with out Emily?

Last night Emily and I went up to see Fraulein in reception time and read a German Play. Fraulein is just as dear as ever. I don't know what we should have done if she had not come back. We are getting on swimmi[n]gly in French. Read one novel—and a long one too—in three recitations. Now we are starting one of Dumas.

We are haveing regular winter we[a]ther now—snow and wind and *cold*—O my! Ada has gone to Chicago to spend Sunday with Edith Bacon. She will be back today and promised to bring me some candy.

I was more than sorry to hear of your finger. How is it now?

I am afraid the Chapel bell has rung and must go and see

Love to all
Adelaide

Tell Duchess to write

14

Adelaide T. Crapsey
[1895]
Kemper Hall, Kenosha, Wisconsin
2 fols.

My dearest Mamma

As the time for the girls to go draws nearer the thought of staying here makes me pretty blue. The number of girls who are to stay here has greatly diminished and you can think how dismal this big place will be with eight or nine of us floating round in it. However you must not worry as we shall probably manage to survive it. The service here yesterday was lovely. I wish you could have seen it. The Chapel was filled and evry single person went up to the alter steps and got a palm. There was one poor lonely man who came with Mrs Grey and she dragged him up to get his. You should have seen him. One hand was half in his pocket so that it looked as though he would very much have liked to put it all in but was afraid to. He walked all over his feet and was altogether about the most rattled young man I ever saw. We were all very sorry for him but couldnt help laughing. Meryn and I led the prosession and succeeded in getting through without any breaks. It was a very long service and we were all very tired when it was over. We sang "All glory laud and honor" five times during the prosession—60 verses—so you can see how long it took everyon[e] to get palms. In the afternoon there was a baptism. Saturday was confirmation. We are all quaking over exams. I guess they will be *awfull.* Emily and I were so surprised to hear of Mr Parkins death. What will Mrs Parkins do? Who are the "A.P.A."s? Emily and I have not the slightest idea. Emily has told you of our hardupedness I think. Our sole possessions are two cents It is all becaus[e] of that beastly bill I told you of. Of course we will have to make an Easter offering next Sunday; so if we could have the money before then we would like it very much. O dear! it makes me so home sick to think we have got to be hear [here] Easter. I dont think June will ever come. Why don't you come out here and spend the vacation? Really I dont think I shall survive if you don't. Love to all

very affectionately
Adelaide

15

Adelaide T. Crapsey
[1895]
Kemper Hall, Kenosha, Wisconsin
2 fols.

My dearest Mamma

We have just finished reading a highly exciting (?) book by Maxwell Grey which we invoked [?] from the town. By we I mean Miss French, Emily, and I. We got the book (a costly freak) under the impression that it was something wildly exciting and though it has turned out to be just the opposite we have had no end of fun over it. It would be almost impossible to read the book to yourself but read aloud it is awfully funny. Just full of padding. Outside scenery always accords with the emotions of the people or forms a picturesque contrast. The clock always ticks on and the /cinders/embers/ tinkle on the hearth under all circumstances. The fire dies down at exactly the right moment. The hero has a voice like the roll of an Atlantic breaker. One of the girls has heart'sease eyes. Mr Grey devotes pages to the description of a dog and a cat and they turn up on every possible occasion. It gets to be perfectly ridiculous. We have had quite a cozy time this vacation. It will come to an end Tuesday. O dear! I wish the snow would keep all the girls away. We have made no end of candy this week. Some for ourselves and some for Sister Francis Anna's Children. We made molasses candy for them and nearly murdered our hands pulling it. Emilys were the worst; they were covered with blisters. To night the girls are making popcorn. I am too lazy to go down however. I wish you could have some of the fudges Miss French + Emily made this morning. Sister Margaret Clare says we will all be ill. I guess Mrs Jennison will be glad when the Hollidays are over. The poor thing gets perfectly wild because we neve[r] get down to breakfast on time. She nearly had a canipition [conniption] one day because we laughed in grace. She is the most unpopular person in the school I guess. She give[s] us all several pains. Emily Washburn and I are [w]racking our brains to get up a ghost for Emilys benefit. You see she has ghosts on the brain and last night dragged me over in her bed, declaring that she heard noises. We are going to give her some first class ghosts tonight. I wish you were having a brighter time at the rectory. What is the matter of the Vestry? Paul said that the Easter offering was $2000. We think that big. Just wait till summer comes. If we dont have a jolly time it wont be our fault. One thing Emily and I are wild to do and that is learn to make our own gowns. Do you think we can? Tell Phil he has owed me a letter for ages. With love to all

Very affectionately
Adelaide

Will you send us Grandma's ad[d]ress.

B

To Family and Friends

1908–1914

1

Adelaide T. Crapsey
1908
en route to Europe
1 fol. [letterhead 'Hamburg-Amerika Linie/Genua-Via Roma, 4/ Telegramm-Addresse HAPAG, GENUA']

Dear Mother—

Gibraltar is nearly here and the rain is pouring down. The coast of Africa is supposed to be in sight but because of the fog it isn't. We've had a fair voyage. No storms but a tremendous swell that has sent the ship from side to side with tiresome regularity. It hasn't been cold at all.

I'm not going to try to write much—Its so hot + stuffy inside—and ones mind doesn't work on shipboard—or mine doesnt.

How I wonder how you all are. Is this going to reach you any where around Christmas? Dont work too hard and have Elizabeth to help out. Everything has been very nice—one voyage is very like another.

Now I'm going to rush out on deck. This is almost the first time I've been here (in the writing room) since we started. Its over the dining room and smells abound.

Heaps of love to you all, I'll send another line from Napels—and really write when we get to Rome.

A merry Christmas + a happy New Year—to you and the children + Mr Seward

Lovingly—Adelaide

2

Adelaide T. Crapsey and Algernon S. Crapsey et. al.
1909
Rome
2 fols.

Dear Mother and Father—and all of the family— I wonder how you all are and what you are all doing. Its about time for you to stop doing anything I should think and take a rest.

As for me, who have done nothing but rest, I am still better, there is still another month for me here in Rome and then I shall go to Fiesole. So far the weather has been very nice, hot in the middle of the day but cool in

the morning and the evening. The tourists however are all going north and there are only really Romans left here.
This week I have been very gay indeed. Fräu' von Heuslins brother was here and he had arranged a trip to some of the smaller places by carrige with Herr von Heuslin and his daughter and it quite suddenly and unexpectedly got itself arranged that I was to go too—for a day—instead of which I didn't get back until Thursday night—we started on Sunday. In that time we went to Viterbo and saw the Villa Lante, on Monday drove to Toscanella and saw there two wonderful churches, then Lake Bolsano then to Monte Fiascone where we had lunch at a dear little inn saw another nice church and drove on to Orivieto reaching there about 8 o'clock. The next morning we looked a little at Orvieto and then went on intending to get to Assissi by train but the trains in true Italian fashion only ran every other day, and we got landed at a most unheard of station for four hours and then stopped at Perugia—getting there at about six in the evening. We spent the evening and the next morning looking at Perugia and in the afternoon went to Assisi, going by train and returning by carrage. Then the next day we drove to Chuisi where I took the train back for Rome. It was great fun. Of course there wasnt time to see much of anything but it was a nice way to get a general view of the country and rather unusual because most people don't care to do such long distances driving. We really had a very entertaining time.

I was sorry I couldn't send you Miss Pritchards address but I didn't write it down when she told me and so of course I forgot it and I am now sending letters by way of Paris. She must be safely in America by now and I hope, for her and for all of you, having not too hot weather.

In the Via Margutta 53 B. everything seems to be as usual. Fräu'lein Römer, Assunta, Rosina, Maddelena, Luigina and Maria being all here and all at least as well as usual. Assunta has been ill but now she is better and betrothed. She would have preferred a policeman but this one will do.

Some day I hope to write really nice letters but you see it isn't happening yet.

With love to you all—and tell Marie I am horrid.

Ever lovingly—Adelaide.

3

Adelaide T. Crapsey
1909

Via Margutta 53B, Rome, Italy
5 fols.

The building is the Palazzi Patrizio where I live (Via Margutta 53B.) My two windows are those with the mark over them. You can see how big they are. The street is really a narrow one—not wide as it looks in the picture.

My dear Mamma,

I am still looking at that money order for $100 with amazement and other mixed feelings. Oh, its plain enough that you were too lovely to have done it—there's no mixture about that feeling, but alas! that it couldn't have gone for some sort of a grand nice time for you and Father or the children. It seems so sad to be spending money on doctors and nourishing food when it might be used for a good time. Well just the same I thank you very much, which seems a very pale acknowledgement for such a lovely gift. But Oh, you ought not to have done it.

By this time you will have had a letter about my plans. I should like too [to] add something more definite but I'm still vague. In a day or two I may manage to get clear. I am still inclined to think that I can manage the summer much more cheaply in America than over here. As for how I am I tried to be clear about that. I seem to be very well, the only difficulty is to get any strength. That is nothing to worry about and I wouldn't write of it if I hadn't to keep considering it in planning what to do. Anyone would be an unmitigated idiot to spend their time and money as I am doing short of necessity.

I enclose just to amuse you two pictures—taken about three weeks apart. You will see by the later one (with the hat) that I am by no means vanishing off the face of the earth. [Added in left margin: They are for a museum pass—or will be sometime—not because I've suddenly taken to being photographed. Do tear them up.]

It seems to me that I deal in unnecessa[ri]ly detailed accounts of my health. After this I'll let it go unmentioned—and you'll know that I [am] getting on very well with ups and downs of course and more slowly than is convenient—and there it all is.

How very futile and selfcentered this must seem to you in the middle of all your work. I'm waiting to hear if you really have started the diet kitchen. That would be the splendidest thing. Father's letters sound as if everything were going well. You will both be glad to wind thing[s] up in May though I should think. That is when you close the winter work isn't it. Father says you and Arthur are going to Cooks Point. Do you really want to go there? There's pretty much of a crowd there now—you know—and the meals really don't vary much.

What do you hear from Paul? Is he getting on fairly well. I feel rather horrid with all this fuss over my health when his is quite twice as bad.

Yesterday—on Saturday—Louise Merritt and all of her family arrived in Rome. They are going to spend a month here which is very nice indeed. It was ever so nice too to see Mrs Porter. She is going to write you about my room. We were so grand the day she came—a lot of lavender—well I dont know what they are, something between a crocus and a fleur-di-lis—had just come in from the country and the room had just been cleaned within an inch of its life. So we were all dusted and decorated and looked most attractive.

Did I tell you that Mrs Willard wrote a nice little note from Egypt offering to come up here from Naples if there was anything she and Mr. Willard could do. That was sweet of her wasn't it—but of course its not in the least necessary. I wrote and sent messages by Mrs Porter.

The rain is pouring down—as usual. We have had only four clear days this month. But it is always that way in March. I don't mind it but it is hard on the people who are trying to see things.

This is another stupid letter. Sometime I may do better. Marie and Father wrote me about your birthday. My letter to you is still here sealed and unsent. It was such a rambling wobbly thing that I hadn't the courage to get it off. I'm so glad it was a nice day—and I know how hard it must have been too.

I won't try to say anything more about the money but you know how I feel.

Lovingly—Adelaide

4

Adelaide T. Crapsey
1909
Rome
6 fols.

Dear Mamma: I have been searching Paris editions of the Herald and the Daily Mail for more news from Rochester but there is nothing to be found. That means I hope that the fires—two of them at once, one paper said—were not too dreadful—at any rate in loss of life. One fire, a telegram in the Herald reported, was in one of the foreign sections—down by the station I seemed to make out. If that is so the Brotherhood must be doing heaps of relief work. There must be still another week or ten days before I can hear directly. I am waiting so anxiously for word.

If I were sure that it wouldn't come in upon a very sad time with you all I could be writing a most lighthearted letter. The weather has been so lovely. Italy is really at times everything that people say it is; enchanting skies, flowers all coming out and everything fresh and clean and beautiful. As for me I'm feeling better than I have for three straight years and its perfectly joyous. I am so sorry that that over a month ago letter of mine worried you. I tried hard not to have it sound worrisome.

The Merrits left yesterday and of course I shall miss them—but wasn't it nice that they were here really so long—a whole month. Oh I must tell you a funny thing. One day Louise wanted to go out to the Protestant Cemetary to see Keat's grave. You know I'm not much of a person for doing things like that and I never had been there. When we got out there we went, by mistake, into the new section and after hunting in vain for the grave we went back to the gate and I was just asking the woman who seemed to be in charge of things, where to go when an American came in—a rather lost looking man (I mean he seemed not to know his way) with a big bunch of carnations and while I was talking to the woman I heard him ask Louise if this were the Protestant Cemetary and how could he find the grave of James Lee. Louise offered him my small amount of Italian so when I had finished about Keats he told me over again what he wanted, and I told the portiere and she showed him the book where all the registrations are; and of course all the time I was hunting in my mind for James Lee because the name was perfectly familiar and then I remembered about Professor Lee so I said to the unknown American—"Is it Professor Lee's grave?" and of course he said yes and then in a brief conversation it came out that I knew the Lees, that I had known them not in Milton [?] but in Rochester—the unknown American had known them at Canandagua [Canandaigua]—why so had I; we had had a cottage there—so had he—our cottage was Vine Cottage and (in a sudden burst of information) my name was Crapsey—Oh! then he knew who I was, and I knew who he was—his name was—Sherman Morse.

Wasn't that odd? Do you remember how we used to watch all the grown up people at the "Stone House"—but of course in all the ten summers we were there I never spoke to Sherman Morse. He was much too grown up, just engaged do you remember. And now after some sixteen years I meet him, in a place where I've never been before and where I'll probably never go again—and on one of the two days that he had in Rome. He had come over with Roosevelt and was returning at once.

A young man across the way is tying his tie with as much thought as I spend over a whole getting dressed from the ground up. His mirror is hung square in the middle of the window and of course he is perfectly visible to every one in this house. It takes him a solid three quarters of an hour to part his hair.

My awnings have just been put up and they will be a great help as it gets warmer. I saw Dr Gauigan yesterday and he said he thought I might perfectly well stay through June—he and I both being of the opinion that its safer to stay where I am than to use up energy packing and travelling and getting used to a new place. Really I'm afraid to budge for fear I'll disturb this present heavenly state of things.

Oh, what do you think of me with a dentist! Now I know what a rubber dam is. Really I was awfully thankful to get the things done. One tooth had been bothering me ever since I left home but I didn't quite dare begin until your hundred came and then I thought that was the best first thing to do with it. As a matter of fact I should soon have been driven to it anyhow as the place was getting worse every day—the nerve was exposed and had to be killed.

I wonder how you all are and what you are doing. Your garden must be starting now, the flowers I mean. Tell Marie I'm really going to write to her. Love to you all and to Mr Seward—and everyone. Remember me to Inez—How does all the domestic machinery go? Lovingly—Adelaide.

5

Algernon S. Crapsey
1909
Rome
2 fols.

Dear Father: I keep sending letters to Rochester—and you keep on staying in East Aurora. You must be an old inhabitant by this time. I hope that I didn't speak disrespectfully of Elbert Hubbard. But his books really are pretty awful aren't they?

Since I have had your last letter and Mother's I've settled down to staying over here a little while longer and I'm going to get settled in England as soon as possible and see what I can do. As I've written

Mother, we leave here on the tenth and reach Paris about the 12th. I'll hear from Mrs. Thomas when I get there. If her plans have gone awry its very likely that Mrs Draper will have a flat where I can have a room.

You must have been having a good[?] time in East Aurora. I wonder what you are planning for the winter. President Eliot I see to my relief has not started a new Movement. Someone told me Elwood Worcester had nervous prostration. There is no news at San Girolomo except that it is cooler.

Yes I have thought about the English climate—but I cant go on paying attention to climate forever. I don't believe either that staying in Rome another year would be of much use. If it didn't do the business in one winter I don't believe it would in two. Not that I don't think it was a very good place to have been last winter—because it was. But I don't think it will hurt to try England. I can always leave if it gets too bad. Of course what I hope to do is to settle down to about five months of study and then come back say in March and look for a job.

Just at this part in my letter the enclosed from Mrs Thomas reached me. I'm inclined to think it the solution of my difficulties. The climate seems splendid, the cost of living splendider. It's near enough London to go in for a week or two when I want to. And it will be a good place to work in—and one where I can be out of doors a great deal. I'm really rather—in fact very—pleased. Then if later I can do more than seems wise now I've always got London and Oxford "handy." I'm writing her—Mrs Thomas—that I'll come as soon as she is ready. I do hope this will seem right to you and Mother. I feel fairly enthusiastic about it. And $5 a week!

This I finish up and send off in a hurry so that you will know my new plan—

Lovingly—Adelaide

6

Adelaide T. Crapsey
1909
[Rome]
3 fols.

Address:
c/o The American Express Co.

11 Rue Scribe
Paris—
France

Dear Mother— I had a georgous long letter from you a few days ago and another one about two days later. By this time you will have had various ones from me. You must not wonder if the letters take a longish time. Italian mails are the most leisurely things on the face of the earth. Your letters I think have reached me safely. The American Express address is always alright to use—though I am sure I gave a direct one here too. Your last letter was addressed just to Piazza Venezia Rome without the Am. Express—so it might quite easily have gone astray.

Mr Seward will have had a letter from me by this time. Not a very brilliant one I am afraid. Its really awfully hard work to write though it seems absurd. I'm sorry about the pencil and the too small writing.

You and Paul and Algy must have had a nice time. But it was too bad that Paul was ill. I do hope he is better now. And Arthur too. What a busy summer you have had! Just as usual.

I am so much interested in what you say about Marie-Louise and I wonder what will come of it. Miss Wheelock's is the kindergarten place isn't it? I thought Marie had given up wanting to do that.
How nice to have Mrs Willard doing baby blankets again. She and Mr Willard were both dear when they were in Rome. Be sure and give them my love and Mrs Watson too.

We leave here on the 10th of September and as I think I wrote you—go to Genoa stop a night or two and then go up to Paris—a 24 hour journey that I rather dread but I'll be glad to get out of Italy for September. When I go to London will depend on Mrs Thomas. I haven't heard from her again so I don't know when she is going to settle or where. But Mrs Draper is going to be in Paris and in London so I'll have some one to be with. She — Mrs Draper — is doing all the travel bother — tickets, hotels and the rest. It is so much nicer than trying to do it myself — and so much cheaper. I am very glad that I can stay over a little longer and you may be sure I'll keep expenses as near the vanishing point as possible.

There is no more news from San Girolamo. We are a very quiet lot. The worst of the heat is over—at least for a while. September is said to be a corking month.

As usual this is a very stupid and empty letter. But you must be used to them by this time. Give my love to Mr Seward. It was perfectly heavenly of him to send the money. I'm so sorry about the delay in thanking him. Remember me to Mr Corris and to Mr. Bragdon. Love to you and all the family—

Lovingly—Adelaide.

7

Adelaide T. Crapsey
1909
Hotel Smith, Genoa, Italy
1 fol. [letterhead `Hôtel Smith/et Pension/Gênes (Italie)/
Chauffage Central—Ascenseur/Lumière Electrique']

Dear Mother: Here as you will see is Genoa. The Hôtel Smith is right on the docks and I can look out on some dozen or so of ships. It almost seems as if I ought to take one of them and return to my native land. We got here yesterday at half after three or so—the journey fairly hot—and through more tunnels than I dreamed existed in the whole world. As soon as we reached the hotel

I took a Bath. [On a separate line, in letters three times as large as her normal hand.]

—the first one since last January—the first really nice big hot one—or since Febuary if you count the lukeish warm things at the A.A.h.H. Anyhow it was long enough ago to make it an Event. The tunnels made it a necessity. I enjoyed it very much—and it was such an excitement that I forgot to be tired from the journey.

Mrs Draper and Mary and Adelaide have gone to the ship. It must be sailing just about now. Then tomorrow the rest of us—all but Adelaide—go on to Paris. We leave at 8 in the morning. As there are five of us we can occupy nearly a whole—perhaps a whole—compartment and it wont be so bad—though nothing makes overland travel in Europe—or anywhere—really joyful.

As yet I haven't seen anything of Genoa. I'm just up I must admit although I woke up early enough. The square in front of the hotel is tram terminus, a place for shipping and everything else noisy. Its a funny little hotel but nice and clean and comfortable—and there is the nicest coffee I've had since I left 678 Averill Avenue—Rochester N.Y.

I wonder how you all are. The family must be reassembling after the summer. I do hope you will find someone nice to help you in the house. Is Marie going away? I am so curious to know what will happen.

When I wrote the last time I forgot to mention some slight earthquake shocks that stired thing[s] up a bit in Siena and Florence and Rome. It was just felt in Fiesole I believe but I didn't wake up for it. The newspaper accounts were, as usual, much exagerated. Though of course it takes only the slightest wiggle to frighten people now.

You are all reading the Cook-Peary fight I suppose. It's flourishing on here. We are still getting English papers two days late so we are always behind in the game.

In Paris I shall hear again from Mrs Thomas I suppose and very soon I'll get over to England and settle down. Its ever so nice to have a definate place and I've grown quite attached to Herne Bay already. I'm not sure whether its because its near water or whether its because its only a pound a week—the latter I think.

Remember me to Mr Seward and everyone and Love to you and all of the family.

Adelaide.

8

Adelaide T. Crapsey, Algernon S. Crapsey et. al.
1909
Hotel des Etats Unis, Paris
5 fols. [4 fols. holograph]

Remember you only need a 2 cent stamp.
c/o—The American Express Co.
5—6 Haymarket
London—England—
(I dont know the Herne Bay address yet—will send it later)
Dear Mother and Father—and all of the family. Here I am safe and sound in Paris. We changed our plans at Genoa—took a train on Saturday night instead of Sunday morning and got here on Sunday afternoon at two oclock. The night journey was what night journeys always are. The train was crowded, everybody packed on top of everyone else. We did not get a whole compartment—nor even all in one. We alternated between suffocating tunnels and icy alps. Sleep of course was out of the question. We kept up our spirits with Marsalla (a very special kind of Italian wine) and weakened coffee at four o'clock in the morning—and some more at six. So you see we lived through it—and even found it amusing in spots. But oh, such dirt and dust! I've really come through most awfully well.

Poor Mary Draper caught cold on the Alps and has been laid up almost ever since.

We are staying in a funny little Latin Quarter hotel—L'Hotel des Etats Unis—(Hotel of the United States)—I have my room and breakfast and dinner for 5.50—the extra 50 is because I have a room alone—the others are in double rooms and get off with five. We lunch out in various small restaurants—a franc is the limit—so I'm living on 6.50 a day. I had hoped for 5—but thats not to be done short of doing ones own housekeeping. Well I'm going down anyhow and when I get to England it will be less than 5.

The place is a[s] clean as can be—and that let me tell you is a rarer thing on this side than on that. There are plain painted pine floors—just little rugs, no carpets, iron beds, good simple furniture—and very good meals. Its really a nice little place.

Mrs Thomas writes that she will be in the cottage and ready for me on the 6th—so I think I shall go straight there and not to London at all. She says the cottage is ever so nice and the air splendid. Fraulein Römer has sent on my trunk from Rome—so I'll be all settled very soon.

As usual I'm not trying to do any sightseeing. We are near the Luxembourg Gardens and I've been there—and to the Museum—also to the Pantheon. Next week I'm going to get over to the Louvre.

How are you all? I expect I'll be hearing in a little while. The winter work is begining and you [will] all be as busy as ever.

The inevitable finances appear on the next page—also I enclose Mrs Draper's account with me up to date. For once you'll have a businesslike statement of my expenses. Isn't it nice of her to do it?—and she's looking after everything here too. I thought it might amuse Mr Seward to see it. Tell him its all his present. Oh, and I enclose too a quaint little letter from Fraü'lein Römer—I thought it might amuse you to see it too.

Love to you all—Adelaide

Cash on hand—	500 francs
Journey up—	133.35
Hotel + lunch—3 weeks—	136.50
Journey to England—	50.00
	319.85

500.00
319.85
180.15 = $36.50. Out of whole must come laundry—tips—the express

charges on my trunk from Rome—the general odds and ends of expenses like stamps and hairpins—the little extra emergency money that its safer to have—and my "seeing Paris" expenses—which I will make mild —almost nonexistent. But I'm awfully afraid I won't have much between me and the world when I get to Herne Bay. Yet I've tried to be as careful as possible and its made it ever so much cheaper traveling in a group. If I could have $50 it would take me along for a little while. It seems too perfectly horrid to be consuming the family resources to this extent.

[fol. 5 in Mrs. Draper's hand]

Adelaide Crapsey To Credit	307.70
Ticket to Paris	87.35
Luggage from San G. to Florence	2.00
Lunch to Genoa - - - -	1.95
Fees at Florence station-	2.75
Excess luggage - - - -	4.20
Fees + omnibus arriving G.	1.15
" " " leaving G.	1.90
Hotel bill + extra dinner	12.45
Bath	2.00
Hotel fees at Genoa - -	3.60
Lunch for Paris train—	1.25
Dinner on train - -	4.50
Pillow - - - - -	.60
Porters, Cab + luggage Paris	2.60
Paris telegram - - - - - - -	60
Cafe au lait - - - -	1.20
Tulle	
Lunch Monday Paris	
Drive in Genoa	95
	130.25

Cr. 307.70
130.25
177.45 Due A. Crapsey

1.35
.80
2.15

(over)

[on verso]
177.45
.95 pins
176.50 Due Adelaide

9

Adelaide T. Crapsey, Algernon S. Crapsey, et al.
[1909, 1910]
Hotel des Etats Unis, Paris
2 fols.

Dear Mother and Father and all of the family:—Here I am still in Paris and still in the Hotel of the United States. Its such a nice little place—too bad Father and I didn't know about it the last time we were here. We would have saved money. But we couldn't have because it didn't exist, at least not under the present management and before then it was like many another Latin Quarter hostelry rather uninhabitable. Monsieur and Madame Penant tell us how it was when they came and we exclaim over it and then we tell them how nice it is now. And so it is and how they work over it! Monsieur Penant does most of the cooking,—and when dinner is over comes up to ask us politely if everything has been right. Delicious we answer. He names the masterpiece of the evening, the steak, the rabbit, the sweet,—he puts his fingertips together, his eyebrows are lifted. . "Ah . . Ah yes that was good—and all the best materials—it costs—but!—if you wish things good . . and in his house—" then we finish up with the assurance that in his house it is always perfection. I really don't see how they do it at the price that they do. Of course most of the people only have rooms here. There are very few for meals. And then alas! they economize on service. Poor man-of-all-work Jean gets up at grey dawn, works till midnight and, I discovered to my horror yesterday, has to answer all the night calls. We feel that conditions need reforming but there doesn't seem to be any way to do it—especially as he and Monsieur and Madame appear to be quite content and very friendly.

I am spending my time in my usual do nothing fashion though I do get in an occassional visit to the Louvre or the Luxembourg or Notre Dame and two or three times we've been to some nice little Latin Quarter Concerts. Also I've had another bath—at the Y.W.C.A! The tubs are nice and there's splendid hot water—but they are so oppressively christian,—the people not the tubs. However a bath is a bath and Helen and I are going again armed with books and a general appearance of deafness to avoid conversation. Mary Draper has gone to England and Mrs Draper, her niece Louise Brigham and Louise's friend Helen Meeker and I are here now. I am planning to go to England about the 10th or 11th—the others have decided to stay on a little longer in Paris. I shall be glad to be settled for the winter and I am awfully glad to hear that you think the plan a good one. Father's note came the other day saying you all approved of it. Herne Bay is six miles from Canterbury. I go to Canterbury by train and drive the rest of the way. That sounds nice and out in the country doesnt it.

How is Mr Seward? Give him my love—and the Moshers too. They must be back by this time. Does Mr Seward still have his nurse? Its a very sensible and comfortable arrangement I should think—I am so glad you managed to find a nice one.

Love to you all. I blush to think how busy you are and I'm doing nothing. Father says Marie is going to High School again. What happened to the Mechancis? I'll be writing again soon—

Affectionately—Adelaide

10

Adelaide T. Crapsey
[1910]
"Hill Crest," Alma Road 1, Herne Bay, Kent
3 fols.

My address here is
"Hill Crest"
Alma Road—1
Herne Bay—Kent
But the Am. Express in London will do just as well. Isn't "Alma Road" awfull!

Dear Mother: Here I am at Herne Bay and settled for another little while. First though let me tell you that Fathers note and check are here and thank you very much. Also I enclose the second Parisian account and I'll tell you about that too—when I've finished about Herne Bay. It turns out to be a fairly large town of the rather awful English sort and also a London summer resort. There is a Parade and bathing machines and all the rest of it. However that, after a first horrified look at it, wont bother us, for we live quite out of it all,—right down by the water and just on the edge of the downs. The cottage is half of a double house; it has—oh but you know about the rooms from Mrs Thomas' letter—but you dont know the rent—which is 12 + 6 for the house and furniture and 1 + 6 for the sheets towels knives + forks etc which makes in American reckoning—$3.50 a week. I ought to add that this is the winter rent. In the Herne Bay "season" its $15 to $20 a week. We have a nice competent, well trained efficient English maid—who is paid—$6 a month! My socialistic conscience doesn't approve but that, it seems, is a good wage in Herne bay. I wish I could slip her or one just like her over to you. The house of course is tiny. The bedrooms small and the beds so large that you have to squeeze around them; the wallpaper, carpets woodwork and the rest by no means a dream of beauty—but $3.50 a week! that would reconcile you to almost anything and then its quite clean—and a whole house to live in instead of one room. Downstairs there is really only one room besides the kitchen—a combination living and dining room. Off the kitchen there is a fair sized scullery with a small place for coal—garret and cellar of course are not. And no bath—however as we hope to get sea baths that its [is] not so bad. There is gas downstairs—not upstairs.

This is the way we are doing—Mrs Thomas has the largest south room for herself and the baby. The other south room is really too small for comfort so I have the next largest one, that faces north, but it has the sea view, a balcony and a fireplace. The other north room I use also—the furniture is shoved against the wall and I have the remaining space for a small writing table. My books are piled on the beaureau. We keep the tin tub in the other south room and go in there for morning baths,—that keeps our own rooms a little clearer. Beatrice (the $6 maid) arrives at about half past seven, gets breakfast and brings it up—we each have it in our own room. Its really easier and leaves downstairs for her to get things brushed up and in order. Then she brings the hot water for my bath—and when I've finished empties the tub and brings up more for Mrs Thomas and Marie. People talk about the simple life and all that—I think life without a little machinery is a very complicated business. Be thankful for your hot + cold water all over the house, your tubs and electric lights and telephones. We have luncheon or rather dinner about twelve or half past—tea at half past four—Beatrice goes home about half past five or six. She leaves the suppertable all set and we use the kitchen so that we can have the other room free and needn't carry things back and forth. Besides there is a fire there and it's nice and warm. We haven't begun fires in the rest of the house yet.

Well—there is the routine that in just about two days we've slipped into and it is so convenient that I think we'll stick to it. Of course we are not really settled yet.

Dont you think my Parisian accounts are most beautiful. I thought they would amuse you all. I had really a very nice little time there—and stayed a few days longer than I expected to. That was because everyones plans were changed because Louise Brigham, Mrs Draper's ni[e]ce came down with typhoid fever. She has been having it all the time and wont be able to move for some time. She is in a nice little American Hospital—Trinity Lodge—and being taken of by a Miss Tripp from the Homoepathic hospital in Rochester. She knows you—had a Remington (Lillian?) case once—says you were most awfully kind. Do you remember her? It sounded so like home to hear her talk. Louise has been getting on as well as anyone with typhoid fever could—so it might all have been worse. Mrs Draper has spent all her afternoons—at the hospital—in the mornings we kept out of doors. Took small boats up and down the Seine once or twice. Our lunches we got at small Latin Quarter restaurants —finally settling down at one special one where we had napkin rings and kept our napkins for a week, a saving of 2 cents a day. You'll see by the accounts that we were getting quite expert at keeping to the franc and even cutting under.

The poor man who figures on the list was a poor soul walking up and down in front of the restaurant in a driving rain. We were trying to be strongminded about street begging but I weakened and gave him a franc—then Mrs Draper and Helen gave in and took a share each. As a matter of fact a penny or two to someone came to be almost a regular part of lunch—but as I usually had such small change with me the little boy with the violin and the blind woman who sang and the rest aren't on the list. Not that are [our] charities were large,—because we were all really and strictly economizing. I had to have my brown dress mended—new selves [sleeves] and yoke—now it will do for another winter. That was $6 material and making. But my one Parisian extravagance—was a pair of made to order corsets—or not really corsets—girdle things that really fit. We had the funniest time over them. We asked the woman if she could make them—she was doubtful—Oh yes she *could* make them but corsets, real corsets, were the proper the only thing to wear, she was eloquent on the subject of corsets. I began to feel as if my past had been a mistake—because I had spent it without corsets—as if my future would be a disaster if I didn't get some at once. However I stood firm—I hadn't, didn't, couldn't, wouldn't wear corsets. Well then she would make me something—something that would please me forever. Well then we got to work—we got rid of steels, we got buttons instead of hooks—we had the lacing loose—in fact we did everything that would strike a Parisian corsetmaker as mere madness,—and the result is excellent. You see she got quite interested in what she called my "miniatures",—and I wish you could have seen the final fitting, when she and her two assistants tried them on. They invented more enthusiastic descriptive terms for that one girdle in five minutes than I could think of in a lifetime for Alps or Cathedrals or Pictures or statues or heroic acts and great events. It really became a Parisian adventure and we were all much amused. Tell Mr Seward—you can tell him can't you even if it is about girdles—that they—I mean it /are /is / my most beloved possession. They didnt cost all of the 30 francs though—only 20 of them but that was quite enough. I am so glad to be at Herne bay where houses are $3.50 a week and there are no temptations.

This letter is dreadfully long. I must stop writing and send it. I don't ask all the questions over again each time—they must get so tiresome to read but I wonder how you all are and what you are all doing. Father says his evening services are to begin and that you are going on splendidly in your department. I do hope you have someone to help you in the house. I wish I could send you Beatrice.

The air here is wonderful—and now its all a gift from you and Father and I'm most grateful.

Lovingly Adelaide.

My love for Mr Seward—this letter is for him too if it amuses him to hear of my mild doings.

11

Algernon S. Crapsey
May 1910
London
6 fols.

Dear Father: Yesterday I had lunch with Mr Kirsher [Kershner] and Miss Chapman—a very nice lunch at a very swagger restaurant—and heard all the latest news from the front. It was very nice to see someone from home. Mr Kershner is taking all sorts of messages to you all. Tell Mother he says she is the most beautiful woman he has ever seen—and everything lovely—which shows him a discerning person. The political fight must have been awfully exciting. I wish I could have seen it.

Today we hear of nothing but the King's death [7 May 1910]. Its as sad a thing as could have happened. All of the people seem to have loved him as much as if he had been an immediate personal friend. The sudd[e]ness of it all adds to the shock. Of course the new King is rather an unknown quantity—and the new Queen entirely overshadowed by the beauty and popularity of Queen Alexandra. I wonder what effect it will have on the present political tangle.

As for my affairs—to go from great things to less—they are a bit tangled to [too] as usual. My work has gone not as fast as I hoped how[ev]er I hope to see where I am by the end of May. I am writing to make first vague inquiries about jobs and suchlike things. Suppose it should turn out a good thing to go back at the end of May or beginning of June? What would you think of it? I'll be looking up chances of work on both sides of the ocean anyhow. Of course its rather hard work getting back into the machine again but I hope for the best and of course I'll let you + Mother know as much as I know myself. Its all indefinite now—even where to look. In the meanwhile I am of course getting on as fast as I can. Every time I think of all the time that I wasted in College English departments I get a bit irritated.

The weather is horrid—grey and cold and bleak—it congeals me—. Its lucky I didn't try London in the winter if this is what it is like in the spring. And at Herne Bay it was so warm that I got all ready for the summer. Now I've gone back to winter things and have another chillblane—if thats the way to spell it. There is nothing to tell—about me I mean. I'm keeping strictly to business and get a little too tired to do other things. The B.M [British Museum reading room] is rather strenuous and I use the little library near here as much as I can. At least I am looking at the outsides of books that I ought to have know[n] long ago.

When Mr Kershner gets back and you see him be sure to tell him how nice it was to see him. Of course I am writing a note too.

This is a combination to you and mother as usual and as usual not worth reading.

I save finances till the last—it makes a bitter end doesnt it. Unfortu[nat]ely expense[s] here in London have gone up and I am having to add 5 shillings a week to my pound. I didn't know what else to do. I saw that Mrs Thomas was getting worried and of course my being with her mustn't mean any expense. We are both agreed that London is no good for us except for this short time when she can look up houses and I can look up books. We'll both leave it most willingly. I enclose on a separate sheet the accounts of the last two checks,—How things mount up—and I sit on them hard all the time! I should think you + Mother would feel hopeless. I do. Let's all pray for a job!—

Lovingly—Adelaide

For 8 weeks—

	£	s	d
4 weeks (Herne Bay)	4	o	o
4 " London	5		
Dresses + Coat	3	3	
3 dresses repaired	1		
1 dress cleaned		1	
Shoes mended		2	6
Hat		3	6
Kimono + slippers—		5	7
Stockings		5	
Veil, gloves, hairpins, nets Etc. Etc Etc		5	
Laundry— (4 weeks)		6	
Looseleave notebook paper, etc		5	
2 taxicabs		2	6
Bus fares		2	6 (about)
3 petticoats (Material and making)		5	
	15	10	7

Cash on hand 75
15
90
77.64
12.36—only as a matter of fact that is to be diminished by the small penny here and tuppence there expenses.

12

Algernon S. Crapsey and Adelaide T. Crapsey
24 May 1910
London
10 fols.

May 24. { The reason for this proud date is that I am at the British Museum and they make you date your book slips—so that I do know for once what the date is.

Dear Father and Mother—

I was ever so glad to have the letter from home last night. When I don't hear I am always afraid that something is going wrong and you aren't telling me about it. You must have been having great times with politics and united Charities. Hurray for Mother on a platform! And thank you very much for the check. Maybe your daughter will manage to get on her own feet again sometime—and her hopes at the present are brighter than usual and for these reasons.

You remember I said that I hoped to get my work in order by the end of May—enough I mean so that I could tell whether it amounted to anything. Well I have been working just as hard as I could and I have got at any rate this far—I have sent to an English Prosodist—a Mr. T.S. Omond—an account of an experiment I have been trying and this very morning came a letter from him from which I will copy the parts that will show you what in general he thinks. I would send the letter but it has a lot of technical discussion in it that I must keep to answer. I ought to say that I wrote first to ask him if I might—and he said yes—politely but not enthusiastically. Of course it took heaps of courage but I couldn't think of anything else to do. [A leaf seems to be missing from Adelaide Crapsey's letter.] ". . . your paper when completed and have no doubt it would be gladly accepted (No pay I fear but prosodists must not look for pecuniary reward!)

I feel sure that it is only on lines like yours that progress can be made."

Then the rest is about technical points—three *large* pages—with to end up with the hope that I will write again soon, that he will be happy to be of use in any way—and that he is obliged to me for letting him see my work.

And I dont pretend to be anything but tremendiously pleased and tremendiously relieved at such a judgement from a man who has been working at the subject for some thirty years or so and who has read practically everything that has been written on it. To tell you the truth I can hardly believe my eyes. I was quite ready to have him cool—or even crushing—and I wasn't going to be hopelessly discour[a]ged even by that. As you know I have worked alone and in an interrupted scrappy sort of way. I might have made all sorts of mistakes—or the whole way of working might have seemed wrong. But you see it has turned out well and I am glad that I finally screwed up my courage to do it—to send him the work I mean. Of course this is by no means the end of my difficulties. But it is the assurance that I have got a useable amount of material. The idea of publishing is most surprising to me. I hadn't dreamed the thing was worked out enough for that—(The M.S. in question by the way is only 19 of these pages in length)—Me in the Modern Language Review is a little funny isn't it? And I am not sure that I want to unless it would be the only means toward getting a job. If I can get a job that will let me go on working a bit longer I would like it better. You see I have so far gone just as carefully as I could and I want to keep on that way. However we'll see. I will be writing again to Mr Omond and I will let you know everything as soon as I know it.

So you see—I am able to say that I think the work amounts to something and that I can go on with it—and this prosodist *will* make it pay—or at least if I can't then I will give it up. Both of you have been perfectly splendid through all this time—and I never can tell you how grateful I am. If I do come out anywhere it will be because you have been so patient over this hard time. It makes me wriggle every time I think of just the money burden of it to you.

Please excuse this scrawly letter—but I wanted to let you know right away. I've said this is private because it really doesnt represent anything definite to talk about outside of ones own family. And the letter is just a private letter that I would only quote in this way to you. Also any talk about publishing still seems to me too vague—and too absurd!—to talk about. So this letter is just for you two and the older ones—the Duchess and Paul—if you think it will interest them It isn't that I am secretive but that one hates to talk much about work in the experimental stage—so all this is strictly for the family.

By the way don't be disturbed if you don't know much what Prosody is. Hardly anyone does.

This is a disjointed scrawl. To tell the truth I've been working very hard and I'm pretty tired. This silly health of mine is most inconvenient.

Please forgive me for not telling all about the funeral and Kings and things. How I wished that I could have changed places with Arthur for that week. The crowds and crepe and long waitings that kept me from seeing much wouldn't have bothered him and he would have had a glorious time—even if it was a funeral.

I do hope you are all well—and that all the work is going on as splendidly as usual. As I know more of my own plans I will let you know. Thank you again for the money and everything

Your loving and grateful daughter
Adelaide.

My best love to Duchess + the Babies if they are there and to all the family and Mr Seward. As soon as I have any definite plans I will write and tell him about it if you think he would find it interesting?

As I read this over I seem to be giving an exaggerrated importance to a not very important thing—but you see this is the first time I've had anything but my own judgement to go by and I really cant help feeling encouraged.

This is a Private letter to you and Father

13

Algernon S. Crapsey
1910
[Cornwall]
1 fol.

Dear Father—

Your last two letters have had splendid news. The incorporation of the Brotherhood is the sign of its solidity and success—and its perfectly great to have your work proving itself in such a way. I don't wonder Olga Nethersole is a deciple [disciple]. Then the other—why I simply gasp over it! And how perfectly beautiful—I can't think of anything in the world that would seem to me better news. Mother with Kodak stock! Well she deserves it—and everything that could happen.

You and Mother are Wonders The best things in the world would be only a little of what you ought to have. And Mr Seward is an angel with you.

These are short notes. I'll be writing more in a day or two—about the summer and everything.

Lovingly and with all the joy in the world—Adelaide.

14

Adelaide T. Crapsey
[August, 1910]

[Cornwall]
1 fol.

Dearest Mother,

You know that, now that I am better, I am trying to put my affairs in order and get back into the working world again. You and Father have been splendid through all this time and I know how much you wish that it weren't necessary to think of the money part of it but of course it is. I think that I am going to be able to work steadily now and in time repay all the money that I have borrowed. But I can't bear to have you wait so long and so Miss Houghton and I have arranged it that I am to owe the money to her instead of to you. Will you put the enclosed amount in your account or in Marie's. After this I am going to try to be a better businesswoman than I have been and perhaps sometime help to make things easier for you and father. I ought to after everything you have done for me.

With dearest love to you and Father and the children—Adelaide.

15

Adelaide T. Crapsey
23 September 1910
Bushey
2 fols.

Dear Mother—Your letter came the day after Miss Houghtons and I meant to answer it at once but now I'm afraid I've let nearly two weeks go without writing, partly because I've been feeling rather horridly and partly because I've been wandering about in an unsettled way. I got back from Cornwall a week ago and found that the Ebury Street rooms had been let. I had to pack and get all my things out in a day. Then I came down here to Bushey where Mrs Thomas has taken me in for a week until the new rooms in Oakley Street are ready—then I had to go back to town again to finish up various things so that there hasn't been much peace and quiet. Miss Harwood is in the country for a week—we shall get into the new rooms by Tuesday or Wednesday I hope.

I've just written to father about what I had better do next—since a fellowship doesn't seem likely at this moment. Suppose I should come home—work there for a little and try to manage a spring term at Cornell?

I would try to get a job at once but I am afraid it would just mean another breakdown. However this is all in the other letter—written to you both of course and you and father can see what you think. I think that my best way is to continue to look after this absurd and unpracticable health of mine and to get solider ground under my feet and then try for something really good rather than to fritter away what small amount of strength I have on no-account things.

It would at any rate be most awfully nice to come home and see you all. I feel as if I had been away centuries. How is all the family and how is Marie? I do hope her back is better.

Cornwall was nice though I didn't do very much. Mrs Watts is being so awfully nice. I think I told you about her.

This was going to be a long letter but I think I'll wait until I am back and settled. I have a floating in mid-air feeling just now and I'm still tired. What a bother health is—or the lack of it. But don't worry about it—its nothing new you know and I am learning how to manage it fairly well. The main thing is not to work very long at a time. Taken in small doses I can get through a good bit. The trouble with a job is that you must work so steadily. That is why I am afraid of trying.

How is your garden and how does the house look. Perhaps I shall see them soon.

Miss Houghton was splendid wasn't she and it is so much better to have things arranged this way. I'm sure I shall get along—in time—but its horrid to be asking the family for money now.

Please forgive this horrid letter. I'll do better next time. Give my love to Mr. Seward. I'm going to write him soon.

With heaps of love. Adelaide

Sept 23, 1910.

16

Adelaide T. Crapsey
11 October 1910
London
2 fols.

Dearest Mother—

Isn't Mr Seward per[f]ectly, perfectly wonderful. Will you tell him so and thank him because it will be a day or two before I can manage a decent letter for myself. We move tomorrow—thank Heaven. It was dear of Mr Seward. I was getting low and [a] little worried. The reason is that I have *had* to get some clothes. "Donato Pietrocupo" simply wont get me through another winter.

I am distractedly trying to think of what is best to do and get through some work that I want to use at once. Horrid of Cornell not to shower a travelling scholarship on me at once.

I do hope that what I said of my health didn't bother you. It was only to explain why I don't undertake more work right away.

Much, more, most and heaps of love to you and Mr Seward. I'll write him soon. This is just to let you know that the money is here and how grateful I am. Do write soon. Is anything going wrong. I do hope not.

Adelaide

You will see Fathers letter so I haven't written the same things over again.

Oct 11, 1910

17

Adelaide T. Crapsey and Algernon S. Crapsey
23 February 1911
Plainfield, New Jersey
3 fols.

Thursday—
Feb—23d

Dearest Mother and Father—

Did you ever know such funny luck! Of course its a great chance to get work at Smith and I felt that it would be flying in the face of providence to refuse but Oh dear me! why did it come just when I want to see you all. Well the spring vacation will be here soon—and the summer one. Thats a comfort. A telegram this morning says to go to Northampton as soon as possible but I'll take the time for a flying trip home whether or no. I'll leave here tonight—(will wire train later)—have Friday + Saturday + perhaps Sunday at home. Can Father wait and go to New York on Saturday? Then I can see him on Friday. The whole thing wont be much but it will be better than nothing wont it? Oh dear! Isnt it all funny. Its what comes of being born a Crapsey!

I would like awfully to go to Cornell to see Professor Sampson. Do you suppose it could be managed on Sunday? Then I would go straight from

Ithaca to Northampton. Will Father look up trains?—Of course if it can't be managed I can write. My Prosody work and the Fellowship at Cornell is the main thing of course but the work at Smith will give me some money now and whats more a very good connection with things academica. After my three years—or nearly—disconnection that is the main thing + really great luck.

Arthur is waiting for this letter and I want it to go at once.

Well—I'll see you all tomorrow morning. I am so dreadfully dreadfully sorry Mother dear to upset things so. And after all the waiting for that slow old steamer! But we must take what the Gods send I suppose.

Love to you all. Can you arrange so that I can see Mrs Watson + Mrs Willard.

And wont I be glad to see you—and *isnt* it funny.

Lovingly, Adelaide.

Today Rachel + I are re-packing and putting clothes in order.

Will wire train later.

18

Adelaide T. Crapsey and Algernon S. Crapsey
24 (?) February 1911
Plainfield, New Jersey
1 fol.

Darling Mother + Dearest Father.

Did you ever know such luck. They've telegraphed to come at once and "take weekend later for family"—I want my family *now!* But I *must* not refuse. I've just had a letter from Miss Lewis. The work is *Poetics* —just what I want—only 13 hours a week—and only *one* course to give—no two—salary $600 from now till the end of the year. You see it would be mad for me to let it go but oh dear oh dear oh dear! Never mind I'll come *very* soon. How I hated to send that telegram. I'm catching a mail. Heaps of love. I'm too disappointed to speak—but I'll come *SOON* —and its a most unusual chance I try to console myself with that—but I could sit down + weep. But I'm coming soon.

Adelaide

19

Miss Van Horn
[1911]
Tyringham, Massachusetts
1 fol. [letterhead: blue 'Tyringham, Mass.']

Tyringham, Mass.
c/o Miss Beulah Cannon

My dear Miss Van Horn—

Will you do something for me—if the College Library is still open? I left two books that I want in the summer—a volume of *Nursery Rhymes* —and *Early English Classical Tragedies.* They are on my desk in the English Seminar—anyone who is there will show you where that is. Will you get them and send them to me—by mail or parcel post whichever is cheapest. And send me the bill for postage and your time. I would be so very much obliged.

Sincerely yours—
Adelaide Crapsey

Will you also send me the exact title and dates of publication of Paul Verrier's book on English metre. You will find it in the catalogue. (College Library)

[In pencil in another hand: 'Essai sur les principes de la métrique anglaise Paris, Welter, 1909 3v']

20

Marie Louise Crapsey
March 1914
Saranac Lake
1 fol.

Dear Marie-Louise— Will you do something for me?— Hunt up a bible + there must be ever so many around the house—and send it to me. I would like the King James version—not any of the revised or authorized or modern reader things. If you will send it on soon I would be awfully obliged. If there isn't one to be found let me know. How are you? Wont you be glad when the spring really comes. I wonder whether you are still going to your classes and if you like the work. If you can find it—send the bible along right away, will you? Yours—

Adelaide

21

Jean Webster
September 1914
Rochester, New York
1 fol.

The enclosed to amuse you— Eleanor Gates being ushered into Rochester under the protection of your more famous name— Mr Corris hopes you wont mind— (He's the Lyceum manager if you happen to remember)

Dear Jean— With the N.Y. opening actually on top of you I can imagine what H. Miller achieves in the way of whirlwinds. Why doesnt he stage himself sometime? He would provide "thrills" aplenty if nothing else. I'm most dreadfully sorry about the headaches. You aren't often so afflicted are you? Is it a danger signal that even you must stop and rest? Yes of course I am pleased about The Witch—the thinnest blade of an opening wedge is the thing that counts now, and the times are all against us. I've only, as I persistently and ineffectually repeat, awfully troubled over the amt. of work you're putting on the things. Do let them go at any rate until the play is launched.

This is a dreadful scribble but I want to get it off—meant to send it earlier but to tell the truth I'm having a pretty wretched time. Cough raging and temperature moving up to a persistent 101— I must get me to a solitary life as rapidly as may be— I've not yet heard from Dr Baldwin about Brown's Mills— I'm fairly sure he didnt know about it and would have to do some asking wh. always takes time. I'm *praying* that it will be all right—

I wish I could do something to help with D-L-L [*Daddy Long-Legs*]— Dont let H.M. do you out of your meals.

Yours—A.

I wish this werent such a scrawl—

22

Jean Webster
19 September 1914
Rochester, New York
2 fols.

Dear Jean— I'm just most awfully glad about the play. The press is certa[i]nly "good"—and Ziegfield who came here on Tuesday told Mr Corris the play was "a complete success" "a perfect knockout"—and if that isn't the voice of the box office I dont know what is. So now your [you're] off!—and I hope your [you're] not dead to celebrate—

If this is unusually inane forgive it. Present breakdown worst of lot— I'm back in bed with a trained nurse and every bit of strength I ever had vanished— Isn't it sort of tiresome. I enclose Dr Baldwin's letter— I've written Dr Hance + will let you know what he says— Paul has been to Brown's Mills + reports the country + air as everything one could wish—"a piece of southern Georgia picked up and put down in between N.Y. + Phila." The Sanatorium was closed (it's a winter place it seems) but Paul says its a nice enough little establishment to look at + in a most lovely grove of pine and oak. It remains to see what the medical opinion of it is. I do hope + pray it will be all right It seems to me I just *must* get settled

Horrid of me to come down in the middle of your success with all my everlasting troubles—Wasnt it all awful the last days + rather fun too especially at the end—a regular grand Broadway first night! I wish I'd been there to see you clutch the "floral tributes"—and all the rest. I wonder whether I'll ever see that play! I suppose you'll tinker for a week or two— I hope not more— Really aren't you all feeling, al[l]owing for natural qualms + such, as if the thing were launched.

Paul says theres a dear little hotel at Browns Mills with delicious cooking— It might be just the place for you to vanish to (when you can) for a few days rest.

Its funny how weak I am— I've never been so weak. Dear me troubles again!

Remember me to everyone—tell me how the play goes—the details I mean

Adelaide

Isnt Dr Baldwin ever so nice about it all—

C

To Esther Lowenthal

1913–1914

1

17 July 1913
Hillcrest Hospital, Pittsfield, Massachusetts
3 fols. 5 pp.

Hillcrest Hospital
Pittsfield— Mass
July 17—1913

Dear E— What do you think of that? But as you see I can still hold a pen! How are you and where are you and what have you been doing? I do hope it has been and is being awfully nice and restful—

Here's telegraphic report of my news. I finished the favorite literature and sent it off on Saturday the 21st of June. I reckoned that it would take P.E.M [Paul Elmer More, editor of *The Nation*] about 3 weeks to get around to reading his surprise and settled back to rest during that time. It came back on Tuesday the 23d of June—but with (not to employ the method of suspense) a really very nice (if in spots funny) letter. The thing was too long for the Nation but I seem to have "hit on a very interesting point"—but the argument was hard to follow (E! that masterpiece of lucidity!) and "it would be a satisfaction to me personally if I could see your argument shorn of all secondary issues and presented in its barest skeleton." Being willing to oblige I sat me down—(after a day or two to get my breath) and ripped the favorite literature up the back and did a condensed version—sending it off to be typed on the 7th of July— I stayed in Tyringham to avoid the interrupting packing + unpacking. Of course in the meanwhile I had written Mr More saying that I would like very much to send the shorter paper—and getting in reply a nice little note with his vacation address—to send the thing to. On the 8th of July as I got out of my bath I leaned over quickly felt a remarkable pain and after a second found it more discrete [discreet] to drop full length on the bathroom floor than to stand up. After a while I got up grabbed a nightdress—and retired again to the floor. No not really fainting—just staving it off by lying flat you know. It was awfully funny. After one moment or two I got back to my room and went to bed and we got—or rather the others got hot water bags + such and it really was a[w]fully funny—and nothing at all serious— Just one of those things you can do by a queer little twist—the filament of a muscel or something broke. But of course we didnt know that + decided not to take chances so in we motored to a doctor— He has turned out to be a very nice sensible person—poked about settled the back as nothing—it was better by that time anyhow—but told me the best thing I could do would be to cut to a hospital for three or four weeks—have some mild treatment, absolute rest etc—and here I am. As a matter of fact I think its been rather a lucky chance. I'm rather tireder than I thought I was and I'm positively thankful to be here.

The new version of the F.L. [Favorite Literature] is back and ready to go as soon as I can look it over. This is my off time so I'm waiting a little. I shall get it off by about the 21st which isnt bad. As a matter of fact I knew that I ought to have a condensed thing like that but I hadn't had time or energy to tackle it— I'm very glad to have done it. There are only 16 pages including synopsis and notes— It doesnt include the whole argument—keeps just to the point of the vocabularies—but I think maybe the other[']s too complicated (for anyone but us!) without a simpler first statement.

Forgive this scribble— I'll be here four weeks anyhow— Isnt it funny—

I'm hoping to hear from you and I'll be furious with fate if you havent had a truly nice time— How has the weather been—

No more at peril! Your—A.C.

By the way this is all *just* for you— about P.E.M [Paul Elmer More] + the paper and all that.

As for the Hospital I'm not going out of my way to keep it a secret— but I'm not going out of my way to publish it in Northampton—would you?

Miss Esther Lowenthal/c/o The American Express Co/Paris—*France*
[readdressed: Madame Gaulier/72 rue de Seine/Paris]
Pittsfield, Mass./9 PM/ Jul 17/1913

2

26 August 1913
Rochester, N.Y.
2 fols. 2 pp.

Dear E— How are you— and what a marvel you've been! The letters and presents! Not that I love the others less but my favorites are the Marietta letter and the paper cutter— George Moore in Tauchnitz is most nice— (The Colonels book is out—with a preface by George)

Are you a bit rested? I do hope so— You'ld be disgusted with me— I'm still playing semi-invilade having added unto myself a fearsome cough and a still more fearsome throat—and no voice to speak of—or rather to speak with— I tried to telephone your family one day—on the theory that my voice was better—it was an untenable theory. Its coming back now though—the voice I mean. Well, all this merely to explain my saying when can you come to see me— instead of when can I come to see you? Do come soon—

How was the voyage back— calm I hope—

Yours A.

Marvelous Marietta + still more marvelous Hope!

Miss Esther Lowenthal/ 14 Buckingham Street/ Rochester—
Rochester, N.Y./ 1 AM/ Aug 26/ 1913

3

17 September 1913
Saranac Lake, N.Y.
4 fols. 5 pp.

Thank you again, most wonderful E for everything—including sandwiches, slippers *and* the Times! You must check this wild life of yours or you'll be bankrupt! I'm under oath to write only a line—and I'll characteristically use it asking you to do something. I left some papers (students papers) lying around in Seelye— Will you gather them in + tear them up? They will be all the bad ones[—] The others were taken by their owners[—]and I dont care to have the whole English department going over them— An unworthy spirit but why not be unworthy! You will find them[—] They are marked with my name I think—but you will recognize them anyhow—they have bibliographies—lists of technical terms etc— on the table opposite Seelye 11 or 12—or else in the drawer marked with Miss Woodwards or my name—we used the same drawer at the end of the year. If you'll do it as soon as you conveniently can my above mentioned unworthy spirit will be most grateful—

You probably heard most of my news from the family. I told Paul to telephone you about my room etc—so I wont try descriptions of things. I'm down flat—dont get up at all—do nothing—one letter a day + that frowned on— A month of this ought to start me on the right road— Dr Baldwin says that the next three months will show what can or can't be done—

Dont forget everything I told you—eggs, steaks, etc— I *wish* I were there— Why didn't this hold off just one year more—since I wasnt dangerous for any one else!

Love to Mary—and the Lady of the House—and C.B. and proper messages to everyone else—

I do hope the household won't be too uneasy + uncomfortable— I'm glad theres at any rate Mary to fall back on— Perhaps there will be some nice new people—

My line is getting to[o] long! Probably I won't write for 10 days or two weeks— They tell me I must keep perfectly still—and so I suppose I must—

Send me the news *and* all the scandal.

Just have my books packed in the tin boxes + stored— I wont be able to use even the ones we choose for 2 or 3 months I am afraid and there is no place here where I can keep them.

Your letter just hear [here] but I mustn't add a bit I'll write as soon as I can—got a temperature yesterday settling Eng A marks + such—so I'm lying low today—

Really everything is being done— Its just a matter of keeping still + waiting—

You are awfully nice about it all—address *Saranac Lake* not Saranac—

Miss Esther Lowenthal/10 West Street/ Northampton—/ Mass.
Saranac Lake, N.Y./1 PM/ Sep 17/1913

4

25 September 1913
Saranac Lake, N.Y.
2 fols. 4 pp.

Isn't the simple joy of Smith over a faculty *gent* too touching! Of course the Drama drew the crowds— That was a foregone conclusion. Poor C.B. and the others with their seminar wrested from them! Don't stop your small bulletins until you grow weary—they beguile empty moments—and so do the Times and the Nation— The days, truth to tell, are rather long.

Why don't you just let the books stay where they are if the L-of-H [Lady of the House] says they may? It will be ages—2 or 3 months before I can have them. Tell Mary I have her letter and will write in a day or two. Also I'll be writing a decent letter to you— This is just a scribble—

No special news of course—one day is ever like unto another— As for health there will be (Paul told you?) no very fundamental news about that until the fatal 3 months are up. As far as surface indications go I'm getting on well—pulse down, temperature down, cough better and at least a little sleep o'nights. I always feel an idiot when I talk about symptoms—

A nice letter from Maude Temple and "The Christmas Garland"— If you are writing will you record their arrival and say I'll write— I do wonder what she is going to think of her work— tell her she must tell us—

I shall probably withdraw my request for the years leave of absence. I dont think it likely that I can get to work next year—teaching I mean—that is from what the Doctors say now—but I'm waiting a little I'll tell Mary and ask her when there is to be a trustees meeting.

Of course I'm not mad about teaching—and if I were giving it up because I had enough money to live without it and spend all my time on metrics that would be one thing—but after all its my profession—and I've put a fair amount of time and energy into it—and its not wholly a festal business to have to chuck it all.

I write on these wretched little cards because my paper is giving out and my nurse hasn't got down town to get me more—

Yours A.C.

Are you being conscientious about the milk and cream?

Miss Esther Lowenthal/ 10 West Street/ Northampton/ Mass
Saranac Lake, N.Y./ 1 PM/ Sep 25/ 1913

5

2 October 1913
Saranac Lake, N.Y.
1 fol. 2 pp.

Thursday Oct 2

Esther! Punch! You've been wicked again— But I forgot all protests in sheer joy at the sight of the nice old cover and in a gay morning pouring [poring] over the innards— I took it, you see, slowly and with discrimination—"savoured" it as Arnold Bennett says (I hate the word)— Its a particularly nice number (Sept 17th) especially as to the delectable newspaper quotations— I call your attention especially to the five pups (p 240) and Mrs Coverdale Bentnick (p 243) I am also your debtor to the extent of several time-beguiling notes and the writing paper. By some queer freak or other I had just remembered that that was in my desk and meant to tell you to use it your self. But it will come in handy—thank you for sending it. You know how heroic it seems to me to "do up" packages—

To think that one had lived to regret faculty meetings. I fairly wept to think of what I had missed—"filthy cabal" and "brutal frankness"— What language wont be flying about before that curriculum gets reformed. Isnt Mrs Eastman too amazing— Mr Bassets comment on the handsome barkeep is a double delight—as being perfect in itself and as coming from Mr Basset—whod'a thought it.

If you and Mary think it perfectly fair to let my application for leave stand of course I'll do it and feel rather relieved—less swing off into space without any connection anywhere. Of course no one knows what the Trustees will say—but we can leave that to them as you say. My mind is beginning to come alive again and I have hopes that I can do some work on the favorite Literature after say another month or two. You know there is still the Carnegie thing to try—in Washington I mean.

Dr. Baldwin is very nice indeed, very quiet—and very cautious. Its a great relief to me to find that he is as careful about his greys as I am. Grey overcoat, grey other things, grey tie and a scarf pin of some cloudy grey crystal— All of this I am sure will be a great help. (These frivolous comments for your ear alone)— I seem to be going on very well—whether its fundamental or not I'll tell you when I know. I'm still on this silly "absolute quiet" regime— I'll be glad when I can at least brush my own hair and take my own bath.

Remember me to the Lady of the House + C.B. and Mary and every one— Some time when you are in the library + think of it tell Miss Tyler it was ever so nice to get her letter—(item—she says Mr Schutz says he's to have 1300 new books)— No more at present in deference to orders—though I really feel perfectly well— Are you keeping up with milk eggs steak at Boydens and all the other things you must do— Really how are you feeling— any less tired than last year or just the same? Yours Adelaide and thank you for everything. [Written in left margin parallel to side of page: 'Lest this seem an unnatural letter I add a request— some time—*any* time will do—*if* its not packed away will you send me the volume of my Chaucer that has Troilus and Cressida (not sure of the spelling) in it—(There are 2 Chaucers one in one volume with horrid fine print and one in 3 vols—)]

Miss Esther Lowenthal/10 West Street/ Northampton—Mass.
Saranac Lake, N.Y./1 PM/ Oct 2/1913

6

15 October 1913
Saranac Lake, N.Y.
1 fol. [on typewritten letter from the *Times* of London] 2 pp.
[Letter from the Subscription Department, *The Times,* Printing House Square, London, E.C. dated October 1st, 1913.]

Miss A. Crapsey,
39, Clinton Ave.
Saranac Lake, N.Y.

Madam,

We have to acknowledge receipt of your instructions relative to the change in your address. We might, however, mention the fact that we cannot trace any subscription registered on your account, neither have we any record of sending papers to you. We assume, therefore, that you are obtaining the paper through an agent. In which case, it will be necessary for you to write him direct.

Yours faithfully,
THE PUBLISHER
M/J [initialled 'JMRA']
[A.C. letter begins at bottom of *Times* letterhead leaf]

Dear E— A quaint letter? I'm glad they did decide to mention the fact—the information is on the whole useful. Will you interview Mr. Bridgman-Lyman-Abbott some time when its *quite* convenient. I told him to renew the subscription—but I dont know whether he did— This last bill wasnt itemized—

Last week I did nothing but curse my fate— It would have made picturesque reading and I'm sorry I hadn't energy enough left to write it all down.

I've meditated luxuriously over the choice of a book— How nice of some one. The Colonel's book I also gathered from a review is mere sober biography— most disappointing from one of his connections. I saw *Vale* announced in one Autumn list. If its really out there's our man. Otherwise what about *The Idiot* — Dostoyef[ends in a scrawl] I cant spell it but you'll recognize it just the same. The new translation is out (there's a copy in the Forbes). I've seen nothing else so far thats been very alluring, have you? I really think The Idiot would be nice—or is it The Idiots—the more the merrier.

Your Times saves my life once a day. It comes usually at about 4 o'clock just when I'm ready to cut the throat of the universe from shere [sheer] boredom and I read it from end to end. I hope there will be a great many murders and scandals this winter. It will be much nicer for me.

I didn't mean to go on and write a whole letter on the back of the august Times correspondence— More later— Be sure to tell me whether it seemed horrid of me to change the sleeping bag—

I'm sure I had something special to tell you but I cant think what—

Yours—A.

Miss Esther Lowenthal/ 10 West Street/ Northampton/ Mass.
Saranac Lake, N.Y./ 6 PM/ Oct 15/ 1913

7

21 October 1913
Saranac Lake, N.Y.
4 fols. 8 pp.

Tues. Oct 21

Dear E— More commissions— You'll hate the sight of my handwriting—but I do believe these are the last and don't do them until its convenient. Will you confront Mccallums with the tangle in their bookkeeping. The receipted bill is the one they sent when you wrote—the other you forwarded the other day— I asked for an itemized bill when I sent my check but they didn't send it + I was too limp to write again—but the $14 must include the items in the 2d bill— Anyhow they sent the 14 one as settling my account in full—so the 2d one must be a mistake. I don't know why the two dont agree in amount. They have tangled up my bills before

And then will you get hold of the nice man in Brandles (*not* Mr Brandle but the other one) and ask him to send me another pot of cream—prescription no [space left for number] Ask him if he will be careful to have it made up properly— the last he sent wasn't good at all. I would write this but I cant be sure of catching the right man by letter.

Ask him to send a copy of the prescription as he makes it up— He sent it once before but I lost it.

Was it a *class* mate of mine who so scorned your technical terms— There was a Julia Lockwood—she goes to Northfield and prayer meetings so of course technical terms wouldn't seem to her vital gripping human things. Shes undoubtedly drenched in sentimental humanitarianism—

and thinks its economics. I wish I could have seen the encounter. Have you noticed that your colle[a]gue is advertized as "authoritative"!

Mary wrote me that you were all going to the Haven House and I have your two little notes (2d here just this minute) announcing departure and return. It was an event that needed chronicling— Shall I enter you for a Carnegie heros medal? You deserve it. What's the "promising looking long envelope?" It hasnt turned up. Was it from England? Mr Omond is my only correspondent who's really adicted to long envelopes. I await with interest!

Mary also wrote me all gaily that she had been lunching or dining with Mary Willard (allumna trustee) and had "thought it would do no harm to mention Paul Elmer Mores interest in my work—also the English metric's experts attitude"—needless to say my hair is grey with horror— You couldnt possible [possibly] on the basis of the letter or two he wrote say that Mr More is any such general thing as "interested in my work"— He's undoubtedly entirely forgotten it by this time. And just because he has been so nice I would make a special point of *never* mentioning Mr Omond—that is without his very special + explicit permission. If she left him as a vague unnamed "expert" its not so bad—I hope she did— Anyhow you know my metrical work isn't yet finished enough to talk about—in public I mean— Lets revert to the silence policy—its safer. I really do feel horridly uncomfortable about Mr More. If I exagerated the amount of interest I thought he was taking it was quite unconscious—its the last thing one would do— I'll be writing Mary tomorrow— In the meanwhile if you see her tell her not to delude innocent trustees with grand but unfortunately non-existent references—

I had read that section of Parkers speech with wide eyes— Do people *still* do that sort of thing!— What do you suppose were the emotions of Judge Callen— but then the whole trial must have been for him one long "emotional crisis"— He must be glad its over.

I've gone laboriously through the lists of Autumn books and found scarcely one alluring title. Have you had better luck? I've noted the collected poems of "A E" and not much else— Nothing to touch the titles you sent from Paris— Oh, *Vale* is at least announced—Appletons.

No news here of course— One day is so like another that its impossible to tell them apart— but I'm really getting on— Dr Baldwin says I can begin gradually to do a few more things. Shall I send a telegram when I take my first bath?

This is a stupid scrawl— Can you read it? A snow storm this morning— *thats* the kind of weather we are having.

I do hope Mary Willard will promptly forget the More allusion—and the expert—

Yours— A.C.

Dont do my horrid commissions (*are* there 2 *ms* in it) until its perfectly convenient—and I do think these are the last. Love to C.B + the Lady of the House—

Miss Esther Lowenthal / 10 West Street / Northampton— Mass.
Saranac Lake, N.Y. / 6 PM / Oct 21 / 1913

8

24 October 1913
Saranac Lake, N.Y.
1 fol. 2 pp.

Dear E— I'm an Idiot— would have written before to give you news but for the beast of a pain right side —nothing serious— I'll write next week—Trustees—leave of absence 1 yr + $200— (20 a month) But I never thought of such a thing!—last I mean—more Latter [later]— How *nice* of your Brother— Pain not as bad as this writing looks— + getting better

Yours A—

So sorry to have bothered you + Mary when you were being bothered enough any how—

Miss Esther Lowenthal/10 West Street/Northampton— Mass.
Saranac Lake, N.Y./5 PM/Oct 24/1913

9

6 November 1913
Saranac Lake, N.Y.
6 fols. 12 pp.

Forgot to consider disposition of the famous 200 Will write tomorrow.

Dear E. There are heaps of things to write—and fresh and inexplicable weights of fatigue have settled down on me and my pen lags and drags. Since all my "symptoms" (hang 'em) are better its hard to say why this should be so but 'tis true 'tis pity etc. The tale of the new room—or the attempted new room deserves doing—but its too long. There were two reasons for the contemplated change—the expense here wh. [which] is scandalous for me I mean and the more amusing psychological fact that my doctor doesn't like my nurse— He said so mildly when he sent me here to begin with— Its evidently been growing on him since and he was most delightful about it the other day—laughing joyously over my agreement with him and the stories I added to his. Now it all has nothing to do with her nursing abilities—its just that she's what he calls "spurious"—I've been meaning to "do" her for you and some day I will— She has two manners—her natural one—and the veneer— Normally she discourses about "society drunks" "dope fiends" and such like— In the other manifestation she affects a careful elegence and distinguishes languidly between people who are some one and the unfortunates who are nobodies— And all the time her pronuciation [pronunciation] is too funny—attack*t*—are attackt—drown*ded*—heart-rendering—all the things you see in burlesque and dont expect to meet in real life—and she blissfully unconscious the while. Well in spite of all this I'm back here for another month— The room is sunny—the other one was a cavern— Miss Lucy knows what to do for me now without being told (even if she doesnt know how to manage what she says)—and its quiet and away from the sense of a lot of other sick people— Also I have special care and while I think I could get on without it I'm going to be self-indulgent for this month— I'm still so wretchedly tired— At the other place (I stayed there 2 nights) there was only one nurse for the whole collection of invalids. All of this about Miss Lucy I've written to no one else and you'd better not mention it— In one minute it would get itself twisted into the quite wrong impression that I've been uncomfortable wh. [which] isnt so at all. I've said absolut[e]ly nothing about it at home though I did try to convey the impression that I wasn't too wildly enthusiastic about Miss Lucy personally. But you see I didn't dwell on it and we—Paul and I—did dwell on all the good points—so that evidently they include her in a rose-coloured view of the case.

I meant to write again about the P.E.M [Paul Elmer More]-Willard episode but after all its over and done with and I've acknowledge[d] my general and special idiocy— I enter only one correction— I didn't say that P.E.M was nice—I said Mr Omond was— I agree with you that he (Mr More) did nothing that was unusual— Dont you see that was just what bothered me—to say that he was interested when he had only read the paper in the course of his ordinary editorial duties. However Mary says she didn't really say he was in any general way interested—only that he had read the papers—a plain statement of fact of course and perfectly all right

You'll probably have the favorite literature on your hands again soon unless you declare your self sick and tired of the poor dear thing. I've decided that I cant bear this absolute inaction much longer and I think just to amuse myself and to have the sense of doing something I'll take the short paper and send it just as it is to Professor Maccauly—Modern Language Review—asking him whether he would consider that paper or one covering the same ground—(he might want more "style"—) and a second one taking up the question of the metrical application of the data it presents. I'll write him a letter and send it to you and you can tell me what you think— He's already rejected one paper of mine you know (—I think I told you didnt I?)—and doesnt believe in what he calls my "isolation of words"—but the coherence of the analysis might make an impression on him— Is it worth trying as a passtime?— If I'm not going to get over being tired I simply must do something to distract my mind! Just to lie still and be aware of black depths of fatigue is too tiresome. I'll do this first instead of the Carnegie thing because it will take longer to hear from England and it wont involve me in any correspondence since Professor Maccauly would probly [probably] just take it or leave it—(the latter most likely.)

Your news about M. Schutz is illuminating— Who in the first place is M. Schutz that all this fuss should be made? And even if he were very much someone wouldnt you think that a feeling of self respect would operate against any such abject concessions? I certainly agree with you that—unless always its a case of real and flagrant incompetence—people whove done long and faithful service have the right to regard themselves as rather permanently settled. I'm afraid there are going to be strange and not always very nice doings before the curriculum (and the Faculty) get reformed. You know this zeal about the members of the Faculty strikes me as being like Miss Lucy "spurious." Its not, do you think, so much the desire to have a splendid Faculty because a splendid faculty is intrinsicilly (spelling?) splendid—but whats wanted is *names*—something "for show"— Is that horrid of me? The only thing that saves it is that its so open and naive—

The Idiot has been life saving. Its such a relief to have something worth reading. The trash Miss Lucy bestows on me! And I get to the desperate place where I read it— I make *The Times* last as long as it will and all this election "you're a liar" has been most amusing and beguiling—and I read the London Times + The Nation + Punch inside out and upside down— and after that and as much meditative contemplation of the ceiling or the scenery as I can manage I'm driven to George Barr

McCutche[o]n and David Graham Phil[l]ips. Have you ever seen any of their amazing stuff.

A longish letter after all— Can you read it— Do tell me how you are—are you getting tired? Do you keep up milk and eggs? How is the internal situation (C.B. etc)? Has any rumor of the Schutz clean sweep reached the place yet. I must start a fresh sheet. Love to L. of H. [Lady of House] C.B. Mary—and remember to any one who asks—I'm officially better—my symptoms [words following written vertically in left margin] warrant that statement—I've an accursed . . . of commissions—They will descend on you soon but always dont do them unless you want to— A

Miss Esther Lowenthal/ 10 West Street/ Northampton— Mass.
Saranac Lake, N.Y./ 6 PM/ Nov 6/ 1913

10

10 November 1913
Saranac Lake, N.Y.
3 fols. 5 pp.

Dear E— Here are the commissions and if you'll be hanged if you'll do them remember I wont wonder but sympathize

(1) Will you ask Mrs. LaFoe to send me a bottle of her lotion— She will know the kind I use. I simply cant find anything up here that does any good. And do, with your prettiest manner thank her for her letter— She wrote me such a quaint, nice one—and tell her how much I miss her treatments and that I hope she is well and Mr laFoe + Gladys—etc etc— Have her send the bottle by express or parcel post which ever is best with bill including carriage—

(2) Will you have them send me by parcel post from the Northampton Commercial College a box of this paper— (Let me recommend it to you—80 cents for 1000—up here its all frightfull expensive)— You'll see by this token that I'm beginning to lag in amunition. And will you at the same time see if you can get Miss Hyde's address. She did my work for me last year and it would be easier if she could go on with it. I think she would perhaps have time after school hours— She's teaching in some High School—"vocational" training!

Don't do these until its convenient—sometime when you are in the neighborhood. Now here's the next thing and its of a vagueness— Where do you suppose I can find out the name of the review devoted quite exclusively to Poetry (poems + the Criticism thereof) of which Stephen Phillips is Editor. It *may* be called The Poetry Review but I'm not sure— I would like to get a copy to see whether there would be any sense in trying the F.L. [Favorite Literature] on it when it has come back from all its other journeys. Also I would like to see it any how. Do you think that description would fetch them at Brentanos or at the new Scribner Bookstore? I'm a little afraid of Mr Lyman. I got him to order for me a copy of the new British Review for the same purpose— I put the order in last *June* and got the thing just the other day— It is I may add The British Review hopelessly stupid—at once thin and stodgy. I'm sending you as sample of its quality the reviews of Irving Babbitt + Mr Schonfeld—both happened to be in that number— Aren't they hopeless—just *dull*

There is a poetry review in Chicago which isnt what I want (Bridgman-Lyman-Abbott would inevitably turn up with that)—and it sticks in my mind that there is a rival English Review. Its the *Stephen Phillips* one I'm after— All this shows scholarly precision, doesnt it!

I enclose your neat list of French books numbered in the order of choice—though I almost think that Floris DeLattre with Byron + Francis Thompson comes second instead of 3d. Remember the Lotts money goes towards these— Oh! Lets be rash and order them all! Only I must be wicked about it—not you.

Everard Meynall's [Meynell's] *Life* of Francis Thompson is at last announced—for this month. And what do you think, without previous warning, its now announced (after we've got the other) that another (a single volumne) edition of the poems is to be issued with the poems in the order of their composition. This which ought to be for sober working purposes is to be an edition de luxe printed in two colours *(why* 2 colours) at probably prohibitive price— Isnt that stupid of them

And next and finally that $200 that I keep forgetting. Why either bank,—as you say it makes no difference— Probably Mr Tucker's since I've been their [there] before—("Mr Tucker's" bank is also precise and scholarly) You agree with me dont you that it (the fortune) is to be gracefully returned if I dont go back? I've mislaid your letter which I think suggested a masterly way of getting it into said bank without coming here— But after all it wont be much trouble to endorse the checks and send them back—that is if you've not carried out the masterly way already— If you have all the better—if you havent dont bother. I'll tell Mary about meaning to give it back—shall I? As for our other sentiments those are a deep dark secret— [A.C. adds a footnote to this insertion: 'I['ve] written Mary saying I mean to return it if I dont get back and asking her if she thinks that the best way— Of course I've said how nice of the Trustees.']

All this about me and my shop— How are you and yours— Have you any people worth looking at in your various crowded courses? And have you yet read your colleagu[e]s book? I count on you to do it justice. Fancy pouring tea for the Rev. Lym. I'm afraid you'll be a hopeless social light by the time I get back—if I ever do. What do you hear from Maud Temple? I somehow fancy that there are bound to be from her first encounter with the actual conditions of teaching interesting reverberations. And how does she stand it physically?

I'm at present sitting up because I'm tired of lying down—bye and bye I'll be lying down because I'm tired of sitting up and either way I write on a portfolio balanced on my knee and I wonder how much torture it is to read it.

I wish I were in Northampton—working—(and fussing sometimes) and taking little walks and having occasional Boyden orgies with you. Last year looks in comparison with this like one dizzy round of pleasures!

The usual messages— Keep up milk and eggs. Arent they awful—
Your A.

Ill remember about Mrs. Bruckner and thank you for thinking of it— Just now I'm not seeing anyone— Its too tiring.

Did I thank you for sending the cold cream— your exhortations worked beautifully—its perfectly made

Miss Esther Lowenthal / 10 West Street / Northampton / Mass
Saranac Lake, N.Y. / 1 PM / Nov 10 / 1913

11

24–25 November 1913
Saranac Lake, N.Y.
6 fols. 6 pp.

Dear E— Such accumulations of things— The Japanese pictures—the Atlantic—the Poetry Review—the catalogues—and the letters— Oh, dont stop sending news—until you grow weary. I was frightfully sorry (to take the last letter first) to hear about Maude— I expected something of the sort—but not quite so soon— Do you hear anything else—more definite?

Did you get the wretched little scrawl I sent you last—one all unworthy of its occassion? My bank account is the blither for your crime— I can only repeat you ought not to and you ought not to! My news—to be as usual egotistic—is as I wrote you most encouraging. Dr Baldwin was really this time (last examination—the day I wrote you) quite different—instead of being non-commuttal [noncommittal] (spelling?) and cautious he was quite openly optimistic. He feels that the throat complication is pretty well in hand—inflamation gone and little sign or danger of tubercular infection. The lungs havent begun to heal yet but they are no worse which is a sign that the disease is loosing [losing] its activity—the famous "arresting" processe. I dont know why I trouble you with these gruesom details—the sum total is that I think he (Dr Baldwin) feels now that the thing's going to be manageable— Of course just how strong I'll ever manage to be—and whether I can get back to a teaching job and if so when—these are all on the knees of the Gods. My fatigue (technical term "prostration") is ever with me—but that I can manage—

I'm writing this sitting up in bed on an out of door porch with heavy woolen gloves on— Can you read a word of it— The "out of-door" treatment means for me—now—from 10 to 4 or 5 or so on an out of door porch—or, if I dont get up from 10 to about 2.30 Then for the last day or two I've dressed and gone out again—another porch—or, blessed relief, a drive—I've had 3 of these for 3 days in succession and thank Heaven for them. After the eternal no movement its the greatest relief. Dr Baldwin says to try things—but of course very slowly, + very gently—which I religiously do. Jean Webster is up here for a few days—got here Saturday morning. Its awfully nice to have some one around— Does it still linger in your mind that you might come for a bit in the holydays [holidays] or between semesters? Horrid of me even to suggest a long journey to a cold place! I'm going to try to stick it out up here unless it gets too impossible. I think Dr Baldwin is awfully good and as I've never had any consecutive medical care I think it would be a good thing to try it. Also the cold is really better if one can stand it. I've got to decide what to do next—whether to stay here—or where to go—this house I mean—I'm glad Jean is up here during the process—

The fav. lit. [favorite literature] hangs fire— I was laid up a week after Dr Baldwin told me I might work—and in the 3 or 4 days since then Ive spent most of my extra energy in dressing and driving.

Interruption—letter from Claude Bragdon and book— Wait till I've opened them— another Man the Cube?

Next door to it *A Primer of Higher Space*—"hot from the press"—but I'm horrid even to smile—he really is so awfully nice. Did I tell you that he (Mr Bragdon—my pronouns are awful this morning—well my hands are cold!)—that he and Mr Tucker wrote me letters that you could just have interchanged—only one used Xian [Christian] Science terms + the other Indian Philosophy— Both awfully sweet nice letters—but it was a little funny wasn't it—

I do hope (to return) that I can get at the metrical stuff in ernest soon—even to the extent o[f] tackling the 2d paper after I get this one off to the Modern Language Review— But of course I'll be guided—well mainly by my pulse, I suppose— How silly! The Poetry Review like the others—thin and stodgy but a degree more provincial more amateurish—(whats happening to intellectual life in England!) Not much good for fav. Lit [favorite literature] I fear— You'll notice the delightful implication that my intellectual life is neither thin, stodgy, provincial nor amateurish!

Next day

This letter only half finished but I'll send it and continue in my next—as to confidences of my chief—Poet Noyes—etcetc—your note of Sunday Evening is meanwhile here—glad you are going to hear Padervisky [Paderewski]—and with C.B.! Dear me! Do tell me about Poet Noyes and Keats.

The cold weather complicates matters— I stay out of doors but so bundled up—(and it will get worse) that any activity esp. [especially] such a one as writing is next to impossible— What a bore—

The Japanese pictures are awfully nice—how did you think of them?—and everything else— more later— *Can* you read this?— Usual messages to every one—and official information that I'm much better—Tell Mary especially—

I *am* so sorry about Maud Temple— Let me know what you hear—How are you yourself— *Dont* join the disabled lot—

More later (though enough here heaven knows) Adelaide—

Man the Cube bound in with Primer of Higher Space— my 3d copy!

Miss Esther Lowenthal / 10 West Street / Northampton / Mass.
Saranac Lake, N.Y./6 PM/Nov 25/1913

12

27 December 1913
Saranac Lake, N.Y.
3 fols. 3 pp.

Dear E— This letter lags way behind my intentions. I meant to have it waiting for you in Rochester when you got there— But as usual!—at least in these days. First—(to get it out of the way) as to my interminable health—or no-health— My new specialist is very much on the job—with Miss Lucy helping. Next Tuesday he comes again to do something—I dont know what—but I fancy it will leave me pretty uncomfortable for a week or two weeks—in fact the whole thing is uncomfortable—too much so I'm afraid to make me a very visitable person— I'm awfully disappointed—but I suppose its mine but to do and die (if boredom killed I'd be many times a corpse) and stick to the one job of getting rid of these afflictions. So lets put off your coming until I feel more like a human being than I do now. Of course I am really very glad that there is a good man up here and that something is being done—have I told you about him—an exuberent boyish person very nice and cheering—says he thinks he can really accomplish something and that it will help get rid of the ghastly fatigue. Well, lets hope so.

How are you and what are you doing by way of gaiety? I'm glad the New York trip was a success— That was a tempting adventure— Othello Talcot[t] Williams and Springfield at 3 AM. It was sensi a? ble not to do it—but Oh what fun if one had enough strength to be reckless and unsensi a? ble— + these I suppose were your sentiments too. I hope the holydays [holidays] will be nice too and refreshing after Nthmpt. [Northampton] I've a lot of things to write about but I must get a letter off to Mother.— I've not had a chance yet to explain all the new complications—

An English Review tumbled down upon me from Brentanos—and beguiled a weary day. You'll be knowing something about it? Thank the giver— Oh, Jean writes me that she's ordered the Atlantic for me—(arent you all nice!)— The french books havent come because when you order books from abroad you must live a long life die and be reincarnated and *then* they may turn up—possibly. I must have dreamed the *Ave* review. Mary sent me *Spring Days*—by the delectable George— Have you read it? If you haven't I'll be tempted to send it to you when you go back. It comes near being diabolically clever—in spots it is—in fact almost all of it is. And no one would read it when it was first published— Its so easy to see why—and so funny.

Has your brother quite recovered from his operation? Wasn't it an unexpected move— that your sister + her husband should go to Rochester? How does she like being back? More later Yours A.

Your two notes from Nthmpt [Northampton] + Rochester just here—on same mail!

Miss Esther Lowenthal/14 Buckingham Street/Rochester— N.Y.
Saranac Lake, N.Y./7-30 P/Dec 27/1913

13

6 January 1914
Saranac Lake, N.Y.
3 fols. 3 pp.

Tuesday

Dear E— Here's a brief scrawl to greet your return to the ever joyous Northampton— *What* did you think of Mothers journey up here! It left me speechless with amazeme[n]t— You'll have heard from her what she think[s] of the place— She seemed to like it very much + to get a little rest + refreshment from the change. It was very gay to have both parents at once I was up only one day while Mother was here so it wasn't in that way very grand and I've been in bed ever since being laid low ahead of time. I do hope that now things are going to be better and it floats in my mind as a possibility that you might get up here at mid-years— Would it be a much longer journey than from Rochester? And how do you[r] examinations come? This is just a vague wish + suggestion with your convenience ever in mind.

The grape fruit arrived yesterday safe and sound and the figs— How nice of you to remember my weaknesses— No, grape fruit don't grow up here— at least they have been so green and sour that I've given them up— Yours are awfully nice—like real grape-fruit. Also I have received from The Book Hunter Shop The Life of Francis Thompson and what can you tell me of that? I can tell you that I was most glad to see it and I've been poring over it ever since— Only E! E! E! . . . how can I invent new ways of saying thank you— What I think of the Life I'll probably babble to you at great length later—

Dont abstain from talking about the popularity problem— Its a real one especially at Smith—and its my problem too—and will be more so if ever I give any elective courses. Miss Tyler writes me that Prof. McCracken is very popular—and gives double and triple *As*. Now how are such as you and I to compete with that!

My new doctor is still and always very nice + gay and encouraging. I must also record that I am much less uncomfortable than I had expected to be—jud[g]ing by my Pittsfield experience. Yes it is that "something is out a place"—its quite direct technical name being "displacement"— I would be more explicit about it but I'm so heathenis[h]ly ignorant that I dont venture to give any information. Its nothing in itself dangerous or actually serious as perhaps you know—but its effects, if nothing is done about it wh. [which] has been my plight, are in terms of contin[u]ous drag and exhaustion rather dire.

More later— Thank L. of H. [Lady of House] + C.B. for the cards + wish you+ them + every one a Happy New Year etc only writing directly to you I'll privately + less optim[i]sti[cal]ly put it that I do hope you won't be too bored and uncomfortable— You were (as usual) much nicer than you ought to have been in sending the fruit + the F.T. [Francis Thompson]— As if you hadn't already sent a million things!

Yours A.

Miss Hanscom (Hunscome?—combe?) sent me a pair of gloves knitted by herself— Will you tell me exactly how to spell her name + her address— Its absurd not to know but I dont—and dont dare write in ignorance of them. Wasn't it awfully nice of her.—Messages to Mrs Woodward— I hope her liver is well again.

Miss Esther Lowenthal/ 10 West Street/Northampton— Mass.
Saranac Lake, N.Y./6 PM/Jan 6/1914

14

13 January 1914
Saranac Lake, N.Y.
1 fol. 3 pp.

Dear E— Villanous luck indeed—that you should have a cold at all and that you should have it at just this moment. I've sent a telegram with my advice— If you could only *be* here without the Journey—that might be safe enough but *two* nights on these trains with a cold— I'm afraid thats just too awfully risky. As my letter has already told you the trains are impossible— Oh dear and Oh dear—but don't run the risk of getting ill—or fastening a long cold on yourself for the rest of the winter— Being ill—or half ill—is too little of a joke to take chances— I feel strongly on the subject!

And all over again— *What* villanous luck—but let's plan for the spring vac. [vacation]— When does it come?

Where did you get your cold (as if that mattered!) and how are you now? And is it milder? It is here—at least for the moment. When the next drop will come no one knows—40 below was a little cold I assure you.

I'm scrawling this to send special by the next mail— If you get suddenly brilliantly well with no danger of relapse a telegram will be enough notice for us—or indeed just your unheralded arrival— But *don't* take chances—and I'm afraid, arent you? there's no getting out of the fact that it would be a chance—

Must get this of[f]— More later—

Adelaide

Special Delivery / For/ Miss Esther Lowenthal/ 10 West Street/ Northampton— Mass—
Saranac Lake, N.Y./ 1 PM/ Jan 13/ 1914

15

19 January 1914
Saranac Lake, N.Y.
1 fol. 3 pp.

Dear Esther— I registered my rage over Adverse Fate and your non-arrival by running a temperature of 102. Its calmed down now but I got nothing done yesterday + this is just a scrawl. Do come whenever you can manage it— Oddly enough the things you had in mind—my fatigue—that I might catch your cold—never entered mine. I was quite whol[l]y occupied with your cold (as exclusively yours) and the chance of its getting much worse if you attempted night trains in this weather. Of course I wont catch it—! Anyhow I hope its by this time gone— As for my fatigue—you know, youve been perfectly right in finding a tone of ever lagging energy in my letters—but its now only fatigue. Before—in that other horrid time—the unfathomable exhaustion got itself crossed with an equally unfathomable restlessness and it was the shattering impact of these two opposites against each other that left me so speechless. That and a certain amount of nervousness, or something of the sort, until I got this new treatment going— But now I'm if tireder—yet nothing more than that and it would be most awfully nice to see you— Its too horrid that this chance has slipped by— as you say its a long time between now + Easter— If you can work out any scheme *(that wont be too hard on you)* do—and let me know at any last minute—or not at all—just walk in— My social engagements are not so thronging that I need time to make arrangements!

I wait to hear of the Faculty Meeting— And I do hope that your cold has nearly vanished

Messages to everyone—

Adelaide

The French books just here—they look alluring—Bless you for their capture—Remember the bill is mine too—as well as the books— I *would* like to see MissLeDuc's—bring it when you come.

Miss Esther Lowenthal/10 West Street/Northampton—/ Mass.
Saranac Lake, N.Y./6 PM/Jan 19/1914

16

24 January 1914
Saranac Lake, N.Y.
1 fol. 1 p.

I do hope your cold is heaps better—

Dear Esther— No you dont bore me—you delight me. Mr Emericks speech is a gem of purest ray serene—nothing less— Miss Benton's unction delectable—the caps and gowns beyond words. As for the situation in the French Department I think it flatly indecent—M. Schiez [sp? Schutz] is evidently making for his promised "clean sweep" isnt he? Well! Well!

This again a scrawl mainly to say that I'm going to post you, tomorrow or Monday, the fav. lit. [favorite literature] with some questions as to a few corrections. Will it too much bore you to go over them and if you approve mail the thing on to Miss Hyde (39 High Street Easthampton) If you dont, keep it until you come up and we can go over it— Dont laugh if I send it to you by registered mail. There is another copy but I cant think w[h]ere or face the bother of looking for it if this should go astray—

Had an Xray picture of my lungs taken this morning— We are probably to try the pneumo-thorax treatment. Do you know about it?

Yours— A.

Miss Esther Lowenthal/10 West Street/ Northampton— Mass.
Saranac Lake, N.Y./1 PM/ Jan 24/ 1914

17

4 February 1914
Saranac Lake, N.Y.
7 fols. 7 pp.

P.S. Read first— [Inserted above the main body of the letter on p. 1] Your note just here—so glad you can come— Since I wrote this (this morning) Dr Baldwin has been in—next pneumothorax on Friday but that wont make the least bit of difference. I may be limp but it will be all the nicer to have someone to beguile the time and then again I may be very gay. Remember warm things for train and a bit of whiskey to guard against chill (though its fairly warm thank heaven) *Come straight here*—the house will be open and your room ready. I wont try to write again— Tomorrow I must get a letter off to Mary. Messages to C.B + Lady of the House— Tell them I don't advize them to pneumothorax— These new dances are a menace to society! It will be awfully nice to see you— Dont let anything happen this time

Dear E. Does it really pass muster—the poor old fav. lit. [favorite literature] It's cheering to hear you anyhow say so. When I think of the crawling way I've worked over it—the length of time I've been at it—it seems to me I must be an idiot and everything I do accordingly idiotic— It was awfully good of you to go over it (I hope you didn't fag at it before you felt rested—there's never any hurry!) I'm glad you like the title— It seems to me the first time I've really found a really satisfactory one. I've scribbled the answers to your suggestions on the paper you sent— "Secondary" I like much better—will you make the change? Would you then also change *main* to *primary* or is that unnecessary? I hope to get at the "notes" in a day or two— Can you stand having these fired at you too? Oh, I'm forgetting to say that I've told Miss Hyde *not* to but [put] in the marginal references + summarys. I thought it safer to do that myself— Thank you for thinking of it just the same. The red ink underlining is to be put in as it is except where I've made the change to black (because thats the normal way of indicating italics in the body of the text)—and havent I at one place made a note to leave out the underlining altogether?—(the second statement of secondary theses—I think—)

I had hoped to have the "notes" ready by this time but my mild prosodic fit was interrupted by the pneumo thorax treatment. Yes its the treatment you speak of—the lung is collapsed—therefore gets an absolute rest—therefore heals more rapidly. It succeeds in 60% of the cases where it is used. Well, we've tried it once— It was rather funny. 1st Much beating of rugs + general clearing of room. 2d— Me fresh from the tub and all scrubbed + clean—Miss Lucy in spick + span uniform—all this in honor of the "surgical" character of the event. 3d— Arrival of Dr Baldwin and Dr Price with gas + things. Most businesslike 4th Jamming of hollow [line drawn from 'hollow' to explanatory note in lower margin: 'Why I dont know whether its hollow or not anyway there is a needle to make a puncture and then the gas goes through—maybe just the hole in you] needle through which the gas goes (or is supposed to go) into me— then ought to come 5th entrance of gas and collapse of lung but what as a matter of fact happened was—nothing! Dr Baldwin tried 3 places and struck each time in [an] adhesion (inner and outer lining or something stuck together) so that the gas wouldnt go in. They worked a little over an hour and by that time we were all tired so we gave it up and now we'll try again. It isn't awfully bad you know though not what one would choose for a diversion. I had a hypodermic injection of morphine and atropine and Dr Baldwin used cocaine for each of the places. The only (slightly) trying thing was doing it all over again 3 times + still getting no where—and I admit that no one cares less for this sort of thing than I do. Somehow when a competent finger goes tapping along my side and a placid meditative voice says—"Now, Price, do you think we can get in here?"—and "in here" is between my own most precious ribs I do feel a bit of a qualm. However everyone was very gay—my "pnemo thorax party" it got called—and chatted most sociably—the patient occassionally lapsing into silence (after her usual fashion)— I report one nice retort— It was getting to be pretty clear that the 3d try was not going to be successful—and I heard Dr Price say gaily— "Well, you know, with one man we tried 57 times" and placidly Dr Baldwin's voice remarking—"Oh, Price is thinking of pickles" (I couldnt see them you know first because my back was turned to them and my arm up (to draw the ribs apart) and second because I always screw my eyes tight shut when any one does anything to me.) Well—now we'll try again—but I dont know when. You see I did feel pretty tired after it—and not being much used to drugs even the small amounts used upset me rather— However I've recovered now—but only to fall into the usual limpness— But that is nearly over too—and I hope for a good day or two soon—and with just two or three good days I would get those notes done.

What catastrophe with your ward-robe!— Your corderroy [corduroy] (spelling?) ought not to [have] given out in that way. As for the matter of your elections—I leave that for a more lucid moment— It's all very puzzling—or rather not puzzling at all. What it amounts to is that the last thing the student body thinks of is the *subject*—they think of moral issues, or emotional excitement, or culture, or widening of their horizon and coming in touch with the world—movements—or heaven knows what else—but *never* the subject—and there you are— More on this thrilling matter later. It is thrilling—or deadening— Which?

I've just had a letter from Mary saying that Miss Jordan is asking whether I expect to get back next year— Somehow I thought I would have at least till March to find out— Mary says to write Miss Jordan as definitely as I can— It wont be very definite—as all I can say is that I still hope to— Of course I shall put it so that she (Miss Jordan) will feel at liberty to take any action that she pleases. I admit I'm a little sorry its come up just now— I had for some reason counted on at least another month before I'd have to think about it.

More later— I mustn't write any more just now— Can you read the horrid scrawl— Pneumo thorax treatment no secret— I'll be writing Miss Jordan + Mary about it. But for the fav. lit. [favorite literature] Lets not say anything about it. Some how I don't feel expansive—

Miss Le ducs book here— Thank you so much— and 6 delicious grape fruit from Rochester with the name of your family on the cover— As everything of the box *but* the cover vanished on the way + the grapefruit (themselves safe and sound) arrived in a mail bag I dont know whether there was a card inside that would have told me whether you yourself or your most nice + thoughtful family sent them— Will you say thank you in the right direction— There'e [They're] awfully nice ones—beautifully bitter and not in the least sharp.

A hideous scrawl— I've some how not quite got around since that "party"—dissapation doesnt agree with me— How are you? Still tired? Do rest and take much nour[i]shment—

Yours Adelaide.

Dont bother to register fav. lit. [favorite literature] for that little distance—

Can you read a word of this?

I havent yet thanked Miss Hascome. If you see her will you convey dust + ashes and apologize.

[Written at right angles to the main body of the letter in the left margin of the page] *Would* you mind telling them at Lymans to renew my Times subscription Remind them its with Lit Supplement

Miss Lucy alluded learnedly the other day to *The Lookout* [*The Watchman?*]— It took me 3 breaths to grasp it + then it took all my fortitude to suppress hysterics.

Miss Esther Lowenthal/ 10 West Street/ Northampton— Mass.
Saranac Lake, N.Y./ 9 PM/ Feb 4/ 1914

18

16 February 1914
Saranac Lake, N.Y.
4 fols. 4 pp.

Dear E. I had meant to get of[f] an earlier note to assure you that I was much refreshed and not at all exhausted by your flying visit. It was awfully nice to see you. I've had your two little notes + postal— I'm glad the journey wasnt bad— It dropped here that night to 40—no 44 below zero and I was afraid you might have had a pretty freezing journey. I'm also glad to here [hear] that you were able to make immediate application of a faculty meeting—surely a cure for any possible fatigue.

I write my news in a hurry. Dr Baldwin in late yesterday afternoon. We are to give up P-T. [Pneumo-Thorax] for the present anyhow and try tuberculin— That is given by injection—perfectly simple of course but it does tend to give one a fever. We'll begin next week— I hope not till Tuesday—or Wednesday. That would give me time to do my notes so that Miss Hyde can be typing them. I'm going to work on them the rest of today + tomorrow— You see *if* the thing does run up a temperature I wont be able to do anything and as they give it—the tuberculin—to begin with every 4 days I might be blocked for several weeks— Of course I may take it like a lamb—but I want to be on the safe side. You see if I could get the thing—fav. lit. [favorite literature]—off soon it would be rather a good thing.

Of course I'm disappointed about the pneumothorax Its too provoking isnt it when everything else is all right to have those horrid adhesions spoil it all. We *may* go back to it—but Dr Baldwin says they have used the incision (spelling?) only a few times and not with brilliant success— Still it's there to try if it seems best— But Dr Baldwin says its "more orthodox"—delightful phrase—to try the tuberculin first.

I dash to fav. lit. [favorite literature]— Gave Miss Lucy notice that I would be doing some extra work today + tomorrow to get it in before beginning tuberculin—explained I had a stenographer working for me + didnt want to hold the work up indefinitely— It was funny to see her dazed incredulous look— "a stenographer—where?"— to wh. [which] I returned placidly— "In Easthampton"— I dont know whether she believes me or not.

I meant to write a much nicer letter than this to celebrate your visit! I've achieved a letter to Miss Jordan—such as it is— Mary has a copy so that she can know just what I said + smooth over my awfullnesses—

Many messages to every one— More—and more lucidly—later. The tuberculin probably wont have any effect at all—any bad effect I mean—but I'll get the work off anyhow.

Yours. A.

Miss Lucy says the worst of Earthquakes—when they are really bad is that they are so often followed by conflágarations [spelled thus]—luck[i]ly ours wasnt bad so we escaped

Miss Esther Lowenthal/ 10 West Street/ Northampton— Mass—
Saranac Lake, N.Y./ 10-30 A/ Feb 16/ 1914

19

? February 1914 [Apparently written between letters postmarked February 16 and February 21]
Saranac Lake, N.Y.
2 fols. 2 pp. [The poem "Lines Addressed To My Left Lung Inconveniently Enamoured of Plant-Life" seems to have been enclosed with the letter.]

Dear E— More fav. lit. [favorite literature]— No tuberculin as yet thank heaven (if I can just have one more day!) and the notes have run themselves off fairly quickly and I hope *fairly* presentably— I dont hope for more. Give them an eagle glance (if you have time) and make any sort of objection that presents itself. I'll write Miss Hyde that you'll send the stuff on—when we finish its contemplation. I'll register it just because I cant face the bother of doing it over again—but I dont think you need to do it— North + Easthampton are too near to allow much chance of loss. I wait with some curios[i]ty to hear from Miss Jordan and The Trustees.—The 19th is the Trustee meeting—and the first night of Jean's play—a busy day.

If tomorrow is vouchsafed me by the Gods and Dr Baldwin I'll get in red-ink summaries and then except for the references for the notes wh. [which] I cant do till these sheets come back (+ wh. wont take a minute) I'm all in apple pie order—

At that moment enter Dr Baldwin—and me piled chin-high with fav. lit! [favorite literature] The tuberculin's in—lets hope it wont give me a fever and that I can still red-ink the master-piece tomorrow. (But then it *ought* to give me a fever) A wild idea I discover on further inquiry so lets hope that it will—and I'll do red-ink anyhow.

More later—I enclose a master-piece in verse for fear you'll be tired with too much prose—

Yours. A.

I think myself that "laking William" is rather nice—if thats the way to spell it—to lake—laking—or lakeing?

I've just heard that Tanner is ill all over again with pneumonia— Oh dear—

Your letter here—more later— Thank you for news from my chief—a masterly summery of your interview.

[Envelope missing]

20

21 February 1914
Saranac Lake, N.Y.
2 fols. 2 pp.

Dear Esther— This is to show you that red-ink and tuberculin are not incompati a? ble. I've the summarys all in— Nothing's left now but the references to the notes. Thank you for writing to Maud. You are sure she wont mind? And tell her that just the littlest note will do—and of course its all just luck and chance. Professor Grandgent may or may not be interested— Its just something to try— Dont let Maud think that I expect much of anything to come of it—or that I will be disappointed or anything like that if nothing does—dont, I mean, let her feel responsible about it. As you know I'm by this time so used just to working along by myself that any other state of things seems to me only vaguely possible.

No—not into the lungs—just a jab anywhere I think—its given just as a morphine or any other injection is. This reverts to tuberculin. So far I've got on very well—almost no fever—nothing at all to count and only one day of feeling rather done up wh. [which] may not have been due to the tuberculin at all. As the doses increase I may feel them a little more— It sticks vaguely in my mind that Dr Baldwin said something about not using much "where there is a pulse like yours"—but I'm not sure. My attention was all on the matter of working next year wh. [which] was also being discussed.

I long for a little chunky brown bible that's somewhere in my book case— But don't try to do it up yourself—get them to do it at Bridgman's—

I begin to get tired—and discreetly retire to my pillows— Hope you havent—or arent—hurrying over the notes— You'll all be having your pictures taken in your new clothes! How I wish I could see the Washington Birthday procession.

Yours— A.

Messages to Mary—C.B. + Lady of the House—

Miss Esther Lowenthal/ 10 West Street/ Northampton— Mass.
Saranac Lake, N.Y./ 6 PM/ Feb 21/ 1914

21

28 February 1914
Saranac Lake, N.Y.
4 fols. 4 pp. [two newspaper clippings enclosed]

Dear Esther— I could scarcely believe my eyes when I saw the notice of Mr Pierce's death in the Times. I didn't see it until Monday evening. The Saturday paper didn't get here until Monday morning and I was feeling rather horrid and didn't look at it until late. It leaves one rather breathless doesnt it—anything as abrupt as that—and what a thing to come crashing across all those small bickerings—

This is just a note— My inconvenient muscular pain came back on Monday—transferred now to my left side—and I spent Monday in bed and for two days after (yesterday + the day before) still felt a little limp but now I've recovered. Its not a terriffic pain you know—but uncomfortable.

The notes came back yesterday—and I'm going to tackle the paper this morning—get note references in etc— And—if I'm up to it—the note to Professor Grandgent tomorrow— Dont expect to be spared that! I'll send it on—when its evolved—for eagle glances. Then whenever Maud feels like working I'll be ready— But don't let her do it when shes not up to it.

I may be halted myself by the usual event—due on Saturday— How are you feeling? Better again?

I've heard nothing at all from the Trustee Meeting—so its probable, as you say, that nothing was done. Well that gives me a little more time in wh. [which] to make a complete recovery.

More later— Don't know how the notes will go— I seem to feel a bit limp—wh. [which] may be end of the month—or yesterdays tuberculin—or just the normal and perpetual worthlessness of me—

Yours A.

I enclose for your amus[e]ment Washington notices of Jean's play. The important thing is that they show a "good press"—after that aren't they delightful! Jean says they reheresed till 4.30 *A.M.* the day night? before the first night in Atlantic City—the leading lady (Ruth Chatterton) down with tonsilitis to add to the pleasure of the occassion.

What shall I do about Mr Pierce's book—just keep it?

Miss Esther Lowenthal/ 10 West Street/ Northampton— Mass.
Saranac Lake, N.Y./ 1 PM/ Feb 28/ 1914

22

5 March 1914
Saranac Lake, N.Y.
1 fol. 2 pp.

Dear Esther— Much to write to you (to say nothing of Professor Grandgent) and everything held up by a damned cold. Your account of my chief a delight— *never* dare not to share such treasures with me—

I thought what Mr Abbott wrote of Mr Pierce very very nice— didn't you and I'm glad that the memorial service was really right and dignified. (Do you remember the *awful* thing my chief wrote when Miss ? (the elecoution one) died?) If you happen to see Mrs Pierce again will you tell her I shall like very much to keep the book— You were awfully nice to say the things for me too when you saw her before— Does C.B. show any signs of . . of what shall I call it—well any sign of anything—or do you still fly from her.

My love to Mary— I've not heard from her or Miss Jordan— or anyone—so I suppose there is nothing to hear.

The paper cutter as delectable a smooth lovely coloured piece of tortise shell as ever I saw— Thank you for it— Fancy your remembering—and you'd given me the little white one

Last week *wretched*—this week with much energy + determination keeping up to the same standard. How are you? Don't suppress *wails* if there are any—

More later Yours A.

Miss Esther Lowenthal/ 10 West Street/ Northampton— Mass.
Saranac Lake, N.Y./ 2-30 P/ Mar 5/ 1914

23

17 March 1914
Saranac Lake, N.Y.
1 fol. 2 pp.

Yes—a *horrid* week—this only a line to say so—more later In the meanwhile bless you for your letters. My cold's better but the temperature sticks closer than a brother—cant get rid of it— tuberculin of course halted—and everything else— Forgive the wail.

Oh your chief! Oh my chief! The immortals must have rocked with laughter when they saw you and me headed for Smith. Nevertheless all I ask of them is that they'll let me be back there and on the job next year. Lifes an odd thing— Hope the profundity + originality of that remark wont stagger you.

Glad you saw the president—a real letter tomorrow or the next day—there are accumulations of things to write about!— Yours A.

Messages to L of H [Lady of House] + C.B. Love to Mary— How is she— I've still heard from no one—officially—so still suppose there is nothing to hear

Miss Esther Lowenthal/ 10 West Street/ Northampton— Mass.
Saranac Lake, N.Y./ 1 PM/ Mar 17/ 1914

24

24 March 1914
Saranac Lake, N.Y.
4 fols. 4 pp.

Dear E.— I can only suggest that M. Schintz was so convinced of the incompetence of his department that he felt it perfectly safe to say anything—in French. If you do manage to lay hands on the famous (or infamous) thing do send it—I'll return it. I'm sure it will be worth saving. But really of all the impossible things I think this the most impossible— It cant be possible (can it?) that Mr Burton knew about it—ahead I mean. What further news of the departure of the bar-keep? Mr Bassett to be the new head of the department I suppose?—if not more black marks for our honored head dont you think so?

—Your letter just here— Well!— No I dont think Mr Hazen's resignation under these circumstances melodramatic in the least— or anything except, as he said, the only thing to do. What *is* going to become of the place— You know it seems to me—the whole situation—really apalling. I dont wonder that C.B. despairs— What does Mary say? But what can anyone say! I think that the root of the matter is that the President simply can't distinguish between whats decent and what isn't— I'm glad that Mr Hazen is in a position to take decided action— Poor Madame Podere-Bauer and Miss Williams and the rest— What can they do! I'll bubble and rage more about all this later—and if it seems outrageous to us who are so little concerned, so little really involved—how must it seem to the people who do really care a great deal— Mary + C.B. and the others.

Next I will bubble and boil and rage about the Nation— Improved and enlarged!— Lets write and suggest a comic supplement.

All of your letters have been lifesaving. Its been rather a horrid month—nearly six weeks in fact— What funny encounters with Mrs Abbots sister—she must be odd. Any more walks with my chief?

As for me—the temperature has now got back to normal—at least it has for 3 days and it will stay there I hope. I begin to feel a little alive again (this disease can make you feel perfectly dead—never knew anything like it) and I hope to have a good 2 weeks or so before the next slump comes. Dr Baldwin came yesterday + was moved to examine my lungs. They are no worse—and no better. Miss Lucy stayed in the room all the time so neither Dr Baldwin nor I attempted any general remarks. Except—to my surprise—he spoke reflectively of pneumo-thorax—with an incision. I thought he had given that up entirely. Still—despite of everything—I *am* getting stronger; theres that much on the credit side. I went out yesterday—sleighing—for the first time in 2 months. And lately (for a few days) I've dressed in the morning—and gone out for a little while (on the porch) then as well as in the afternoon. The cough is ever with me— If only I could get rid of that. But I'll be back at work next year—see if I'm not.

Maud Temple sent me a French book (Laure)— Will you thank her— Its horrid [o]f me not to write myself. And must I join the Modern Lang.

Asn? [Modern Language Association] Its odd how these things daunt me—they are mere meaningless routine—and I simply crumple up in front of them.

I know there are a lot of other things to write about—they've been accumulating for a long time— I'll send a second installment— Give my love to L of H [Lady of House] + C.B. + Mary. How are you? You dont neglect eggs + cream I hope—

Yours A.

The brown bible only because its the only bible I have— Is it packed miles deep under things? I would send home for one but they would infallable [infallibly] send me an authorzized [authorized] version or revised version or Modern Readers—they are all lying about the house—and the little brown one is Simon pure King James. But dont do anything thats any trouble—*please.* If its under a lot of things let me know + I'll write home with underlined directions

Miss Esther Lowenthal/ 10 West Street/ Northampton— Mass—
[forwarded to: The Bryn Mawr Club/ East 40th St near Lexington Av/ New York City]
Saranac Lake, N Y./ 6 PM/ Mar 24 1914
Northampton, Mass/ 3-30 P/ Mar 25/ 1914

25

[end of March] 1914
Saranac Lake, N.Y.
4 fols. 4 pp.

Sunday Morning.

Dear Esther— I had no notion that the spring vac. [vacation] was at hand— Time has ceased to exist for me— I live a long, limitless vague, indefinite unending—What? Eternity? Well I hope better things of Eternity or if it can't do any better than this it had better stop at once. Your note from N.Y is here. I'm glad Maud seems better— Yes the work happening on—or finding—the play was great luck from every point of view. Tell me about Bryn Mawr—did you get any new light on academic puzzles?

Bless you for the H[enry] James. I had seen it announced, read notices and thought wistfully of it;—even meditated getting it but as I've just allowed myself $3.75 worth of Willy Yeats I felt that I mustnt. It seems to me that its the part of mere decency to suggest that after I've finished the "Notes" [*Notes of a Son and Brother* or *Notes on Novelists*, both published in 1914] they (it) can be returned to you. You can then read at leisure and not depend on a library copy. Next year, in your book shelves, it will be accessi ?a? ble to both of us. Unless you forbid I'll act on my own brilliant suggestion—though I warn you I shall myself amble through the book in proper leisur[e]ly fashion. Its far too nice to hurry over. I've begun it— It seems to me so far quite superlative and again bless you for sending it. The diet of 10th rate books from the library here palls— More about Willy Yeats later. By the way I re-read the George Moore in the English Review and withdraw my coolness— I think I decidedly like it. It does "take liberties" with Lady Gregory and Yeats—but one gets the sense of G.M. as really stirred—(Not of course that it disturbs his suave and impudent manner) by the fact that Lady Gregrory and Yeats have themselves taken liberties—as for instance with Kuno Meyer's translations. I like that thrust immensly. Its so Gregory-Yeatsish to sponge on real and solid scholarship with no credit given—or (that's the worst) felt. I'm not saying that "Willy" cant do a pretty thing or two in English verse, and I think he'll count as, at certain points, significant though they may be rather neutral and negative points—but I would like to know what he thinks of his own poetry when he takes [?] the few pages of Kuno Meyer's translations from Ancient Irish Poetry.

I hope your gossip with Mr Seligman was satisfactory and amusing and I hope you'll man[a]ge this time to see Mr Moore. I count on you to report all illuminating remarks—especially all illuminating indescretions—

I still feel fairly well and hope to tackle the fav. lit. [favorite literature] this week— It's really all ready— but there is the proper sort of letter to Professor Grandgent to be managed—

I do hope the vac. [vacation] will be really refreshing— The Schintz-Hazen cauldron will still be bubbling when you get back I suppose—

Yours A.

Never mind about the bible—Marie-Louise sent me one—

[Envelope missing]

26

7 April 1914
Saranac Lake, N.Y.

11 fols. 11 pp. [two letters from M. L. Burton, President of Smith College, to the Rev. A. S. Crapsey, dated 13 January 1914 and 23 January 1914, enclosed]

Dear Esther— Without apology I plunge into the history of my latest calamity. You and Mary probably know of it already at any rate in part— Here's my account of all of it and the usual question as trailer— Well, now whats to be done.

The enclosed letters mother sent to me, in the most casual fashion, on Friday morning. When I read them I felt as if the sky were tumbling down about my head. I've never been so amazed in my life—in fact I'm still breathless. What happened evidently was this, Dr Burton sent the first letter (dated you'll notice *Jan* 13) to Father. Father was away and Mother instead of doing automatically the only thing to do—namely send the letter on to me—called in Dr Jewett asked him to consult Dr Baldwin and then write Dr Burton. In the meanwhile Father returned, was taken into consultation—and Dr Jewett first and then Father wrote Dr Burton definitely giving up my position for next year. After this Father, as far as I can make out, forgot all about the transaction and Mother put the letters away (forgetting about them too probably!)—and by no breath or sign of any description was it intimated to me that anything had been done.

In the meanwhile as you know my chief, through Mary, sent me the question Dr Burton had asked father—that is how I was getting on and what chance there was of my being at work next year. I answered as you know—my answer being as I now discover utter nonsense since Dr Burton already had Dr Jewetts answer as decidedly settling everything. This Miss Jordan must also have discovered when she reported to Dr Burton. (Its an illumination that Dr Burton hadn't before told her that he had himself written?) As you know I was puzzled over having nothing in answer to my letter to Miss Jordan and then decided that it was simply because no special action had been taken by the Trustees and that the date I had fixed for a final decision was satisfactory. Being essentially a placid soul I let it go at that— Now its clear that Miss Jordan didn't write—because what could she write? From the two letters—Dr Jewetts and mine—it was only too apparent that while my elders and betters had decided what I was to do the decision was being "kept from" me and I was being allowed to think that I could go on (or perhaps go on) with my work by way of keeping me cheered up or heaven knows what. She (Miss Jordan) couldn't of course tell me what was being so elaborately (and so damnably) concealed—neither could she make any reply to my question (as to whether April would be too late for a decision) because as a question it had no real existence— So there she was and like a sensible woman she did nothing. Mary I think must have been in the same perdicament—since Miss Jordan problaly told her what had happened—and I fancy that Mary must have told you—

When it comes to saying what I think of the whole thing I'm simply bereft of words. It seems to me utterly unbelievably [unbelievable] that such a decision should have been made without consulting me—and that it should then have been "kept from" me for two whole months. Now I've not only got to face what I dreaded beyond everything else—another year without work—but instead of making the decision for myself like a reasonable human being (and I knew perfectly well that such a decision loomed pretty threatenin[g]ly before me) I've just been arbitrarily sand-bagged with it. That is the worst thing that could have happened—has happened in the worst possibly [possible] way—and I feel utterly disheartened and discouraged.

Father turned up on Saturday and I've explained to him with some lucidity (though truly Esther, I wasnt horrid about it) how it all seems to me. I think I converted him to my view of the matter— But of what use is that now.

There are of course still various things that aren't clear. I'm most anxious to see Dr Baldwin and I shall most straightly ask him whether he didn't tell me because Dr Jewett and Mother asked him not to. I cant imagine his following the idiotic "keep it from her policy" for any other reason. Also I'll put to him various things that I havent yet explained—things that would have had a bearing on the question of my working next year. To Dr Baldwin, you know as to most laymen, all teaching is alike. He thinks of it, I've made out, in preparatory or high school terms. I feel pretty sure that he thinks that I must be in a class room at a given time say 8.30 or 9 and teach steadily till 4— The more flexible hours of colleg[e] in work—the whole difference in the character of the teaching—that doesnt exist for him. I haven't explained—I thought it time enough to do it when the matter came up finally—wh. [which] I expected would be this or next week. Its not, as I told Father, that I'm sure all of those things would have made a difference but that I had at any rate the right to present them for what they were worth.

However the practical politics of the affair lie now, not here, but in Northampton. You'll notice that Dr Burton's deep disappointment is that hes not to have me "another year"— What does that mean? I found that it was Father's aimiable idea that he had simply postponed my return for a year. Again I pointed out to him that what he had in effect done was to resign my position for me permane[n]tly—since I can see no reason why it should be held open for me any longer. What is my next move—just to send in a formal resignation? Will you and Mary take consul [counsel] and let me have your light on it all

And oh, do you really think it was quite necessary to have all this happen? It gives me the most insecure, exposed feeling. From what unexpected corner will the next bolt be shot!

More later—this just a first dazed exclamation over the thing. I hope that its not shrill or excited—I've not meant it to be—that its to any extent that you please hurt and bewildered I dont pretend to deny— It seems to me so incomprehensi a? ble that anyone should have done exactly this sort of thing to exactly me.

Your nice little New York notes are here—and the netts [?]— There is a new patient in the house— Love to Mary—but I'm writting her too

Wearily yours A.

All this of course for you and Mary and no one else— that is the extent to wh. [which] I feel devistated by the facts themselves— dear me, I'm the only person who hasnt known/it/them/!

I must I suppose manage a letter to Miss Jordan—and seem dimly to see myself taking, as the only way out, a slightly jocose tone—to the extent that is of some reference to the overperturbation of my family (after the way of families) etc etc—

Arrives Dr Browe [sp?]—no—man for the other patient

I've written more briefly to Mary—telling her you would arrive with these 11 pages of detail—if you both can stand it!

Miss Esther Lowenthal/ 10 West Street/Northampton— Mass
Saranac Lake, N.Y./1 PM/Apr 7/1914

27

20–21 April 1914
Saranac Lake, N.Y.
8 fols. 8 pp.

Dear E.— *Two* copies of *Vale* on one and the same mail. One came from Clarence Brown in Rochester and one from Bridgman's. This is the fruit I take it, of your vigerous and widespread ordering. It was great fun having the two arrive—it seemed so ample, so luxurious—but after all I suppose for reading purposes one is suffic[i]ent. I await your orders. Shall I send one to you? or return it—and if so to which B? Brown or Bridgman? I blessed you for its (or their) arrival— These days are none too gay.

When did I last write you and what? If I'm repeating things just skip them. I agree with you and Mary that in the muddle of my affairs the least said the better. It really needs some explanation I suppose that my formal resignation didn't go in at the time the other letters were written but one can just blandly ignore that. I'll have to write a note in returning the $200—wh. [which] also would naturally have been done earlier but again I can ignore— Thats the only necessary writing I fancy. It seems to me a little unfinished, a little less than polite, to drift off into space without mentioning it to my former chief but as she is so little punctilleous it will probably seem to her the more natural procedure. I've seen Dr Baldwin twice though rather hurridely each time— He's unusually busy just now. The first time I asked him about the thing and he looked completely puzzled. On fuller explanation he said he had absolutely no recollection of having been asked anything about my working next year—but he could look up his correspondence. His own admirable answer and summary to the thing itself was "No, I've not been lying to you". Today he told me that he had looked it up and, as he thought, he had not been consulted at all. Well! Well!—

As for the other part of it—whether I can work—why no. The conclusion is the same but I would have chosen a different manner of arriving at it. The thing that ends me, you see, is the cough etc. That simply *will* not stop and while it lasts I cant do anything that will take me out among people. We just glanced at the question of how I am and what I'm to do—I put in my main declaration wh. [which] is just this—that if its chronic tuberculosis why thats what it is and I'm just going to go ahead, find a way of living thats as little invalidish as possible, get what I can out of things and let it go at that. You know Dr Baldwin is awfully nice— Instead of the usual professional psuedo-optomism etc he just said— "Yes, that would be my philosophy."

When he has time he's going to talk places and things with me. You see if there were a good chance or a fair chance of making an "arrested case" of me I would stay up here but with only an off chance it doesnt seem to me worth while. I'll have to stick to a sanatarium way of life of course—one can't, since the thing is infectious, wander where one will— but I can find, or at least hunt for, something less expensive, more liveable and less arctic than this. Jean had begun before any of this came up investigat[ing] a place in Poughkeepsie— But I dont know. Its all in the air now, I shant make any move or change until the end of May anyhow.

This is all horrid and muddled. I'm writing out of doors with a very cold and stiff hand—and a mind not wildly brilliant. Every thing seems rather complicated and difficult—wh. [which] is an extremely silly sentence—skip it.

Your batch of college news lives up to the proper scandelous standards I think it a great mistake to give the Dean the ABC Eng. The students don't take it seriously and there is no earthly reason why they should. M. Shin[t]z ought to be dropped into the nearest body of water thats deep enough to drown him. Why dont the students abolish the faculty entirely? Their latest demands as per your report are delicious.

I'm awfully sorry about Elizabeth Adams— I do hope she'll pull around without a real smash. If she would just rest a bit— How she's kept it up as she has is beyond me.

How is your hat and how are you? Are you keeping up milk + eggs as you ought too [to?]. More later— I'm sorry this is such a scrawl—

What is going to happen in Mexico— and Oh, what did you think of Asquith's move in the Ulster crisis—wasnt it a nice one—

The next morning

I ought to tear this up and start over again but I wont. Perhaps you can make some sense out of it and I'll write more lucidly later. I'll be writing more soon especially to ask the proper way to return the 200— Shall I draw a check for whats been paid—and then they can shut off the future installments.

Well—its somehow all a little disconcerting. "Invalid" isnt a word I'm attached to. It was amusing, and nice, to see Dr Baldwin chose the very farthest mountain top to look it [at] when he said it. Love to Mary—

Yours—A.

Tell me about *Vale.* I'm returning to you Miss LeDuc's book— It ought to have gone to her with a note and instead of that I just weakly ask you to be polite for me. How nice of Maud Temple to have my work in mind— I must get at it soon.

Miss Esther Lowenthal/ 10 West Street/ Northampton— Mass.
Saranac Lake, N.Y./ 1 PM/ Apr 21/ 1914

28

6 May 1914
Saranac Lake, N.Y.
3 fols. 3 pp.

Dear Esther—Just a scrawl to tell you what youve anyhow guessed that I'm rather done and down—cough devilish for the last 3 or 4 weeks, now a head cold and a temper[a]tu[r]e to get rid of—wherefore I'm back in bed again— Its awfully nice to get your Northampton chroniclings— I'll be writing a decent letter one of these days— At present I've reverted to "drastic" rest—because next week I am going to do the fav. lit. [favorite literature] letter to Professor Grandgent or die—therefore it behooves me to take active—or rather inactive measures to get rid of my affliction or calm them at any rate

I'm awfully sorry about Elizabeth Adams— Is it a regular smashing nervous breakdown? To what extent are people worried? She had a pretty bad breakdown once before you know. Dear me—a sad world!

I got a letter off to Mary about resignations etc—also asked her about a place called Wheaton College— Marie Louise wants to go away for a year or two— Do you know any place?— I think you'll guess the requirements—something between a school + a college and not dreadfully in fact not at all expensive. Marie Louise has found a place in Illinois I think the climate much too severe and the routine much too hard for any one as little strong as M-L. So I'm anxious to supply a counter-suggestion. I think a place near Boston would be nice— Wish I were more intelligent about these things.

Ever so many things to write about— some letters started but I gave out before the end— Rachel up here for a day—*so* cheerful and breezy + everything nice— The Revue Bleu letter amazing beyond belief— Shall I return to Miss LeDuc— Aren't the suffragettes too much— Why of all men chop up Henry!

I fall back on pillows to "rest"—loathsome word—temp. [temperature] not awfully high—only between 100 + 101 but steady there even in morning so ones supposed to do something about it. One of these days I wont do anything about it I'll just let it temp.

Your hat must be a ma[r]vel— The new patient gone thank heaven!— He came as a "good" case requiring no care— As a matter of fact he had an abscess (sp?) on the lung + gangrene had set in! Ugh! One would have been (w)?racked with sympathy but his character was so much worse than his illness that there was never any chance for it. I'll "do" it for you when I'm "normal" again.

No indeed the cough isn't bound to stop sometime. Like the brook + the Bensons it can go on and on fo[re]ver More later— Yours—A.

Miss Esther Lowenthal/ 10 West Street/ Northampton— Mass.
Saranac Lake, N.Y./ 6 PM/ May 6/ 1914

29

7 May 1914
Saranac Lake, N.Y.
2 fols. 2 pp.

Dear Esther—What of this? I feel rather at sea as to just the kind of letter to write and therefore send this on for your scrutiny. Scorn it without scruple. (Jolly lot of ss?)— Also will you be an angel and deposit the enclosed $20 to my famous Northampton account? You see the first payment I put in the bank here and I've kept forgetting to transfer it. Then with the money all there—I'll send the letter—if you approve it— and so endeth the Smith Chapter. Or do you suppose I'll be hunting for a job there the year after next? I asked Dr Baldwin what faint chance there might be, not of being well of course—but just well enough to get on—by that time. He said all dubiously—"Well it will depend on whether the cough stops"— *Whether* it will stop—in a another year + a half! Oh *hang* the cough!

Still in bed— The weather too dismal—and no sign of anything better. Its been damp & dark + rainy ever since it stopped snowing.

What news from E.K.A. and how is Mrs Abbott. I'm glad to hear of your novel and hammock mood— I hope you indulged it a little in loafing even minus the proper equipment.

The student-summary of Mr Burtons career at Smith I think delightful— and Hull [?] and a Million Dollars is no slouch of a 4 [11?] years crop, is it?

Behold I flop.
Yours—A.

I'm much absorbed in Marie's problem— I do wish I could find just the right place—

Wave the enclosed before Mary if you feel doubtful— Yes— Lyman sent me the Vale bill—I didnt pay it though Heaven knows why I shouldnt— I sent the 2d copy to E.K.A. as you said

Miss Esther Lowenthal/ 10 West Street/ Northampton— Mass.
Saranac Lake, N.Y./ 6 PM/ May 7/ 1914

30

11 May 1914
Saranac Lake, N.Y.
4 fols. 4 pp.

Dear E— Glad you approve. I thought myself that the first phrase was a masterpiece of double meaning. How, by the way, do you spell unluck*ily*— ily? yly?— The check's to be made out to the treasurer isnt it? All this time I've been meaning to write you a last will and testament letter about my Northampton belongings. Sell the desk to the L of H [Lady of House] by all means. The only other thing I own is I believe the small stand for books— Have you any use for that—if you have wont you *please* take it. If you haven't throw it in with the desk for full measure or dispose of it in any other way. The book case, you know, is yours. Then for the books— Can't you have a man in from some where to pack those that are left—and will the L of H [Lady of House] let them stay in the cellar—or better can you have them stored somewhere—until I know where to have them sent? It will be awfully nice to have you come up here "on your way home"—if I'm still here. But really I'm going to move as soon as some suitable tomb or other can be found. I dont in the least know though when that will be. Jean + Rachel are investigating—as soon as I hear anything I'll tell you. You see I do want to settle down somewhere and have my books and at least try to work a little. I'm sure I can find something much more reasonable than any of the places up here. Up here they deal exclusively in very small rooms at very high prices—wh. [which] seems to me a bad combination. It's just possible that I'll go down to Rochester, stay for 3 or 4 weeks and go to the new place from there— What do you think of that?

As a matter of fact a good deal depends on this silly temperature + things. Dr Baldwin came in on Saturday.— Said a journey wouldn't be "good form" in my present dilapidated state—an amusing application of the phrase? To my great surprise he harked back to pneumothorax again—I thought it dead and buried. But he talked a little of trying it with an incision— Its awfully funny— He's frankly perfectly unenthusiastic and so am I. Its just a matter of well, theres something we might try— I don't know whether he'll let it drop or what. As a matter of fact I dont believe it would do a bit of good.

I'm still pretty much laid up—Havent been out of my room for days—and heres a resolution gone. I just wasnt going to bother you with another commission but heaven knows when I'm going to get out and Miss Lucy's taste doesn't some how appeal to me— What I need is a dressing gown—mine ar[e] all draggeld + wintry. Could you bear to stop in at the Womans shop + see what they have— I remember some silk things last year that weren't so very expensive 6 or 7 dollars—something like that. It seems to me they have in these days pretty powdery flowery designs. Would something like that be nice?— I've had so many just plain colours— Have it pinkish rather than blueish— I look less ill in pink. I would be awfully obliged if you'll do it—go over 6 or 7 if you must to get anything decent—but as little as possible— And Oh yes—add a pair of garters if you dont mind— Miss Lucy says they have none in Saranac Lake + no elastic decent enough to use. She went for some and came back with an odd thing of straps + things—quite useless. I feel most ignom[in]ious—I wasn't going to bother you again but I seem to be just stuck in my room and the things I have are so forlorn by this time.

Its, as usual, a bleak grey morning. I've never known such gloomy weather— How are you and what new news rends the Northamptonic Universe— The rest of the week I devote to Professor Grandgent— The silly part of it is that it wouldn't take me more than an hour or two to do the thing if I could just get started. Are you going to venture Marietta—?

Yours—Adelaide

What do you think of Miss Davis and her conspiracy?

I am afraid I left some things in the desk-drawers— Would you mind emptying them? Just how awful a muddle there is I dont know— But be *sure* to get someone to do all the other book packing. I'm sure there are men to do it.

Miss Esther Lowenthal/ 10 West Street/ Northampton— Mass.
Saranac Lake, N.Y./ 6 PM/ May 11/ 1914

31

16 May 1914
Saranac Lake, N.Y.
4 fols. 4 pp. [Advertisement for *Blast* enclosed]

Dear Esther— Will this do at all? Dont hesitate to say no— Its been the devil's own week but I just went ahead + tried anyhow— the results how[e]ver are probably fit only for the wastepaper basket. Its fearfully humiliating to have to work so hard over a perfectly simple letter— My intellectual self respect is trailing in the dust— Do you think I am always going to be an idiot? It seems a sad fate. Anyhow tell me what you think of the letter—is that enough—or ought I to say anything more—except the polite flourish at the end. I wonder how much flourish is necessary in these circles. Need I do much protesting as to extreme goodness of the learned professor (who ever he is to be) in squandering his valuable time etc etc. I dont much like the phrase "find a hearing for" but I wanted something that didn't suggest a demand for immediate publication and couldnt think of anything else.

Had we any reason for hurling this at particularly Professor Grandgent (or is it Dr. or Mr?) except that Maud suggested a letter to him? All professors + such are, alas, to me equally unknown— And if Maud still feels like writing the note I suppose Professor Grandgent will do as well as another. Tell Maud not to bother with anything but the smallest note—and as I said before not to feel the least responsibility about the thing. There's probably nothing in it— The C.B. connection doesnt seem to me promising (does it to you?)—and I would rather not use it. . . Your way of thinking too I fancy.

I'm still in my room—for the last two or three days flat in bed again. Its a gay life. Thank you for not hating me + my commissions. The paper is here—done up by your own hands I judged—(with gratitude + compunction). Did you take from your own store? Don't tell me you are still using the first lot we ordered. Do choose the dressing-gown. I know I'll like it—much more than anything that at present I could choose for myself. Miss Lucy is this morning going to send me up some indian baskets so that I can choose one in which to conceal various of the parts of my "invalids" paraphenalia (Good Lord, Why did I try to spell such a word)— She asked me if I would like one "with pink trimmings"!

Fancy you bothering to get the desk sold to students. I thought the L of H [Lady of House] was wanting it to furnish my old palatial appartment. *Dont* bother about anything else— And why, oh, why didnt you take the stand long ago if you had the least use for it. Have I said how magnificent I think the Ency. Brit. [Encyclopedia Britannica]— What a grand present—

Your latest news as to Dean + general internal situation most depressing— Miss Benton is proba[b]ly the silliest person now living.

I [I'm] most anxious to get some information about Wheaton for Marie Louise and Mary is evidently too busy + preocupied to write. Do you suppose Miss TeHow would know about it—she's a New England person—or Miss Baker? The catalogues etc look promising and Father says the building, equipment + that part of it seem very good. It has a large endowment and charges only $450 a year—a magni[fi]cently good point in Crapsey considerations. Unless there is something that is a hidden scandel it seems to be just the place Marie is looking for. I do most awfully want her to get in the right place and have the right sort of time.

Do go to see Marietta + Hope and then tell me about it. And the Virginia trip sounds promising even with the disadvantage of the return journey. My plans are still in the vague— Its mainly the difficulty of finding the right place.

All of this written in bed—cant imagine why I've had this horrid slump— Yours Adelaide.

Dont you really think you would get some real rest and refreshment by going to Virginia with Janet Thornton— Do think of it. It really seems to me a nice thing to do—

[Clipping, advertisement for *Blast* enclosed. Pencil note in Adelaide Crapsey's hand on clipping: 'Rather delightful, dont you think so— We must have it! I'll order it + have it for your entertainment']

Miss Esther Lowenthal/ 10 West Street/ Northampton— Mass.
Saranac Lake, N.Y./6 PM/May 16/1914

32

19 May 1914
Saranac Lake, N.Y.
1 fol. 4 pp.

Dear Esther— Letter to Hon. Pres. [Honorable President] at last off— I made out check for magnif[i]cent sum of $160.00 to include May payment. Heaven send that amount really is in the bank— there is no reason why it shouldnt be but I never seem to feel sure of any of my accounts. They seem my[s]terious things. What do you say to a bank when you want them to send you your canceled checks + things? I've never had to ask[;] the "statement" (?) has always turned up of itself but the bank here seems to need a special request. Wouldn't it have been fun to return that 200 in $20 per month installments— Why didnt I think of it—or did I once before mention so gay a project.

What about Virginia— I'm hoping you'll go. . That is if you would really get some rest and fun out of it. If I should find my new place in time to move around about Commence[me]nt time would you pay me your visit there (wherever it is it would be nearer than here) + help me settle? There is still, I may add, no tomb in sight.

If flowery dressing gowns are hard to find dont persue them. I mentioned them only because I seemed to remember seeing a lot of them last year. Yes I know—long sleeves are a vain dream— Please dont take a lot of trouble— You are not Hercules you know and this is a fairly busy time of the year—as I remember it! It seems a million billion years since I was alive and on the job—(or half alive any how).

How are you?

Yours A.

Miss Esther Lowenthal/ 10 West Street/ Northampton— Mass.
Saranac Lake, N.Y./ 6 PM/ May 19/ 1914

Textual Appendices

Materials for This Edition

The holograph manuscripts at Rochester are in five groups: ninety-three leaves of loose holographs on a variety of papers; the manuscript volume "Verse," assembled after the poet's death by Esther Lowenthal; the Academy notebook; the CO-OP notebook; and miscellaneous notes including Crapsey's selections and arrangements of her poems for a proposed copy. Three groups of author-corrected typescripts found in the Adelaide Crapsey papers at Rochester include: a typewritten copy of sixty-three poems, the "Presentation copy"; seventeen leaves identical in paper, type, and holes to the Presentation copy; three full-sized and twenty half-sized leaves of poems in elite type on Imperiale Parchment. Precise bibliographical descriptions of these Rochester materials and their provenance are provided in the present editor's "The Poems of Adelaide Crapsey: A Critical Edition with an Introduction and Notes" (Ph.D. diss., University of Rochester, 1971) available from University Microfilms, Ann Arbor, Michigan.

In 1973 another significant group of Crapsey manuscripts was discovered in the collection of Mr. and Mrs. Ralph Connor of LaGrangeville, New York. Mrs. Connor is the daughter of Jean Webster McKinney, and the manuscripts apparently are those in the possession of Jean Webster McKinney at the time of her death in 1916. The Connor collection of Crapsey manuscripts consists in part of 113 leaves of holograph copies or author-corrected typewritten copies of poems, including fourteen poems previously unknown and unpublished, and six holograph versions of poems heretofore available only in printed texts of doubtful authority or in copies in the handwriting of Esther Lowenthal ("For Lucas Cranach's *Eve*," "The Elgin Marbles," "The Fiddler," "Grain Field," "The Guarded Wound," and "Fate Defied.") The loose holographs in the Connor collection strongly resemble those at the University of Rochester in their various inks and papers and the author-corrected typed copies of poems are in the same type and on the same papers. Nonpoetic holographs in the Connor collection include lists of poems and tentative tables of contents; lists of characters, scenes, stage diagrams, blockings, and fragments of a dialogue for a projected play; prose paragraphs; one letter to Jean Webster, two draft letters to publishers, and the draft of a letter to Professor Grandgent.

Most of the extant holographs are fair copies or semifinal

drafts. Rough drafts of most of the poems are missing: whether they were systematically destroyed by the poet is impossible to say. Little remains of the shaping poetic process, and the manuscripts prove disappointing, on the whole, to those interested in the entire poetic genesis. Sometimes rough drafts are of a poem also represented by a fair copy, of "Snow" and "Madness," for example. Other drafts are of unfinished poems existing only in this form: "Fresher / Than spring's new scents," or "Grave Digger Catch," of which the only holograph copy is entirely deleted. It seems possible that, when Crapsey had found something close to the final form of a poem, she made one or more fair copies and destroyed the earlier versions. For some poems, she made a later fair copy of a poem written years before: one poem existing in both forms is "To Anacreon. On His Age." Poems of which several very different versions survive may be those for which she never worked out a satisfactory final form, for example, "The Two Mothers."

Textual Notes on the Poems

The copy-text for each poem is listed as A and may be an author-corrected typewritten copy, a fair copy, a semifinal draft, or a rough draft. The copy-text of a completed poem existing in more than one copy is the version that most completely fulfills the final intentions of the author. Only for unfinished poems, where the principle of fulfilling the author's intentions becomes invalid, is the selection of the copy-text made for other reasons. Sometimes, as for "Thou art not friendly sleep," the copy-text is the latest version. For other poems, such as "Nor moon,/Nor stars," the copy-text is the version that provides a comprehensible poem. Following the identification of the copy-text, A, other extant versions are listed as B, C, D, and so forth. Manuscripts from the Connor collection are identified as such; all other materials are now at the University of Rochester. Substantive variants in the copy-text, if any, are noted after the list of extant versions.

"Verse"

PART I

Birth-Moment

A. Presentation copy fols. 5 and 6: elite type and ink
B. Typed copy: elite type and pencil on 3 half-fols. Imperiale Parchment stapled in upper left corner
C. Typed copy: elite type and pencil on 3 half-fols. Imperiale Parchment
D. MS. Vol. "Verse" fols. 6–8: ink on The Danish Bond
E. Holograph: ink on 3 half-fols. Universal CB Co.
F. Holograph: ink and pencil on 2 fols. Standard one hundred page quires, with marks [â] above stressed syllables
G. Holograph: ink and pencil on 2 fols. Standard one hundred page quires with marks [â] above stressed syllables and the number of stressed and unstressed syllables entered in ruled pencil columns at left

The Mother Exultant

A. Presentation copy fols. 7–9: elite type and ink
B. Typed copy: elite type and pencil on 3 fols. Imperiale Parchment
C. Typed copy: elite type and pencil on 3 half-fols. Imperiale Parchment

D. MS. Vol. "Verse" fols. 9–11: ink on The Danish Bond
E. Holograph: ink on The Danish Bond
F. Holograph: ink and pencil on 2 fols. Extra Strong Leslie's Mill, with marks [â] above some stressed syllables
G. Holograph: pencil on Standard one hundred page quires, on verso of fol. 1 of I, with marks [â] above stressed and unstressed syllables
H. Holograph: ink and pencil on 3 fols. Universal CB Co. with marks [â] above stressed syllables and syllable counts entered in ruled vertical columns at left of line
I. Holograph: ink and pencil on 3 fols. Standard one hundred page quires, with marks [â] above stressed syllables and syllable counts at left of lines
J. Holograph: ink and pencil on 4 fols. with marks [â, ā] above stressed and unstressed syllables and syllable counts at left of lines in stanzas 1-3
K. Holograph: ink on 5 fols.

John Keats (February 1820–February 1821)

A. Presentation copy fol. 10
B. Typed copy: elite type on Berkshire Type Writer Paper USA
C. MS. Vol. "Verse" fol. 12: ink on Gloucester Ledger
D. Holograph: ink and pencil on 2 fols. Charing [Cross]
E. Holograph: ink and pencil on graph paper, with title, syllable counts, marks [â] over stressed syllables, and diagram of stressed and unstressed syllables and syllable counts at right. Occasional words or parts of words are underlined or otherwise marked in pencil. The significance of these markings is not clear.
F. Holograph: ink and pencil on graph paper, with title and marks [â] over some stressed syllables
G. Holograph: ink on graph paper
H. Holograph: ink and pencil on graph paper with title, syllable counts, marks [â] over stressed syllables, and two lines in pencil on verso: 'Enveil her in thy tender dusks, O Night / And give her rest who nowhere else finds rest'
I. Holograph: ink and pencil on graph paper, 'Agony' in pencil at left of l. 13
J. Holograph: ink and pencil on graph paper
K. Holograph: ink and pencil on graph paper of final stanza with marks [â] above some stressed syllables

19. Even thy careful nurse,]
'Ever thy careful nurse' post copy-text variant in 1915 edition of *Verse*

CINQUAINS

November Night

A. Presentation copy fol. 12
B. Typed copy: elite type on half-fol. Imperiale Parchment
C. Typed copy: elite type on half-fol. Imperiale Parchment [Connor]
D. MS. Vol. "Verse" fol. 14: ink on Hurds

Release

A. Presentation copy fol. 13
B. Typed copy: elite type on half-fol. Imperiale Parchment
C. Typed copy: elite type on half-fol. Imperiale Parchment [Connor]
D. MS. Vol. "Verse" fol. 15r: ink on Hurds, 'With grea' on fol. 15v

Triad

A. Presentation copy fol. 14
B. Typed copy: elite type on half-fol. Imperiale Parchment
C. Typed copy: elite type on half-fol. Imperiale Parchment [Connor]
D. MS. Vol. "Verse" fol. 16: ink
E. Holograph notebook: Academy fol. 1r ink

Snow

A. Presentation copy fol. 15
B. MS. Vol. "Verse" fol. 17: ink
C. Holograph: ink on half-fol.
D. Holograph: pencil on half-fol. Weymouth with "Winter" on verso and marks [â] over stressed syllables
E. Holograph: pencil on folded fol. Weymouth with two versions of "Nor moon" and many starts of "Snow" on verso
F. Holograph: pencil on folded fol. Weymouth above E
G. Holograph: ink on folded fol. Wemouth with "Nor moon" and ll. 1–4 of "Chimes" and marks [â] over some stressed syllables
H. Holograph: ink on folded fol. Weymouth above G, marks [â] over some stressed syllables
I. Holograph: ink on Weymouth beneath two versions of "Nor moon" and many starts of "Snow" with E and F on verso, mark [â] over one stressed syllable
The ink starts of three or more words, but of three lines or less appearing on the single fol. of Weymouth with I are given below.
J. 'Look up!
The first'
['first' deleted and 'keen' inserted beneath, 'first' written after 'keen', 'bre' deleted after 'first' and 'breat' written on next line]
K. 'Look up
The keen first breath,'
L. 'Look up!
The'
M. 'Look up
O sage, the wi'
N. 'Look up
With sudden breath
The keen, and wintry wind'
O. 'Look up!
From hill top blown,'
[both lines deleted]

P. 'Look up!
It comes the first'
[line 2 deleted]
Q. 'Look up
The earliest wind
Of winter'
R. 'Loop [*p* probably a slip of the pen for *k* as Crapsey thought ahead to 'up'] up! and scent'
S. 'Look up! / And'

Anguish

A. Presentation copy fol. 16
B. Typed copy: elite type on half-fol. Imperiale Parchment
C. Typed copy: elite type on half-fol. Imperiale Parchment [Connor]
D. MS. Vol. "Verse" fol. 18: ink on Hurds
E. MS. Vol. "Verse" fol. 25v: ink on Hurds, no title,
'Keep thou
Thy tearless watch
All night bu'

Trapped

A. Presentation copy fol. 17
B. Typed copy: elite type on half-fol. Imperiale Parchment
C. Typed copy: elite type on half-fol. Imperiale Parchment [Connor]
D. MS. Vol. "Verse" fol. 19: ink on Hurds

Moon-shadows

A. Presentation copy fol. 18
B. Typed copy: elite type on half-fol. Imperiale Parchment
C. Typed copy: elite type on half-fol. Imperiale Parchment [Connor]
D. MS. Vol. "Verse" fol. 20: ink on Hurds

Susanna And The Elders

A. Presentation copy fol. 19
B. Holograph: ink on Persian Bond [Connor]

Youth

A. Presentation copy fol. 20
B. Typed copy: elite type on half-fol. Imperiale Parchment
C. Typed copy: elite type on half-fol. Imperiale Parchment [Connor]
D. MS. Vol. "Verse" fol. 21: ink on Hurds

Languor After Pain

A. Typed copy: elite type on Berkshire Type Writer Paper USA
B. Holograph: ink on half-fol. blue [Connor]

The Guarded Wound

A. Holograph: ink on half-fol. blue [Connor]

Winter

A. Presentation copy fol. 21
B. MS. Vol. "Verse" fol. 22: ink on Yokena Bond
C. Holograph: pencil on half-fol. Weymouth, accented syllables marked [â]. When C is turned top-to-bottom, a note in pencil is at the top:
'Technical?
Scientific Exposition: an introductory course—'

Night Winds

A. Typed copy: elite type on Berkshire Type Writer Paper USA
B. Holograph: ink on half-fol. blue [Connor]

Arbutus

A. Typed copy: elite type on Berkshire Type Writer Paper USA
B. Holograph: ink on half-fol. blue [Connor]

Roma Aeterna

A. Typed copy: elite type on Berkshire Type Writer Paper USA
B. Holograph: ink on half-fol. blue [Connor]

"He's killed the may and he's laid her by / To bear the red rose company."

A. Presentation copy fol. 22
B. Typed copy: elite type on half-fol. Imperiale Parchment
C. Typed copy: elite type on half-fol. Imperiale Parchment [Connor]
D. MS. Vol. "Verse" fol. 23: ink on Hurds

Amaze

A. Presentation copy fol. 23
B. Typed copy: elite type on half-fol. Imperiale Parchment
C. Typed copy: elite type on half-fol. Imperiale Parchment [Connor]
D. MS. Vol. "Verse" fol. 24r: ink on Hurds, 'I know' on verso

Shadow

A. Presentation copy fol. 24
B. Typed copy: elite type and ink on half-fol. Imperiale Parchment
C. Typed copy: elite type on half-fol. Imperiale Parchment [Connor]
D. MS. Vol. "Verse" fol. 25r: ink on Hurds, on fol. 25v, 'Keep thou / Thy tearless watch / All night bu[t]' ("Anguish")

Madness

A. Presentation copy fol. 25
B. Typed copy: elite type on Berkshire Type Writer Paper USA
C. Holograph: ink on half-fol. Bunker Hill Ledger [Connor]
D. MS. Vol. "Verse" fol. 26: ink, undeciphered watermark
E. Holograph: ink on Hurds, with stressed syllables marked [â], lines 1–3 deleted, F on verso
F. Holograph: ink on Hurds, E on verso
G. Holograph: pencil on fol. with "Warning" and "The Changed Request," stressed syllables marked [â]

The Warning

A. Presentation copy fol. 26
B. Typed copy: elite type on Berkshire Type Writer Paper USA
C. MS. Vol. "Verse" fol. 27: ink on Berkshire Bond U.S.A.
D. Holograph: ink on half-fol. Bunker Hill Ledger [Connor]
E. Holograph: pencil on fol. beneath pencil draft of "Madness" with "The Changed Request" on verso

Saying of Il Haboul

A. Presentation copy fol. 29: elite type and ink
B. Holograph: ink on half-fol. blue [Connor]

Il Haboul] 'Il f—' B
Guardian . . . Armour] omitted B
Prophet's] typed 'Prophets" typed apostrophe erased and apostrophe inserted before *s* in ink A

Fate Defied

A. Holograph: ink on half-fol. blue [Connor]

The Death of Holofernes

A. Presentation copy fol. 28
B. Holograph: ink on half-fol. blue [Connor]

Laurel In The Berkshires

A. Presentation copy fol. 29
B. MS. Vol. "Verse" fol. 28: ink on Persian Bond
Laurel In The Berkshires] Laurel in Tyringham B'

Niagara

A. Presentation copy fol. 30
B. Typed copy: elite type on Berkshire Type Writer Paper USA
C. MS. Vol. "Verse" fol. 29: ink on half-fol. blue
D. Holograph: ink on half-fol. blue [Connor]

The Grand Canyon

A. Presentation copy fol. 31
B. Typed copy: elite type on Berkshire Type Writer Paper USA
C. Holograph: ink on half-fol. blue [Connor]

Now Barabbas Was A Robber

A. Presentation copy fol. 32
B. MS. Vol. "Verse" fol. 30: ink on half-fol. blue

Refuge in Darkness

A. Presentation copy fol. 33
B. Holograph: ink on half-fol. blue [Connor]

PART II

To Walter Savage Landor

A. Presentation copy fol. 35
B. MS. Vol. "Verse" fol. 35: ink on Weymouth
C. Holograph notebook: Academy fol. 2r ink
D. Holograph notebook: CO-OP fol. 4r ink

The Pledge

A. Presentation copy fol. 36
B. MS. Vol. "Verse" fol. 36: ink on Cornell CO-OP
C. Holograph notebook: CO-OP 12r ink
D. Holograph notebook: CO-OP 13r ink
E. Holograph notebook: CO-OP 15r ink
F. Holograph: ink on Consols Bond [Connor]

Hypnos, God of Sleep

A. Presentation copy fol. 37
B. MS. Vol. "Verse" fol. 37: ink on The Danish Bond
C. Holograph notebook: CO-OP fol. 18r ink
D. Holograph notebook: CO-OP fol. 1r ink

Expenses

A. Presentation copy fol. 38
B. Holograph: ink on Berkshire Bond U.S.A.
C. Holograph: ink on blue
D. MS. Vol. "Verse" fol. 38: ink on Cornell CO-OP
E. Holograph notebook: Academy fol. 10r ink

Adventure

A. Presentation copy fol. 39
B. Holograph: ink on three-quarter fol. Consols Bond [Connor]
C. MS. Vol. "Verse" fol. 40: ink

On Seeing Weather-Beaten Trees

A. Presentation copy fol. 68
B. Typed copy: elite type on Berkshire Type Writer Paper USA
C. MS. Vol. "Verse" fol. 39: ink on Berkshire Bond U.S.A.
D. Holograph: ink on blue
E. Holograph notebook: Academy fol. 45r ink, marks [â] above stressed syllables
F. Holograph: ink on half-fol. Weymouth beneath "The truth is male"

Warning To The Mighty

A. Presentation copy fol. 69: elite type and ink
B. MS. Vol. "Verse" fol. 73: ink on half-fol. blue
C. Holograph: ink on half-fol. Berkshire Bond U.S.A. [Connor]
D. Holograph: ink on half-fol. blue [Connor]

Oh, Lady, Let The Sad Tears Fall

A. Presentation copy fol. 70
B. Holograph: ink on half-fol. blue [Connor]

Dirge

A. Presentation copy fol. 71
B. Typed copy: elite type on Berkshire Type Writer Paper USA
C. Holograph: ink on half-fol. blue [Connor]

The Sun-Dial

A. Presentation copy fol. 72
B. MS. Vol. "Verse" fol. 41: ink on Persian Bond

The Entombment

A. Presentation copy fol. 40: elite type and ink
B. Holograph: ink on half-fol. blue [Connor]

Autumn

A. Presentation copy fol. 41: elite type and ink
B. Holograph: ink on half-fol. blue with some stress marks [Connor]
C. Holograph: ink on half-fol. blue with numbers above some lines [Connor]

Ah me. . Alas. .

A. Presentation copy fol. 42: elite type and ink
B. MS. Vol. "Verse" fol. 43: ink on Berkshire Bond U.S.A.
C. Holograph notebook: CO-OP fol. 2r ink, marks [â] above stressed syllables and number of stressed syllables at left of each line
D. Holograph notebook: CO-OP fol. 30r ink and pencil, eight lines, marks [â] above stressed syllables and number of stressed syllables written at left of line, pencil 'McClure's' in lower left corner
E. Holograph: ink on blue

12. what] *w* inserted in ink over erasure A

Perfume of Youth (Girl's Song)

A. Presentation copy fol. 43
B. Typed copy: elite type on Berkshire Type Writer Paper USA
C. MS. Vol. "Verse" fol. 44: ink
D. Holograph: ink and pencil on The Danish Bond
E. Holograph notebook: CO-OP fol. 21r ink and pencil

Rapunzel

A. Presentation copy fol. 44
B. Holograph: ink on Berkshire Bond U.S.A.
C. MS. Vol. "Verse" fol. 45: ink on Bunker Hill Ledger
D. Holograph notebook: Academy 47r ink

Narcissus

A. Presentation copy fol. 45
B. Holograph: ink on half-fol. blue [Connor]
C. Holograph: ink on half-fol. blue [Connor]

Vendor's Song

A. Presentation copy fol. 46
B. Holograph: ink on C. & P. Co. [Connor]

AVIS

A. Presentation copy fol. 47: elite type with pencil and ink
B. Typed copy: elite type and ink
C. MS. Vol. "Verse" fol. 46: ink
D. Holograph notebook: CO-OP fol. 16r ink
E. Holograph: ink and pencil on The Danish Bond

A has a holograph note in pencil below the poem: '(This has for starting point "Belle Aliz matin leva")'.

A holograph copy of this source appears in ink on fol. 6v of the Academy notebook:

Belle Aliz matin leva,
Son corps vêtit et para,
En un verger elle entra,
Cinq fleurettes y trouva
Un chapelet fait en a
  De roses fleuries.
Pour Dieu! Sortez vous de là
Vous qui n'aimez mie

Doom

A. Presentation copy fol. 48
B. Holograph: ink on half-fol. blue
C. MS. Vol. "Verse" fol. 47: ink on Berkshire Bond U.S.A.
D. Holograph: ink on half-fol. blue [Connor]

Grain Field

A. Holograph: ink on folded fol. blue [Connor]
B. Holograph: ink on folded fol. blue with A [Connor]
C. Holograph: ink on folded fol. blue [Connor]
D. Holograph: ink on folded fol. blue with C [Connor]

Song

A. Presentation copy fol. 49
B. Holograph: ink on half-fol. blue [Connor]
C. Holograph: ink on Eaton's Highland Linen [Connor]
D. Typed copy: elite type and pencil on Imperiale Parchment [Connor]

Pierrot

A. Presentation copy fol. 50

B. Holograph: ink on Berkshire Bond U.S.A.
C. MS. Vol. "Verse" fol. 48: ink on Bunker Hill Ledger
D. Holograph: four words 'Pierrot is dead / Pierrot' deleted, ink on Japan Bond
E. Holograph: five words (one word deleted) 'Pierrot was dying / Columbine, Harlequin' 'is' written over 'was', 'Columbine' deleted, ink on Japan Bond with D

The Monk In The Garden

A. Presentation copy fol. 51
B. MS. Vol. "Verse" fol. 49: ink on blue

The Mourner

A. Presentation copy fol. 52
B. Typed copy: pica type and ink on Japan Bond [Connor]
C. Holograph: ink on blue [Connor]

Night

A. Presentation copy fol. 53
B. Typed copy: elite type, ink and pencil on Berkshire Type Writer Paper USA
C. Holograph: ink on Berkshire Bond U.S.A.
D. MS. Vol. "Verse" fol. 52: ink on blue

Harvesters' Song

A. Presentation copy fol. 54: elite type and pencil
B. Typed copy: elite type and ink on Berkshire Type Writer Paper USA
C. Holograph: ink on half-fol. blue [Connor]
A has a pencil note beneath the poem: '(This is from an Italian peasant song)'.

ROSE-MARY OF THE ANGELS

A. Presentation copy fol. 55
B. Typed copy: elite type on Berkshire Type Writer Paper USA
C. Holograph: ink on Cornell CO-OP
D. MS. Vol. "Verse" fol. 53: ink on The Danish Bond
E. Holograph notebook: CO-OP notebook fol. 10r ink and pencil

Angélique

A. Presentation copy fol. 56: elite type and ink
B. Typed copy: elite type and ink on Berkshire Type Writer Paper USA
C. MS. Vol. "Verse" fol. 54: ink on Berkshire Bond U.S.A.
D. Holograph: ink on Roman Bond

Chimes

A. Presentation copy fol. 57

B. Holograph: ink and pencil on Bunker Hill Ledger
C. MS. Vol. "Verse" fol. 55: ink on Berkshire Bond U.S.A.
D. Holograph notebook: Academy fol. 46r ll. 1-4 ink
E. Holograph: ll. 1-4 in pencil on same fol. Weymouth with F, stressed syllables marked [â]
F. Holograph: ll. 1-4 in pencil on same fol. Weymouth with E, stressed syllables marked [â]

Mad-Song

A. Presentation copy fol. 58: elite type and ink
B. MS. Vol. "Verse" fol. 56: ink on Consols Bond
C. Holograph: ink and pencil on Consols Bond

The Witch

A. Presentation copy fol. 59
B. MS. Vol. "Verse" fol. 58: ink on Berkshire Bond U.S.A.
C. Holograph: ink and pencil on Bunker Hill Ledger

Cry Of The Nymph To Eros

A. Presentation copy fol. 60: elite type and ink
B. Typed copy: elite type and ink on Berkshire Type Writer Paper USA
C. Holograph: ink on Imperiale Parchment
D. Holograph: ink on Berkshire Bond U.S.A.
E. Holograph: ink on half-sheet Gloucester Ledger, marks [â] above stressed syllables
F. MS. Vol. "Verse" fol. 59: ink on Cornell CO-OP
G. Holograph notebook: CO-OP fols. 5r and 6r ink, marks [â and ā] above stressed syllables ll. 6–11 and mark [ā] above stressed syllables in ll. 13–16

Cradle-Song

A. Presentation copy fol. 61: elite type and ink

To Man Who Goes Seeking Immortality Bidding Him Look Nearer Home

A. Presentation copy fol. 62
B. Holograph: ink on Berkshire Bond U.S.A.
C. MS. Vol. "Verse" fol. 60: ink on Bunker Hill Ledger
D. Holograph notebook: Academy fol. 43r ink

The Lonely Death

A. Presentation copy fol. 63
B. Holograph: ink on Eaton's Highland Linen [Connor]
C. Holograph: ink on half-fol. blue [Connor]

Lo, All The Way

A. Presentation copy fol. 64: elite type and ink
B. Holograph: ink on blue [Connor]
C. Holograph: ink on half-fol. blue [Connor]

The Crucifixion

A. Presentation copy fol. 65
B. Holograph: ink on Berkshire Bond U.S.A. [Connor]
C. Holograph: ink on blue [Connor]
D. Holograph: ink on half-fol. blue [Connor]
E. Holograph: ink on blue (first four lines) [Connor]

The Immortal Residue

A. Presentation copy fol. 66
B. MS. Vol. "Verse" fol. 74: ink and pencil on half-fol. blue
C. Holograph: ink on white [Connor]

Additional Poems I

To The Dead In The Grave-Yard Under My Window:—Written in A Moment of Exasperation

A. MS. Vol. "Verse" fols. 50 and 51: ink on Textile Bond
B. Holograph: ink on 2 fols. Berkshire Bond Type Writer Paper USA.
C. Holograph: ink on 3 half-fols. blue [Connor]
D. Holograph: ll. 1–4 ink on Berkshire Type Writer Paper USA [Connor]
35. To] 'And' deleted and 'To' interlined above A

To An Unfaithful Lover

A. Holograph: ink on Berkshire Bond U.S.A.
B. Holograph: ink on half-fol. blue [Connor]
C. Typed copy: elite type on half-fol. Imperiale Parchment [Connor]
D. Typed copy: elite type on Berkshire Type Writer Paper USA [Connor]
4. eternity's] 'eternities' A

To A Hermit Thrush

A. MS. Vol. "Verse" fol. 33: ink on Berkshire Bond U.S.A.
B. Typed copy: elite type and pencil on Imperiale Parchment
C. Holograph: ink on half-fol. blue [Connor]
D. Typed copy: elite type on Berkshire Type Writer Paper USA [Connor]

The Source

A. MS. Vol. "Verse" fol. 32: ink on Berkshire Bond U.S.A.

For Lucas Cranach's *Eve*

A. Holograph: ink on half-fol. blue [Connor]
B. Typed copy: elite type on Berkshire Type Writer Paper USA [Connor]

Blue Hyacinths.

A. MS. Vol. "Verse" fol. 31: ink on half-fol. blue

Fresher/ Than spring's new scents

A. Holograph: pencil on Weymouth with stressed syllables marked [â]
B. Holograph: pencil on Weymouth above A with some stressed syllables marked [â]

2. spring's] 'springs' A
3. winter's earliest] 'winters earliest' A
breath] 'breath' is unclear in A, the *r* seems to be missing and the top of the *a* is not closed

Why have/ I thought the dew

A. Copy in handwriting of Esther Lowenthal. The French source is Michel Revon's *Anthologie de la Littérature Japonaise des Origines au XXe siècle* published in Paris in 1910. The tanka by Satô Yoshikiyo (1118–1190) is given in footnote 3 on page 145:

Comment ai-je pu penser
Que la rosée
Etait chose éphémère,
Quand moi-même sur l'herbe
Je resterai si peu de temps?

Adelaide Crapsey's holograph copy of Revon's translation is among her miscellaneous notes in the Adelaide Crapsey Papers.

Lunatick.

A. Holograph: ink on blue [Connor]

2. slip,] 'creep,' with 'slip' inserted above 'creep,' A

Thou are not friendly sleep that hath delayed

A. Holograph: ink on Japan Bond
B. Holograph: ink on Japan Bond
C. Holograph: ink on Japan Bond above B with stressed syllables marked [â]
D. Holograph: five-word start, 'Thou art not friendly sleep' ink on Japan Bond beneath B

3. Estranged from eyes] 'Estranged from eyes' written beneath poem A
4. Makes blind to dawn.] 'Turns blind to dawn.' with 'Turns' deleted and 'Makes' inserted below A

Nor moon,/ Nor stars . . the dark . . and in

A. Holograph: ink on Weymouth with stressed syllables marked [â] in lines 1 and 2.
B. Holograph: ink on same fol. Weymouth with A, with stressed syllables marked [â] in line 3
C. Holograph: ink on Weymouth, with two versions of "Snow" and two versions of ll. 1–4 of "Chimes"

3. the grey] 'the grey ghost glimmer' with 'ghost glimmer' deleted A
6. Cypresses.] 'Cypresse' A

Old Love

A. MS. Vol. "Verse" fol. 42: ink on Textile Bond

My Birds That Fly No Longer

A. MS. Vol. "Verse" fol. 57: ink
B. Holograph: ink on notepaper
C. Holograph: 3 lines in ink on verso of B, deleted in pencil

2. heavens] 'heaven's' A

The Elgin Marbles

A. Holograph: ink on half-fol. blue [Connor]
B. Typed copy: elite type on Berkshire Type Writer Paper USA [Connor]

Safe.

A. Holograph notebook: CO-OP fol. 22r ink
B. Holograph notebook: Academy fol. 15v ink

Sad of Heart.

A. MS. Vol. "Verse" fol. 69: ink on Cornell CO-OP
B. Holograph notebook: Academy 23v ink
C. Holograph notebook: Academy 5v ink and pencil

The Event.

A. MS. Vol. "Verse" fol. 71r: ink, 'There is a joy in grief when peace dwells in the bosom of the sad—Ossian' ink on verso
B. Holograph notebook: CO-OP fol. 25r ink and pencil

The Companions

A. MS. Vol. "Verse" fol. 72: ink
B. Holograph: ink on blue [Connor]

Epigram

A. Holograph: ink on Eaton's Highland Linen [Connor]

You Nor I Nor Nobody Knows

A. Holograph: ink on Berkshire Bond U.S.A. [Connor]
B. Holograph: ink on half-fol. blue [Connor]
C. Holograph: ink on Berkshire Type Writer Paper USA [Connor]

The Proud Poet

A. Holograph: ink on State Bond [Connor]

3. ladies'] ladie's A

The Plaint

A. Holograph: ink on Eaton's Highland Linen [Connor]

5. a] 'thy' deleted and 'a' inserted above A
6. A] 'Thy' deleted and 'A' inserted at left A

Endymion.

A. Holograph: ink on Cornell CO-OP

What news comrade upon the mountain top

A. Holograph: ink, 8 lines written as poetry, with stressed syllables marked [â] in ll. 4, 6, and 7
B. Holograph: ink, below A, 3 lines written as poetry
C. Holograph: ink and pencil, 11 lines written as poetry, with stressed and unstressed syllables marked [â] and groups of syllables or feet divided by vertical lines
D. Holograph: ink, 11 lines written as prose, with A and B on verso

4. Heaven's Hunter:] 'Heavens Hunter:' A
7. Saw you young Cynthia threading her] 'Saw you young Cynthia threading' A
8. Silver way among the stars] A ends with 'stars'
9. [yearned o'er him,] 'yearned a him' with 'leaned to him' interlined above D
10. The winds] 'All the winds', 'All' deleted in ink C
'All the great winds', 'All' and 'great' deleted in ink D

11. You in] 'In' with 'You' inserted in pencil before 'In' C
    'in' D
    night,] 'dark,' D
    they] 'the' D
    told you of the] C ends with 'the'
12. Hath your soul followed thence] 'And in the silence of' interlined above and deleted, 'Hath dawn—loneliest of dawns' interlined above and 'of dawns' deleted D
14. Envisaged] 'And envisaging', 'And' deleted and 'ed' written over 'ing' D

Now doth blue-kirtled night relume the stars

A. Holograph: ink on blue [Connor]
B. Holograph: ink on blue [Connor]

2. Bidding] 'Biding' A

Tears.

A. Holograph: eight lines in ink, with title, and the number of syllables (10, 9, 10, 10, 9, 10, 9, 10) in ink at the left of each line. These numbers are deleted in pencil, and pencil marks for stressed syllables [â] are inserted throughout. Ink dots throughout and some vertical lines in pencil divide groups of syllables.
B. Holograph: eight lines in ink, on the same fol. with A. Heavy vertical lines in ink divide groups of syllables. These lines sometimes cover punctuation marks and letters. Syllable counts for ll. 1–3 appear at the left of these lines.
C. Holograph: four lines in pencil, on the same fol. with A and B, with each line divided into halves. Part of C extends over ll. 1–2 of B.

John-a-dreams—

A. MS. Vol. "Verse" fol. 66: ink on Cornell CO-OP
B. Holograph: ink and pencil on Extra Strong Leslie's Mill, several stressed syllables marked [â] in pencil, some feet divided by vertical lines in pencil

1. feet,] foot, B
4. In] 'Through' deleted and 'In' interlined above in pencil A
12. Blessed, ultimate] 'Blessed, shining' with 'shining' enclosed in brackets and 'ultimate' inserted beneath poem A

Incantation.

A. MS. Vol. "Verse" fol. 64: ink and pencil on Cornell CO-OP
   (You must say it. . . .)] MS. gives this as a footnote to '*O mia Luna! Porta mi fortuna!*'
   In the MS. an alternate form of l. 1 'tender blue of fading twilight sky', is written beneath the poem in pencil.

Milking Time

A. MS. Vol. "Verse" fol. 61: ink on half-fol. blue
B. Holograph: ink on half-fol. blue [Connor]
C. Holograph: ink on half-fol. blue [Connor]
D. Holograph: ink on Berkshire Type Writer Paper USA [Connor]

The Fiddler

A. Holograph: ink on 3 fols. blue with holes in upper left corners [Connor]
B. Holograph: ink on 3 fols. blue [Connor]
C. Holograph: ll. 49–54, ink on half-fol. blue [Connor]

Aubade.

A. Holograph notebook: ink and pencil on CO-OP fol. 8r
B. Holograph notebook: ink on CO-OP fol. 7r with stressed syllables marked [â] in ll. 1–8 and the number of stressed syllables (5, 5, 2, 3, 7, 4, 6, 4) written at left of lines
C. Holograph notebook: ink and pencil on CO-OP fol. 17r with stressed syllables marked
D. Holograph: ink and pencil on Charing [Cross] with stressed syllables marked [â] in ll. 3–8 and the number of stressed syllables (5, 5, 2, 3, 7, 4, 6, 5) written at left of lines, 'Hasten b' on verso
E. Holograph: ink and pencil on Charing [Cross]
F. Holograph: ink on Oceana Fine, "I offer my self to you as cool water in cup of crystal" on verso
G. Holograph: ink on Oceana Fine [Connor]

4. For see, while] 'see' interlined in pencil above deleted 'look' A

The Parting.

A. Holograph: ink on blue [Connor]

12. sentience] senscience A

As I Went

A. MS. Vol. "Verse" fol. 70: ink on half-fol. Textile Bond
B. Holograph: ink on half-fol. Textile Bond

As I Went] 'I hear' deleted beneath title A

Additional Poems II

Lines Addressed to My Left Lung Inconveniently Enamoured of Plant-Life

A. Holograph: ink on folded fol. blue
B. Holograph: ink on half-fol. blue [Connor]
Lines Addressed to My Left Lung] 'Lines Lines Addressed to My Left Lung' A

5. erewhile] 'ere while' A

Lament

A. Holograph: ink and pencil on Bunker Hill Ledger [Connor]

Lament] 'The lamenting maiden—' in ink deleted and 'Lament' inserted above in pencil A

Grave Digger Catch

A. Holograph: ink on notepaper [Connor]
The entire poem is deleted.

11. bed] 'bed' written over 'grave' A

The Song of Choice.

A. Holograph: ink on 3 fols. Gloucester Ledger, marks [â] above most stressed syllables in ll. 1–47, number of stressed syllables written at left of ll. 1–47
B. Holograph: ink on 3 fols. Oceana Fine [Connor]
C. Holograph: ink and pencil on 3 fols. white [Connor]

2. win] 'win' written over 'woo' A
10. yourself] 'your self' A
18. darkling] 'darkling' written over undeciphered word A
26. alone] 'alone' written over 'at dawn' A
32. overcast] 'over cast' A
34. other saith] written 'other lover saith', 'lover' deleted A
42. keen] 'keen' written over undeciphered word A

The Two Mothers

A. Holograph: ink on 2 half-fols. blue
B. Holograph: pencil on Yokena Bond, 23 lines
C. Holograph: pencil on Yokena Bond, 'abbc' at left of ll. 1–4
D. Holograph: pencil on Yokena Bond, 22 lines and erased lines
E. Holograph: pencil on Yokena Bond, 13 lines
F. Holograph: pencil on Yokena Bond above E

G. MS. Vol. "Verse" fol. 34: ink and pencil on Consols Bond, deleted draft fragment of ll. 19–24

10 ff. B, C, D, and E give one or more stanzas not found in A:

B. 'Restlessly,
Up and down
Wandered she,
All alone:

All alone
In Eden's bowers
Wandered she
Gathering flowers—

The lily, the violet and the rose—
(Why do I gather these she said)
So strang[e] a rose of white and red)

And nard and thorn and small wild rose
and all dew drenc[h]ed by a hidden pond [entire line deleted]
and a flower the colour of noon day sky
Eve's heart named them Mary's eyes [entire line deleted]'

C. 'Restlessly
Up and down
Wandered she
All alone,
All alone
In Eden's bowers
Wandered she
Gathering flowers—

The lily, the violet and the rose,
Why do I gather these she said
So strang[e] a rose of white and red
And triple [undeciphered word underlined]
Of the lily pale and full
The violets purple and sweet'
[Last three lines written over erased lines.]

D. 'Restlessly
Up and down
Wandered she
All alone.
All alone
In Edens bowers
Wandered she
Gathering flowers—

The lilly the violet and the rose
Why do I gather these she said
So strange a rose of white and red
And the lily pale and tall [line erased]
And the violet small [line erased]
Are these for [? four undeciphered words] [line erased]?
I do not know' [line erased]

E. 'Restlessly
Up and down
Wandered she
All alone'

The Expulsion

A. Holograph: ink on half-fol. blue [Connor]

6. thee?] 'thee, / Adam?' 'Adam?' deleted and question mark inserted following 'thee,' A

Dooms-day

A. Holograph: ink on half-fol. blue [Connor]
ll. 1-4 rewritten below first version A
Various attempts at continuation are inserted and then deleted below the two copies of the first four lines:
(a) 'Thou wilt not miss the mark
My soul will laugh to see'
(b) 'Neither thy praise nor blame
A-wry will go but str[a]ight'
(c) 'Thy conducts warp and war'

I offer my self to you as cool water in cup of crystal

A. Holograph: ink on Oceana Fine, "Aubade." on verso

5. A subtle] inscription appears to be 'Asuble' A
7. two] 'tw' A
8. thou] not clear A
Thirsty] This is a conjectural reading of an inscription which lacks one or more letters: the word begins 'thi' and these letters are followed by what may be three or four additional letters including one descender but without an ascender. The conjectural reading 'thirsting' has been inserted in pencil by Esther Lowenthal, but this reading is without authority.

Evil.

A. Holograph notebook: ink on CO-OP fol. 36r

6. curious] inscription unclear, 'curious' is preceded by a *c* and a second mark which appears to be a catch of the penpoint rather than any letter A

La Morte

A. Holograph: ink on Berkshire Type Writer Paper USA, torn into eight pieces and five pieces taped back together
B. Holograph notebook: CO-OP fol. 29r two shades of ink. The number of stressed syllables in each line is written at the left of the line and there are marks [â] over the stressed syllables throughout.
C. Holograph: ink on folded fol. Extra Strong Leslie's Mill

La Morte] no title [torn away?] A
4. gold's] 'golds' A

Girl Fleeing Love

A. Typed copy: elite type on Berkshire Type Writer Paper USA [Connor]
B. Holograph: ink on half-fol. blue [Connor]

It's oh, my dear, the sun shines clear

A. Holograph: ink on Eaton's Highland Linen [Connor]

3. it's] its A
5. it's] its A
6. it's] its A

Clotilda Sings

A. Holograph: ink on half-fol. blue [Connor]
B. MS. Vol. "Verse" fol. 34: ll. 7–11, ink on Consols Bond with deleted lines from "The Two Mothers." The lines are not underlined are not are punctuated.

Journey's End.

A. MS. Vol. "Verse" fol. 67: ink and pencil on Cornell CO-OP
B. Holograph: ink on Imperiale Parchment

8. this] 'this' may be 'the' written over 'his' A

There's a gay girl laughing

A. MS. Vol. "Verse" fol. 68: ink on Cornell CO-OP
B. Holograph: ink on Imperiale Parchment

Champagne.

A. Holograph notebook: ink on CO-OP fol. 31r

The Black-mailing Ruffian.

A. Holograph: ink on Persian Bond
B. Holograph notebook: Academy fol. 44r ink

4. crooked-up] 'croocked up' A

Bob White.

A. MS. Vol. "Verse" fol. 62: ink and pencil on Cornell CO-OP

4. is] 'grows' deleted and 'is' interlined above in pencil A
14. The] 'For' deleted and 'The' inserted A
15. glorious] 'radiant?' in darker ink at right of line A

An Early Christian Hymn

A. Holograph: ink on folded fol. Weymouth, 'How doth the rampi' on verso

3. his] 'this' deleted and 'his' interlined above A

Non Solo.

A. MS. Vol. "Verse" fol. 63: ink and pencil on Cornell CO-OP

4. love] 'like' deleted and 'love' interlined above in pencil A
6. like] 'love' deleted and 'like' interlined above in pencil A

To Anacreon on His Age.

A. Holograph notebook: CO-OP fols. 33r and 34r ink and pencil
B. Holograph: ink and pencil on 2 fols.

Traces of the Rustic in Amos

A. Holograph: ink on folded fol. Berkshire Bond U.S.A.

9. rural Prophet] inserted over erasure A
15. interlined above deleted 'With what prophetic mournful clamour' A
17. blushing] interlined above deleted 'must they' A

Truthful Love.

A. MS. Vol. "Verse" fol. 65: ink on Cornell CO-OP

6. cries] 'crys' A

Beneath the poem, not aligned with the two stanzas, are the words 'Oh Smiling-Eyes and Darling-Heart' and 'Oh Smiling-eyes and Darling-heart'. They may be experiments with possible titles or with the form of the first line.

The Golden Princess.

A. Holograph: ink and pencil on graph paper

3. the laughing] 'the flowered, laughing', 'flowered,' deleted in pencil and 'laughing' enclosed in pencil parentheses A

The changed request

A. Holograph: pencil and ink, "Madness" and "Warning" on verso

O que m'importe] 'Oqe m'importe' A
2. lad] written over undeciphered word A
6. he grows wise] interlined in ink above 'wise he grows' in pencil A

Undergraduate Poems

Loneliness.

Vassar Miscellany, 28, No. 2 (Nov. 1898), 71.

Time Flies.

Vassar Miscellany, 28, No. 2 (Nov. 1898), 94.

The Heart of a Maid.

Vassar Miscellany, 28, No. 3 (Dec. 1898), 137.

Repentance.

Vassar Miscellany, 28, No. 5 (Feb. 1899), 229.

8. chansonettes.] printed 'chausonettes.'

Hail Mary!

Vassar Miscellany, 29, No. 3 (Dec. 1899), 148.

Charms (Cherokee Indians)

A. Holograph: ink on 2 fols. Imperiale Parchment

(1) Love Charm—
21. Let loneliness leave its mark upon her.] 'Let loneliness wait upon her.', 'wait upon her.' deleted and 'leave its mark' interlined above,'upon her.' inserted following A

Notes

Life

1. *Vassarion* (Poughkeepsie: Vassar College, 1901), p. 101.
2. *Vassar Miscellany* 44 (1915): 414.
3. *Adelaide Crapsey*, (Boston: Bruce Humphries, 1933), p. 28.
4. Blake McKelvey, *Rochester: The Quest for Quality 1890–1925* (Cambridge: Harvard University Press, 1956), p. 145.
5. Algernon Sidney Crapsey, *The Last of the Heretics* (New York: Knopf, 1924), p.183.
6. *Ibid.*, p. 194.
7. *Ibid.*, p. vii.
8. McKelvey, *Rochester*, p. 125.
9. *Ibid.*, p. 133.
10. *Ibid.*, p. 45.
11. *Ibid.*, p. 46.
12. *Ibid.*
13. *Ibid.*, p. 134.
14. Stated in an interview, 4 May 1969.
15. Crapsey, *The Last of the Heretics*, p. 260.
16. *Ibid.*, p. 264.
17. McKelvey, *Rochester*, p. 139.
18. Mary Delia Lewis, "Adelaide Crapsey," *Smith College Monthly* 23 (1915): 114.
19. "Adelaide Crapsey's Poems," *New Republic* 33 (1923): 258.
20. Letter from Dora Schatz (Mrs. Nathan), Hartford, Connecticut, n.d., cited by Sister M. Edwardine O'Connor, "Adelaide Crapsey: A Biographical Study," (Master's thesis, Notre Dame University, 1931), pp. 30–31.
21. Telephone conversation during an interview with Arthur H. Crapsey, Jr., on 4 May 1969.
22. The lines, in a letter addressed to John Adams Lowe, then director of the Rochester Public Library, dated 30 April 1944, are now in the local history collection of the Rochester Public Library.
23. Claude Bragdon, *More Lives Than One* (New York: Knopf, 1938), p. 258.
24. Claude Bragdon, *Merely Players* (New York: Knopf, 1929), p. 208.
25. *Ibid.*, pp. 206 and 209.
26. Bragdon, *More Lives Than One*, p. 258.

Previous Criticism of the Poems

1. Claude Bragdon, Foreword to *Verse* (Rochester: Manas Press, 1915), p. 11.
2. *Poets and Their Art* (New York: Macmillan, 1926), pp. 137–138.
3. "The Great Adventure," *Poetry: A Magazine of Verse*, 10 (1917): 317.

4. *The Letters of Carl Sandburg,* ed. Herbert Mitgang (New York: Harcourt, Brace & World, 1969), p. 115.
5. Sandburg, *Letters,* p. 124.
6. Carl Sandburg, *Cornhuskers* (New York: Holt, 1918), p. 48.
7. Louis Untermeyer, ed. *Modern American Poetry: A Critical Anthology* (New York: Harcourt, Brace, 1919), pp. 205–206; *The Pursuit of Poetry: A Guide to Its Understanding and Appreciation With an Explanation of Its Forms and a Dictionary of Poetic Terms* (New York: Simon and Schuster, 1969), p. 181.
8. *Forms of Discovery: Critical and Historical Essays on the Forms of the Short Poem in English* (Chicago: Alan Swallow, 1967), p. 329.
9. *The Encyclopedia of Poetry and Poetics,* ed. Alex Preminger (Princeton: Princeton University Press, 1965), p. 126.
10. "Adelaide Crapsey's Poems," *New Republic* 33 (1923), 258.
11. "Adelaide Crapsey: A Biographical Study" (M.A. thesis, Notre Dame University, 1931), pp. 26–27.
12. K. L. Goodwin, "William Soutar, Adelaide Crapsey, and Imagism," *Studies in Scottish Literature* 3 (1965): 96–100. See also William Soutar, *Collected Poems,* ed. Hugh Mac Diarmid (London: Andrew Dakers, 1948), pp. 243–252, 299–309, 319–342.
13. Osborn, *Adelaide Crapsey,* pp. 108-109.
14. O'Connor, "Adelaide Crapsey: A Biographical Study," p. 26.
15. Osborn, *Adelaide Crapsey,* p. 109.
16. Earl Miner, *The Japanese Tradition in British and American Literature* (Princeton: Princeton University Press, 1958), p. 188.
17. William N. Porter, trans. *A Hundred Verses From Old Japan: Being a Translation of the Hyaku-Nin-Isshiu* (Oxford: Clarendon Press, 1909), p. 85.
18. "Adelaide Crapsey and Michel Revon: Their Connection with Japanese Literature," trans. Yoshiaki Arai, *University of Osaka College of Commerce Anniversary Festschrift,* n.d., n.p.
19. Yone Noguchi, *From the Eastern Sea* (New York: Mitchell Kennerley, 1910), p. 67.
20. Michel Revon, *Anthologie de la Littérature Japonaise des Origines au XXe Siècle* (Paris: Delagrave, 1910), p. 145, n. 3.
21. Revon, *Anthologie,* p. 108.
22. *Ibid.,* p. 108, n. 1.
23. *Ibid.,* p. 383 and p. 383, n. 2.
24. Ezra Pound, "Vorticism," *Fortnightly Review* NS 573 (1914): 462.
25. Miner, *The Japanese Tradition,* p. 188.
26. Revon, *Anthologie,* p. 133.
27. *Ibid.,* p. 133, n. 2.
28. Miner, *The Japanese Tradition,* p. 189.
29. Donald Keene, *Japanese Literature: An Introduction for Western Readers* (New York: Grove Press, 1955), p. 21.
30. Revon, *Anthologie,* p. 397.
31. William Pratt, ed., *The Imagist Poem: Modern Poetry in Miniature* (New York: Dutton, 1963), pp. 121–122.
32. Babette Deutsch, *Poetry in Our Time* (New York: Holt, 1952), p. 84.
33. Yvor Winters, *Primitivism and Decadence: A Study of American Experimental Poetry* (Arrow Editions, 1937) in *In Defense of Reason* (Denver: Alan Swallow, 1947), p. 104, n. 1.
34. Winters, *Forms of Discovery,* p. 329.

35. Yvor Winters, *The Anatomy of Nonsense* (New Directions, 1943) in *In Defense of Reason* (Denver: Alan Swallow, 1947), p. 568.
36. Yvor Winters and Kenneth Fields, eds. *Quest for Reality: An Anthology of Short Poems in English* (Chicago: Alan Swallow, 1969), pp. 121–122.
37. Ian Fletcher, "Adelaide Crapsey's *Cinquains*," *ADAM International Review* 35 (1970); 62–64; and G. S. Fraser, "Two Rochester Muses," *ADAM International Review* 35 (1970): 4–11.

Toward a Critical Revaluation

1. Ezra Pound, "Vorticism," *Fortnightly Review*, 573: 461–471. The article often mentions the July issue of *Blast*.
2. *Ibid.*, p. 462.
3. *Ibid.*, p. 464.
4. *Ibid.*, p. 467.
5. Keene, *Japanese Literature*, pp. 40–41.
6. Pound, "Vorticism," p. 467.
7. Revon, *Anthologie*, p. 94.
8. Keene, *Japanese Literature*, pp. 38–39.
9. *Ibid.*, p. 29.
10. *Ibid.*, pp. 28–29.
11. *Ibid.*, p. 46.
12. Winters, *Forms of Discovery*, p. 330.
13. René Dubos and Jean Dubos, "Consumption and the Romantic Age," in *Curiosities of Medicine*, ed. Berton Roueché (New York: Berkeley Medallion Books, 1964), p. 52.
14. Keene, *Japanese Literature*, pp. 28–29.
15. Robert Bridges, *Milton's Prosody: An Examination of the Rules of the Blank Verse in Milton's Later Poems, with an Account of the Versification of Samson Agonistes* (Oxford: Clarendon Press, 1893), p. 68.
16. An excellent account of the mutual indebtedness is given by Jean-George Ritz in *Robert Bridges and Gerard Hopkins 1863–1889: A Literary Friendship* (London: Oxford University Press, 1960).
17. Bridges, *Milton's Prosody*, p. 68.
18. *Ibid.*, p. 72.
19. Keene, *Japanese Literature*, p. 15.
20. Miner, *The Japanese Tradition*, p. 101.
21. Iona Opie and Peter Opie, eds., *The Oxford Dictionary of Nursery Rhymes* (Oxford: Oxford University Press, 1952), p. 137.
22. Winters, *Forms of Discovery*, pp. 330–331.

A Note on the Present Text of the Poems

1. See "The Materials for This Edition," in the Textual Appendices.
2. *The Editing of Emily Dickinson: A Reconsideration* (University of Wisconsin Press: Madison, 1967), p. 142.

Poems

1. Walter Savage Landor (1775–1864) lived at Fiesole, a village near Florence, from 1858 until 1864.
2. In the spring and summer of 1692, nineteen persons were hanged at Salem and one person was pressed to death. No witches were burned.
3. Mark 15:39, Matthew 27:54.
4. *Hamlet* II.ii. 593-596:
   Yet I,
   A dull and muddy-mettled rascal, peak
   Like John-a-dreams, unpregnant of my cause,
   And can say nothing!
5. A "cushy cow" (ll. 8 and 19) is a cow without horns.
6. A "silver tee" (ll. 10 and 21) is a silver cow tie.

Bibliography

Manuscript Materials

LaGrangeville, New York. Collection of Mr. and Mrs. Ralph Connor. Adelaide Crapsey manuscripts and letters from Jean Webster to Glenn Ford McKinney.

Rochester, New York. Rochester Public Library. Algernon Sidney Crapsey papers.

Rochester, New York. University of Rochester Library. Claude Fayette Bragdon papers.

Rochester, New York. University of Rochester Library. Adelaide Crapsey papers.

Published Sources

Bragdon, Claude Fayette. *Merely Players.* New York: Knopf, 1929.

——. *More Lives Than One.* New York: Knopf, 1938.

Bridges, Robert. *Milton's Prosody: An Examination of the Rules of the Blank Verse in Milton's Later Poems, with an Account of the Versification of Samson Agonistes,* Oxford: Clarendon Press, 1893.

Crapsey, Adelaide. *A Study in English Metrics.* New York: Knopf, 1918.

——. "A Girl to Love." *Vassar Miscellany* 27 (1897): 59–63.

——. "An Insane Episode." *Vassarion 99,* Baltimore: Williams & Wilkins, 1899, pp. 118–126.

——. "The Knowledge He Gained." *Vassar Miscellany* 27 (1898): 396–399.

——. "Milord and Milady." *Vassar Miscellany* 29 (1900): 223–229.

——. "Mr. Percival Poynton and a Pig." *Vassar Miscellany* 29 (1899); 36–50.

——, ed. *Vassarion.* Poughkeepsie: Vassar College, 1901.

——. *Verse.* Rochester, New York: Manas Press, 1915.

——. *Verse.* New York: Knopf, 1922.

——. *Verse.* New York: Knopf, 1926.

——. *Verse.* New York: Knopf, 1929.

——. *Verse.* New York: Knopf, 1934.

——. *Verse.* New York: Knopf, 1938.

——. "The Witch." *Century Illustrated Magazine* 89 (November 1914): 128.

Crapsey, Algernon Sidney. *The Last of the Heretics.* New York: Knopf, 1924.

——. *Religion and Politics.* New York: Thomas Whittaker, 1905.

Fletcher, Ian. "Adelaide Crapsey's Cinquains." *ADAM International Review* 35 (1970): 62–64.

Fraser, G. S. "Two Rochester Muses." *ADAM International Review* 35 (1970): 4–11.

Goodwin, K. L. *The Influence of Ezra Pound.* London: Oxford University Press, 1966.

——. "William Soutar, Adelaide Grapsey, and Imagism." *Studies in Scottish Literature* 3 (1965): 96–100.

Henderson, Alice Corbin. "The Great Adventure." *Poetry: A Magazine of Verse* 10 (1917): 316–319.

Kawanami, Hideo. "Adelaide Crapsey and Michel Revon: Their Connection with Japanese

Literature," translated for the editor by Yoshiaki Arai. *University of Osaka College of Commerce Anniversary Festschrift*, n.d.

Keene, Donald. *Japanese Literature: An Introduction for Western Readers*. New York: Grove Press, 1955.

McKelvey, Blake. *Rochester: The Quest for Quality, 1890–1925*. Cambridge, Mass.: Harvard University Press, 1956.

McKinney, Jean Webster. *Daddy Long-Legs*. New York: Century, 1912.

——. "Foreword Upon the Poems of Adelaide Crapsey." *Vassar Miscellany* 44 (1915): 414–415.

Miner, Earl. *The Japanese Tradition in British and American Literature*. Princeton: Princeton University Press, 1958.

Monroe, Harriet. *Poets and Their Art*. New York: Macmillan, 1926.

Nicholl, Louise Townsend. "Adelaide Crapsey's Poems." *New Republic* 33 (1923): 258.

Noguchi, Yone. *From the Eastern Sea*. New York: Mitchell Kennerley, 1910.

O'Connor, Mary Edwardine. "Adelaide Crapsey: A Biographical Study." Master's thesis, University of Notre Dame, 1931.

Omond, T. S. *A Study of Metre*. 1903. Reprint. London: Alexander Moring, 1920.

Osborn, Mary Elizabeth. *Adelaide Crapsey*. Boston: Bruce Humphries, 1933.

Porter, William N., trans. *A Hundred Verses from Old Japan: Being a Translation of the Hyaku-Nin-Isshiu*. Oxford: Clarendon Press, 1909.

Pound, Ezra. "Vorticism." *Fortnightly Review* 573 (1914): 461–471.

Pratt, William, ed. *The Imagist Poem: Modern Poetry in Miniature*. New York: Dutton, 1963.

Revon, Michel. *Anthologie de la Littérature Japonaise des Origines au XXe siècle*. Paris: Delagrave, 1910.

Sandburg, Carl. *Cornhuskers*. New York: Holt, 1918.

——. *The Letters of Carl Sandburg*. Ed. Herbert Mitgang. New York: Harcourt, Brace, 1968.

Untermeyer, Louis, ed. *Modern American Poetry*. New York: Harcourt, Brace, 1919.

——. *The New Era in American Poetry*. New York: Henry Holt, 1919.

——. *The Pursuit of Poetry: A Guide to Its Understanding and Appreciation with an Explanation of Its Forms and a Dictionary of Poetic Terms*. New York: Simon and Schuster, 1969.

Winters, Yvor. *Forms of Discovery: Critical and Historical Essays on the Forms of the Short Poem in English*. Chicago: Alan Swallow, 1967.

——. *In Defense of Reason*. Denver: Alan Swallow, 1947.

Winters, Yvor, and Kenneth Fields. *Quest for Reality: An Anthology of Short Poems in English*. Chicago: Alan Swallow, 1969.

Index of Titles or First Lines